SAIT KITTS

AND NEVIS

INVESTMENT AND BUSINESS GUIDE

VOLUME 1

STRATEGIC AND PRACTICAL INFORMATION

International Business Publications, USA
Washington DC, USA – St. Kitts & Nevis

ST.KITTS & NEVIS

INVESTMENT AND BUSINESS GUIDE

VOLUME 1 STRATEGIC AND PRACTICAL INFORMATION

UPDATED ANNUALLY

We express our sincere gratitude to all government agencies and international organizations which provided information and other materials for this guide

2012 Edition Updated Reprint International Business Publications, USA
ISBN

For customer service and information, please contact:

in the USA: **International Business Publications, USA**
P.O.Box 15343, Washington, DC 20003
Phone: (202) 546-2103, Fax: (202) 546-3275.
E-mail: rusric@erols.com

Printed in the USA

SAINT KITTS

AND NEVIS

INVESTMENT AND BUSINESS GUIDE

VOLUME 1

STRATEGIC AND PRACTICAL INFORMATION

TABLE OF CONTENTS

STRATEGIC AND DEVELOPMENT PROFILES

Capital (and largest city)	Basseterre 17°18′N 62°44′W17.3°N 62.733°W
Official language(s)	English
Demonym	Kittitian (or, Alternatively, Kittian), Nevisian
Government	Parliamentary democracy and Federal constitutional monarchy
- Monarch	Elizabeth II
- Governor-General	Sir Cuthbert Sebastian
- Prime Minister	Dr. Denzil Douglas
	Independence
- from the United Kingdom	19 September 1983
	Area
- Total	261 km^2 (207th) 104 sq mi
- Water (%)	negligible
	Population
- July 2005 estimate	51,300 (209th)
- Density	164/km^2 (64th) 424/sq mi
GDP (PPP)	2010 estimate
- Total	$723 million[1]
- Per capita	$13,124[1]
GDP (nominal)	2009 estimate
- Total	$557 million[1]
- Per capita	$10,315[1]
HDI (2007)	▼0.838 (high) (62nd)
Currency	East Caribbean dollar (XCD)
Time zone	(UTC-4)
Drives on the	left
ISO 3166 code	KN
Internet TLD	.kn
Calling code	+1-869

SAINT KITTS AND NEVIS PROFILE

The **Federation of Saint Kitts and Nevis** also known as the **Federation of Saint Christopher and Nevis**),[2] located in the Leeward Islands, is a federal two-island nation in the West Indies. It is the smallest sovereign state in the Americas, in both area and population.

The capital city and headquarters of government for the federated state is Basseterre on the larger island of Saint Kitts. The smaller state of Nevis lies about 2 miles (3 km) southeast of Saint Kitts, across a shallow channel called "The Narrows".

Historically, the British dependency of Anguilla was also a part of this union, which was then known collectively as Saint Christopher-Nevis-Anguilla. Saint Kitts and Nevis are geographically part of the Leeward Islands. To the north-northwest lie the islands of Sint Eustatius, Saba, Saint Barthélemy, Saint-Martin/Sint Maarten and Anguilla. To the east and northeast are Antigua and Barbuda, and to the southeast is the small uninhabited island of Redonda, and the island of Montserrat, which currently has an active volcano (see Soufrière Hills).

Saint Kitts and Nevis were among the first islands in the Caribbean to be settled by Europeans. Saint Kitts was home to the first English and French colonies in the Caribbean.

GEOGRAPHY

Location: Caribbean, islands in the Caribbean Sea, about one-third of the way from Puerto Rico to Trinidad and Tobago
Geographic coordinates: 17 20 N, 62 45 W
Map references: Central America and the Caribbean

Area:
total: 269 sq km
land: 269 sq km
water: 0 sq km

Area—comparative: 1.5 times the size of Washington, DC
Land boundaries: 0 km
Coastline: 135 km

Maritime claims:
continental shelf: 200 nm or to the edge of the continental margin
territorial sea: 12 nm
contiguous zone: 24 nm
exclusive economic zone: 200 nm

Climate: subtropical tempered by constant sea breezes; little seasonal temperature variation; rainy season (May to November)

Terrain: volcanic with mountainous interiors

Elevation extremes:
lowest point: Caribbean Sea 0 m
highest point: Mount Liamuiga 1,156 m

Natural resources: NEGL

Land use:
arable land: 22%
permanent crops: 17%
permanent pastures: 3%
forests and woodland: 17%
other: 41%

Natural hazards: hurricanes (July to October)

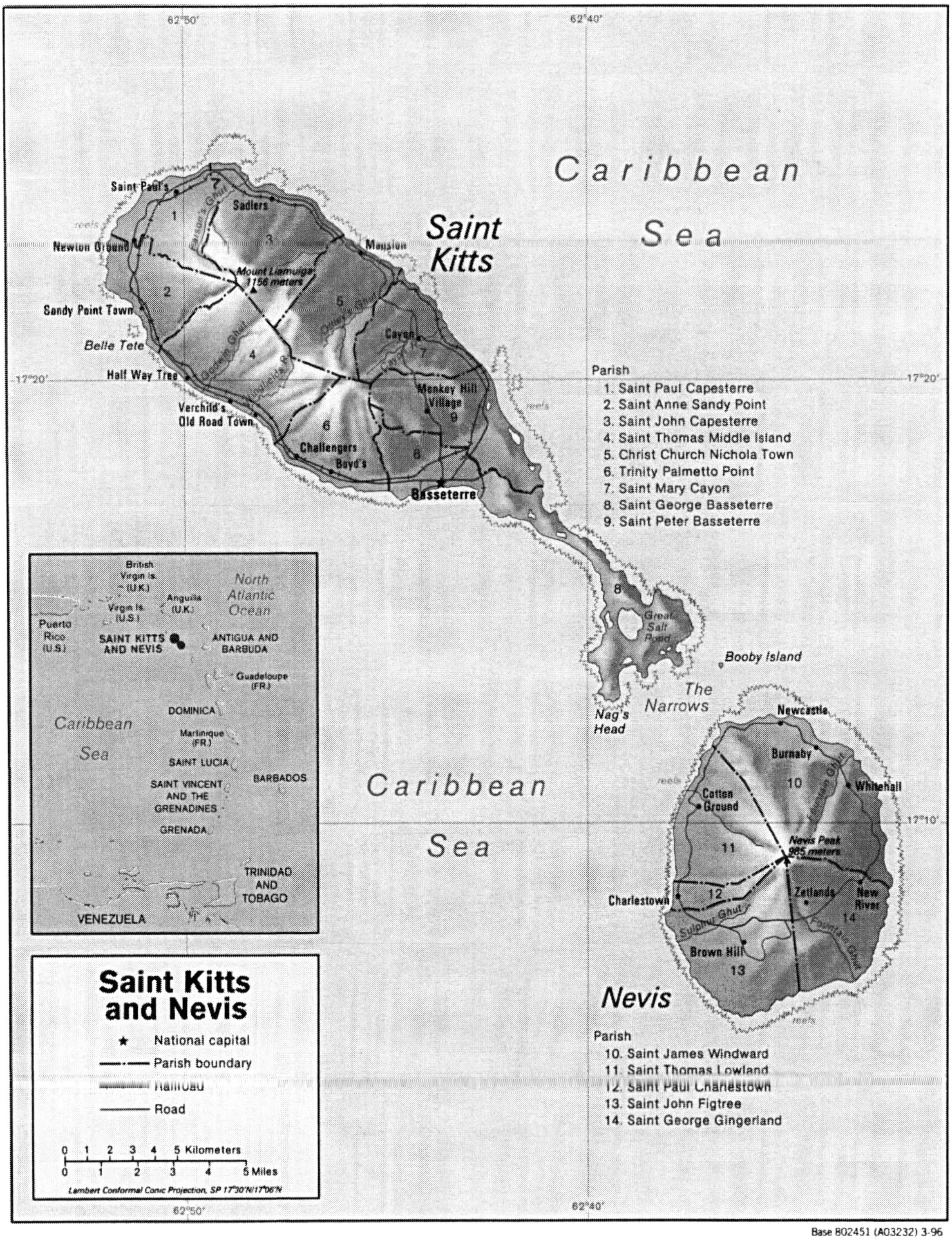
Caribbean Sea
Saint Kitts
Saint Paul's
Sadlers
Newton Ground
Mansion
Mount Liamuiga 1156 meters
Sandy Point Town
Belle Tete
Cayon
Half Way Tree
Monkey Hill Village
Verchild's
Old Road Town
Challengers
Boyd's
Basseterre
Parish
1. Saint Paul Capesterre
2. Saint Anne Sandy Point
3. Saint John Capesterre
4. Saint Thomas Middle Island
5. Christ Church Nichola Town
6. Trinity Palmetto Point
7. Saint Mary Cayon
8. Saint George Basseterre
9. Saint Peter Basseterre
Great Salt Pond
Booby Island
The Narrows
Nag's Head
Newcastle
Burnaby
Whitehall
Cotton Ground
Nevis Peak 985 meters
Charlestown
Zetlands
New River
Brown Hill
Nevis
Parish
10. Saint James Windward
11. Saint Thomas Lowland
12. Saint Paul Charlestown
13. Saint John Figtree
14. Saint George Gingerland
British Virgin Is. (U.K.)
Virgin Is. (U.S.)
Anguilla (U.K.)
North Atlantic Ocean
Puerto Rico (U.S.)
SAINT KITTS AND NEVIS
ANTIGUA AND BARBUDA
Guadeloupe (FR.)
DOMINICA
Martinique (FR.)
SAINT LUCIA
BARBADOS
SAINT VINCENT AND THE GRENADINES
GRENADA
TRINIDAD AND TOBAGO
VENEZUELA
Saint Kitts and Nevis
National capital
Parish boundary
Railroad
Road
Kilometers
Miles
Lambert Conformal Conic Projection, SP 17°30'N/17°06'N
Base 802451 (A03232) 3-96

Environment—international agreements:
party to: Biodiversity, Climate Change, Desertification, Endangered Species, Hazardous Wastes, Law of the Sea, Ozone Layer Protection, Whaling
signed, but not ratified: none of the selected agreements

PEOPLE

Population: 42,838

Age structure:
0-14 years: 33% (male 7,178; female 6,826)
15-64 years: 61% (male 13,226; female 13,083)
65 years and over: 6% (male 1,020; female 1,505)

Population growth rate: 1.34%
Birth rate: 22.6 births/1,000 population
Death rate: 8.15 deaths/1,000 population
Net migration rate: -1.05 migrant(s)/1,000 population

Sex ratio:
at birth: 1.06 male(s)/female
under 15 years: 1.05 male(s)/female
15-64 years: 1.01 male(s)/female
65 years and over: 0.68 male(s)/female
total population: 1 male(s)/female

Infant mortality rate: 17.39 deaths/1,000 live births

Life expectancy at birth:
total population: 67.94 years
male: 64.87 years
female: 71.21 years

Total fertility rate: 2.42 children born/woman

Nationality:
noun: Kittitian(s), Nevisian(s)
adjective: Kittitian, Nevisian

Ethnic groups: black
Religions: Anglican, other Protestant sects, Roman Catholic
Languages: English

Literacy:
definition: age 15 and over has ever attended school
total population: 97%
male: 97% *female:* 98%

GOVERNMENT

Country name:
conventional long form: Federation of Saint Kitts and Nevis

conventional short form: Saint Kitts and Nevis
former: Federation of Saint Christopher and Nevis

Data code: SC
Government type: constitutional monarchy
Capital: Basseterre

Administrative divisions: 14 parishes; Christ Church Nichola Town, Saint Anne Sandy Point, Saint George Basseterre, Saint George Gingerland, Saint James Windward, Saint John Capisterre, Saint John Figtree, Saint Mary Cayon, Saint Paul Capisterre, Saint Paul Charlestown, Saint Peter Basseterre, Saint Thomas Lowland, Saint Thomas Middle Island, Trinity Palmetto Point

Independence: 19 September 1983 (from UK)
National holiday: Independence Day, 19 September (1983)
Constitution: 19 September 1983
Legal system: based on English common law
Suffrage: 18 years of age; universal

Executive branch:

chief of state: Queen ELIZABETH II (since 6 February 1952); represented by Governor General Cuthbert Montraville SEBASTIAN (since 1 January 1996)

head of government: Prime Minister Dr. Denzil DOUGLAS (since 6 July 1995); Deputy Prime Minister Sam CONDOR (since 6 July 1995)

cabinet: Cabinet appointed by the governor general in consultation with the prime minister

elections: the monarchy is hereditary; the governor general appointed by the monarch; following legislative elections, the leader of the majority party or leader of a majority coalition usually appointed prime minister by the governor general; deputy prime minister appointed by the governor general

Legislative branch:

nicameral National Assembly (14 seats, 3 appointed and 11 popularly elected from single-member constituencies; members serve five-year terms)

elections: last held on 25 January 2010 (next to be held by 2015)

election results: percent of vote by party - NA; seats by party - SKNLP 6, CCM 2, PAM 2, NRP

Judicial branch: Eastern Caribbean Supreme Court (based on Saint Lucia) (one judge of the Supreme Court resides in Saint Kitts)

Political parties and leaders: People's Action Movement or PAM [Dr. Kennedy SIMMONDS]; Saint Kitts and Nevis Labor Party or SKNLP [Dr. Denzil DOUGLAS]; Nevis Reformation Party or NRP [Joseph PARRY]; Concerned Citizens Movement or CCM [Vance AMORY]

International organization participation: ACP, C, Caricom, CDB, ECLAC, FAO, G-77, IBRD, ICFTU, ICRM, IDA, IFAD, IFC, IFRCS, ILO, IMF, Interpol, IOC, OAS, OECS, OPANAL, OPCW, UN, UNCTAD, UNESCO, UNIDO, UPU, WCL, WHO, WIPO, WTrO

Diplomatic representation in the US:
chief of mission: Ambassador Edwards ERSTEIN
chancery: 3216 New Mexico Avenue NW, Washington, DC 20016
telephone: [1] (202) 686-2636
FAX: [1] (202) 686-5740

Diplomatic representation from the US: the US does not have an embassy in Saint Kitts and Nevis; US interests are monitored by the embassy in Bridgetown (Barbados)

Flag description: divided diagonally from the lower hoist side by a broad black band bearing two white, five-pointed stars; the black band is edged in yellow; the upper triangle is green, the lower triangle is red

ECONOMY

Economy - overview:,
The economy of Saint Kitts and Nevis is heavily dependent upon tourism revenues, which has replaced sugar, the traditional mainstay of the economy until the 1970s. Following the 2005 harvest, the government closed the sugar industry after decades of losses of 3-4% of GDP annually. To compensate for employment losses, the government has embarked on a program to diversify the agricultural sector and to stimulate other sectors of the economy, such as tourism, export-oriented manufacturing, and offshore banking. More than 200,000 tourists visited the islands in 2009. Like other tourist destinations in the Caribbean, St. Kitts and Nevis is vulnerable to damage from natural disasters and shifts in tourism demand. The current government is constrained by one of the world's highest public debt burdens equivalent to roughly 185% of GDP, largely attributable to public enterprise losses.

,
GDP (purchasing power parity):,
$918 million (est.)

country comparison to the world: 202
$904.2 million (est.)
$917.8 million (est.)
note: data are in 2011 US dollars

,
GDP (official exchange rate):,
$700 million (est.)

,
GDP - real growth rate:,
1.5% (est.)

country comparison to the world: 173
-1.5% (est.)
-4.4% (est.)

,
GDP - per capita (PPP):,
$16,400 (est.)

country comparison to the world: 71
$16,500 (est.)
$17,100 (est.)
note: data are in 2011 US dollars

,
GDP - composition by sector:,
agriculture: 2.4%
industry: 22.7%
services: 74.8% (est.)

,
Labor force:,
18,170 (June 1995)

country comparison to the world: 208

,
Unemployment rate:,
4.5% (1997)

country comparison to the world: 41

,
Population below poverty line:,
NA%

,
Household income or consumption by percentage share:,
lowest 10%: NA%
highest 10%: NA%

,
Investment (gross fixed):,
39% of GDP (est.)

country comparison to the world: 13

,
Budget:,
revenues: $222.2 million
expenditures: $222.2 million (est.)

,
Taxes and other revenues:,
31.7% of GDP (est.)

country comparison to the world: 80

,
Budget surplus (+) or deficit (-):,
0% of GDP (est.)

country comparison to the world: 42

,
Public debt:,
185% of GDP (est.)

country comparison to the world: 3

,
Inflation rate (consumer prices):,
4.6% (est.)

country comparison to the world: 110
0.5% (est.)

,
Central bank discount rate:,
6.5% (31 December 2009)

country comparison to the world: 60
6.5% (31 December 2008)

,
Commercial bank prime lending rate:,

9.1% (31 December 2011 est.)

country comparison to the world: 119
8.625% (31 December 2010 est.)

,

Stock of narrow money:,
$128.4 million (31 December 2011 est.)

country comparison to the world: 184
$113.8 million (31 December 2010 est.)

,

Stock of broad money:,
$879.1 million (31 December 2010 est.)

country comparison to the world: 171
$823.8 million (31 December 2009 est.)

,

Stock of domestic credit:,
$777.8 million (31 December 2011 est.)

country comparison to the world: 162
$703.7 million (31 December 2010 est.)

,

Market value of publicly traded shares:,
$623.9 million (31 December 2010)

country comparison to the world: 108
$648 million (31 December 2009)
$595.2 million (31 December 2008)

,

Agriculture - products:,
sugarcane, rice, yams, vegetables, bananas; fish

,

Industries:,
tourism, cotton, salt, copra, clothing, footwear, beverages

,

Industrial production growth rate:,
NA%

,

Electricity - production:,
130 million kWh (est.)

country comparison to the world: 188

,

Electricity - consumption:,
120.9 million kWh (est.)

country comparison to the world: 191

,

Electricity - exports:,
0 kWh (est.)

,

Electricity - imports:,
0 kWh (est.)

,

Oil - production:,
0 bbl/day (est.)

country comparison to the world: 129

,

Oil - consumption:,
2,000 bbl/day (est.)

country comparison to the world: 191

,
Oil - exports:,
0 bbl/day (est.)

country comparison to the world: 206

,
Oil - imports:,
1,699 bbl/day (est.)

country comparison to the world: 184

,
Natural gas - production:,
0 cu m (est.)

country comparison to the world: 119

,
Natural gas - consumption:,
0 cu m (est.)

country comparison to the world: 124

,
Natural gas - exports:,
0 cu m (est.)

country comparison to the world: 172

,
Natural gas - imports:,
0 cu m (est.)

country comparison to the world: 122

,
Natural gas - proved reserves:,
0 cu m (1 January 2011 est.)

country comparison to the world: 185

,
Current account balance:,
-$154.4 million (est.)

country comparison to the world: 79
-$140.5 million (est.)

,
Exports:,
$63.1 million (est.)

country comparison to the world: 197
$61.7 million (est.)

,
Exports - commodities:,
machinery, food, electronics, beverages, tobacco

,
Exports - partners:,
US 56.5%, Canada 9.2%, Azerbaijan 5% (2010)

,
Imports:,
$315.7 million (est.)

country comparison to the world: 194

$292.7 million (est.)

,
Imports - commodities:,
machinery, manufactures, food, fuels

,
Imports - partners:,
US 39.5%, Trinidad and Tobago 17%, Poland 4.7%, Barbados 4% (2010)

,
Reserves of foreign exchange and gold:,
$100 million (31 December 2011 est.)

country comparison to the world: 173
$168.9 million (31 December 2010 est.)

,
Debt - external:,
$211.3 million (31 December 2011 est.)

country comparison to the world: 179
$215.8 million (31 December 2010 est.)

,
Exchange rates:,
East Caribbean dollars (XCD) per US dollar -
2.7 (est.)
2.7 (est.)
2.7 (2009)

COMMUNICATIONS

Telephones - main lines in use: 20,600 (2010)
country comparison to the world: 192

Telephones - mobile cellular: 84,600
country comparison to the world: 192

Telephone system:

general assessment: good interisland and international connections
domestic: interisland links via Eastern Caribbean Fiber Optic cable; construction of enhanced wireless infrastructure launched in November 2004; fixed-line teledensity about 40 per 100 persons; mobile-cellular teledensity is roughly 160 per 100 persons
international: country code - 1-869; connected internationally by the East Caribbean Fiber Optic System (ECFS) and Southern Caribbean fiber optic system (SCF) submarine cables
Broadcast media:

the government operates a national television network that broadcasts on 2 channels; cable subscription services provide access to local and international channels; the government operates a national radio network; a mix of government-owned and privately-owned broadcasters operate roughly 15 radio stations (2007)

Internet country code: .kn
Internet hosts: 51
country comparison to the world: 210

Internet users:17,000
country comparison to the world: 197

TRANSPORTATION

Railways: *total:* 58 km
narrow gauge: 58 km 0.762-m gauge on Saint Kitts to serve sugarcane plantations
Highways: *total:* 320 km *paved:* 136 km *unpaved:* 184 km
Ports and harbors: Basseterre, Charlestown
Merchant marine: none
Airports: 2
Airports—with paved runways:
total: 2 *1,524 to 2,437 m:* 1 *914 to 1,523 m:* 1

MILITARY

Military branches: Royal Saint Kitts and Nevis Defense Force, Royal Saint Kitts and Nevis Police Force, Coast Guard

TRANSNATIONAL ISSUES

Disputes—international: none
Illicit drugs: transshipment points for South American drugs destined for the US

STRATEGIC INFORMATION FOR CONDUCTING BUSINESS

Official Name: Federation of St. Kitts and Nevis

PROFILE

Geography
Area: St. Kitts 168 sq. km. (65 sq. mi.); Nevis 93 sq. km. (36 sq. mi.).
Cities: *Capital*--Basseterre (pop. about 15,000).
Terrain: Generally mountainous; highest elevations are 1,156 m. (3,792 ft.) at Mt. Liamuiga on St. Kitts and 985 m; (3,232 ft.) at Nevis peak on Nevis.
Climate: Tropical.

People
Nationality: *Noun and adjective*--Kittitian(s), Nevisian(s).
Population (2007): 39,129.
Annual population growth rate (2007): 1%.
Ethnic groups: Predominantly of African origin; some of British, Portuguese, and Lebanese descent.
Religions: Principally Anglican, with Evangelical Protestant and Roman Catholic minorities.
Languages: English (official).
Education (2005): *Adult literacy*--97.8%.
Health (2007): *Infant mortality rate*--14.5/1,000. *Life expectancy*--men 68 years; women 72 years.
Unemployment (2006): 5.1%.

Government
Type: Parliamentary democracy; independent sovereign state within the Commonwealth.
Constitution: 1983.
Independence: September 19, 1983.
Branches: *Executive*--governor general (representing Queen Elizabeth II, head of state), prime minister (head of government), cabinet. *Legislative*--bicameral Parliament. *Judicial*--magistrate's courts, Eastern Caribbean Supreme Court (High Court and Court of Appeals), final appeal to Privy Council in London.
Administrative subdivisions: 14 parishes.
Political parties: St. Kitts and Nevis Labour Party (ruling), People's Action Movement (PAM), Concerned Citizens Movement (a Nevis-based party), and Nevis Reformation Party.
Suffrage: Universal at 18.

Economy
GDP (2007): $477.4 million.
GDP growth rate (2006): 5.8%.
Per capita GDP (2006): $8,546.
Inflation (2006): 5.25%.
Natural resources: Negligible.
Agriculture: Rice, yams, bananas, fish, cotton, peanuts, vegetables.
Industry: Financial and business services, tourism, construction, clothing, footwear, beverages, and tobacco.
Trade (2006): *Exports*--$31 million (merchandise) and $139 million (commercial services). *Major markets*--United States (91.9%), EU (3.0%), Trinidad and Tobago (2%), Netherlands Antilles (0.8%), St. Vincent and the Grenadines (0.3%). *Imports*--$210 million (merchandise) and $87

million (commercial services). *Major suppliers*--United States (57.9%), Trinidad and Tobago (14.1%), European Union (9.3%), Japan (3.8%), and Barbados (2.8%).
Official exchange rate: EC$2.70 = U.S. $1.

HISTORY

At the time of European discovery, Carib Indians inhabited the islands of St. Kitts and Nevis. Christopher Columbus landed on the larger island in 1493 on his second voyage and named it after St. Christopher, his patron saint. Columbus also discovered Nevis on his second voyage, reportedly calling it Nevis because of its resemblance to a snowcapped mountain (in Spanish, "nuestra senora de las nieves" or our lady of the snows). European settlement did not officially begin until 1623-24, when first English, then French settlers arrived on St. Christopher's Island, whose name the English shortened to St. Kitts Island. As the first English colony in the Caribbean, St. Kitts served as a base for further colonization in the region.

The English and French held St. Kitts jointly from 1628 to 1713. During the 17th century, intermittent warfare between French and English settlers ravaged the island's economy. Meanwhile Nevis, settled by English settlers in 1628, grew prosperous under English rule. St. Kitts was ceded to Great Britain by the Treaty of Utrecht in 1713. The French seized both St. Kitts and Nevis in 1782. The Treaty of Paris in 1783 definitively awarded both islands to Britain. They were part of the colony of the Leeward Islands from 1871-1956, and of the West Indies Federation from 1958-62. In 1967, together with Anguilla, they became a self-governing state in association with Great Britain; Anguilla seceded late that year and remains a British dependency. The Federation of St. Kitts and Nevis attained full independence on September 19, 1983.

GOVERNMENT AND POLITICAL CONDITIONS

As head of state, Queen Elizabeth II is represented in St. Kitts and Nevis by a governor general, who acts on the advice of the prime minister and the cabinet. The prime minister is the leader of the majority party of the House of Representatives, and the cabinet conducts affairs of state. St. Kitts and Nevis has a bicameral legislature: An 11-member Senate appointed by the governor general (mainly on the advice of the prime minister and the leader of the opposition); and an 11-member popularly elected House of Representatives which has eight St. Kitts seats and three Nevis seats. The prime minister and the cabinet are responsible to the Parliament.

St. Kitts and Nevis has enjoyed a long history of free and fair elections, although the outcome of elections in 1993 was strongly protested by the opposition and the Eastern Caribbean Regional Security System (RSS) was briefly deployed to restore order. The elections in 1995 were contested by the two major parties, the ruling People's Action Movement (PAM) and the St. Kitts and Nevis Labour Party. Labour won seven of the 11 seats, with Dr. Denzil Douglas becoming prime minister. In the 2010 elections, Denzil Douglas and the Labour Party were returned to power, winning six of the eight seats allotted to St. Kitts in the Parliament. The Nevis-based Concerned Citizens Movement (CCM) won two seats, the Nevis Reformation Party (NRP) won one seat, and the PAM party won two seats. The next elections are constitutionally due by November 2015.

The constitution gives Nevis considerable autonomy. Nevis has an island assembly, a premier, and a deputy governor general. Under certain specified conditions, it may secede from the federation. In accordance with its rights under the Constitution, in 1996 the Nevis Island Administration under the Concerned Citizens' Movement (CCM) of Premier Vance Amory initiated steps towards secession from the Federation, the most recent being a referendum in 1998 that failed to secure the required two-thirds majority for secession. Constitutional safeguards include freedom of speech, press, worship, movement, and association. Like its neighbors in the English-speaking Caribbean, St. Kitts and Nevis has an excellent human rights record. Its judicial system is modeled on British practice and procedure and its jurisprudence on English common law. In the July 10, 2006 Nevis elections for the Nevis Island Administration, the NRP won three of the five seats; the CCM won two. The NRP's Joseph Parry assumed the premiership of Nevis. While opposing secession, the government acknowledged the constitutional rights of Nevisians to determine their future independence. Premier Parry won reelection in the July 2011 poll. The opposition has challenged the results in court and a resolution is pending.

Principal Government Officials
Chief of State--Queen Elizabeth II
Governor General--Cuthbert M. Sebastian
Prime Minister and Minister of Finance, Sustainable Development, Information and Technology, Tourism, Culture and Sports--Denzil L. Douglas
Minister of Foreign Affairs and Education--Sam Condor
Ambassador to the United States and Permanent Representative to the OAS--Jacinth L. Henry-Martin
Permanent Representative to the UN--Delano Bart
Principal Nevis Island Government Official, Premier--Joseph Parry

The embassy of St. Kitts and Nevis is located at 3216 New Mexico Ave., NW, Washington, DC 20016 (tel. 202-686-2636).

ECONOMY

St. Kitts and Nevis was the last sugar monoculture in the Eastern Caribbean until the government decided to close the sugar industry in 2005, after decades of losses at the state-run sugar company. To compensate for the loss of the sugar industry, the Government of St. Kitts and Nevis has begun exploring alternative energy uses for sugar cane. The United States and Brazil have agreed to develop biofuels programs in the region.

The economy of St. Kitts and Nevis experienced strong growth for most of the 1990s, but hurricanes in 1998 and 1999 and the September 11, 2001 terrorist attacks hurt the tourism-dependent economy. Economic growth picked up in 2004, with a real GDP growth rate of 6.4%, followed by 4.1% growth in 2005. The GDP growth rate rose to 5.8% in 2006, mostly as a result of diversification into tourism and construction related to the Cricket World Cup. Tourism has shown the greatest growth and is now a major foreign exchange earner for St. Kitts and Nevis, as evidenced by an 83% increase in foreign direct investment in a range of tourism-related projects. Recent significant investment included a 648-room Marriott hotel and convention center that opened in December 2002, as well as 2007 plans for "Christophe Harbor," a U.S. investor-funded $500 million resort project. The government instituted a program of investment incentives for businesses considering the possibility of locating in St. Kitts or Nevis, encouraging domestic and foreign private investment. Government policies provide liberal tax holidays, duty-free import of equipment and materials, and subsidies for training provided to local personnel.

However, the debt of public enterprises has increased, and total public and publicly guaranteed debt reached $290,740,000 in 2006. Consumer prices have risen marginally over the past few years. The rate of inflation, as measured by the change in the CPI, rose on average by 5.3% in 2006, compared with 3.6% in 2005 and 2.3% in 2004.

St. Kitts and Nevis is a member of the Eastern Caribbean Currency Union (ECCU). The Eastern Caribbean Central Bank (ECCB) issues the Eastern Caribbean dollar (EC$) for all members of the ECCU. The ECCB also manages monetary policy, and regulates and supervises commercial banking activities in its member countries. The ECCB has kept the EC$ pegged at EC$2.7 to U.S. $1.

FOREIGN RELATIONS

St. Kitts and Nevis maintains diplomatic relations with the United States, Canada, the United Kingdom, France, Russia, Taiwan, Cuba, and South Korea, as well as with many Latin American countries and neighboring Eastern Caribbean states. It is a member of the Commonwealth, the United Nations, the World Bank and the International Monetary Fund, the Organization of American States, the Organization of Eastern Caribbean States, the Eastern Caribbean Regional Security System (RSS), and the Caribbean Community and Common Market (CARICOM). The Eastern Caribbean Central Bank is headquartered in St. Kitts. St. Kitts and Nevis has chosen to recognize Taiwan instead of the People's Republic of China.

U.S.-ST. KITTS AND NEVIS RELATIONS

Since St. Kitts and Nevis attained full independence in 1983, relations with the United States have been friendly. The United States seeks to help St. Kitts and Nevis develop economically and to help strengthen its moderate, democratic, parliamentary form of government. St. Kitts and Nevis is a beneficiary of the U.S. Caribbean Basin Initiative. U.S. assistance is primarily channeled through multilateral agencies such as the World Bank and the Caribbean Development Bank (CDB), as well as the U.S. Agency for International Development (USAID) office in Bridgetown, Barbados. In addition, St. Kitts and Nevis benefits from U.S. military exercises and humanitarian civic action construction projects.

St. Kitts and Nevis is strategically placed in the Leeward Islands, near maritime transport lanes of major importance to the United States. St. Kitts and Nevis' location close to Puerto Rico and the U.S. Virgin Islands makes the two-island federation attractive to narcotics traffickers. To counter this threat, the Government of St. Kitts and Nevis cooperates with the United States in the fight against illegal narcotics. In 1995, the government signed a maritime law enforcement treaty with the United States, later amended with an overflight/order-to-land amendment in 1996. St. Kitts and Nevis also signed an updated extradition treaty with the United States in 1996, and a mutual legal assistance treaty in 1997.

St. Kitts and Nevis is a popular American tourist destination. In the aftermath of September 11, 2001, tourism declined, but the islands have seen growing numbers of visitors in recent years. Fewer than 1,000 U.S. citizens reside on the island, although students and staff of Ross University Veterinary School and the Medical University of the Americas (Nevis) constitute a significant population of U.S. citizens.

The United States maintains no official presence in St. Kitts and Nevis. The Ambassador and Embassy officers are resident in Barbados and frequently travel to St. Kitts and Nevis. A U.S. consular agent residing in nearby Antigua, however, assists U.S. citizens in St. Kitts and Nevis.

Principal U.S. Embassy Officials (resident in Barbados unless otherwise noted)
Ambassador--vacant
Charge d'Affaires for the Eastern Caribbean--Christopher J. Sandrolini
Political/Economic Chief--Brian E. Greaney
Consul General--Eugene P. Sweeney
Commercial Affairs--Gregory A. Floyd
Public Affairs Officer--Rebecca Ross
Peace Corps Country Director--Kevin Carley (resident in St. Lucia)

The **U.S. Embassy** in Barbados is located in the Wildey Business Park, Wildey, St. Michael (tel: 246-227-4000; fax: 246-429-5246).

TRAVEL AND BUSINESS INFORMATION

Travel Alerts, Travel Warnings, Trip Registration
The U.S. Department of State's Consular Information Program advises Americans traveling and residing abroad through Country Specific Information, Travel Alerts, and Travel Warnings. **Country Specific Information** exists for all countries and includes information on entry and exit requirements, currency regulations, health conditions, safety and security, crime, political disturbances, and the addresses of the U.S. embassies and consulates abroad. **Travel Alerts** are issued to disseminate information quickly about terrorist threats and other relatively short-term conditions overseas that pose significant risks to the security of American travelers. **Travel Warnings** are issued when the State Department recommends that Americans avoid travel to a certain country because the situation is dangerous or unstable.

For the latest security information, Americans living and traveling abroad should regularly monitor the Department's Bureau of Consular Affairs Internet web site at http://travel.state.gov, where current Worldwide Caution, Travel Alerts, and Travel Warnings can be found. The travel.state.gov website also includes information about passports, tips for planning a safe trip abroad and more. More travel-related information also is available at http://www.usa.gov/Citizen/Topics/Travel/International.shtml.

INFORMATION ON THE ACCREDITATION PROCESS IN ST. KITTS AND NEVIS

The Accreditation Process in St. Kitts and Nevis is guided by two Acts passed in the National Assembly, viz:

1. The Saint Christopher and Nevis Accreditation of Institutions Act, 1999 (No. 21 of 1999)

2. The Saint Christopher and Nevis Accreditation of Institutions (Amendment) Act, 2001 (No.9 of 2001)

Under the above Acts, an Accreditation Board has been established. All tertiary institutions wishing to operate in St. Kitts and Nevis are required by law to apply to the Accreditation Board. Only those institutions that are registered with and accredited by the Accreditation Board can legally claim to be accredited by the Government of St. Kitts and Nevis.

LIST OF ACCREDITED INSTITUTIONS

The Accreditation Board recognizes the following five (5) institutions in St. Kitts and Nevis as being accredited by the Government of St. Kitts and Nevis:

The Clarence Fitzroy Bryant College. This is the National College.

Ross University School of Veterinary Medicine. Fully accredited.

Berne University International Graduate School. Fully accredited, renewable. A review will be held later this year.

International University of Health Sciences (IUHS). Currently has provisional accreditation; a review for full accreditation will be held later this year.

Windsor University School of Medicine. Currently has provisional accreditation; a review for full accreditation will be held later this year.

No other tertiary level institution that claims to be operating in St. Kitts and Nevis is accredited by the Government of St. Kitts and Nevis, as at 3rd May, 2002.

ST CHRISTOPHER AND NEVIS ACCREDITATION BOARD

Application For Accreditation

Guidelines

The Accreditation Process is shown in Figure 1.

Institutions that are applying for accreditation for the first time must submit information and documents required under Section A: **Basic Information to be Provided;** and Section B: **Matters to be Considered by the Board** to be submitted in triplicate.

Section C: Institutional Self-Study and Section D: Site visit are optional for the first application. However, they will be required for follow-up review exercises.

Fees

1. In view of the international concerns regarding money laundering, all institutions applying for accreditation will be subjected to a due diligence check on its principal officers and/or Board Members. Each institution will be required to pay US$1000.00 to cover the costs of the due diligence check, for U S addresses, and US$1500.00 for addresses outside of the United States.

2. Initial applications for accreditation: **US$2000.00** to be submitted along with the application.

3. Review and site visit.

All expenses for the site visit will be met by the institution. An appropriate budget will be prepared by the Board and submitted to the institution.

Cheques should be made payable to: **Accountant General for Accreditation Board** and sent to the Chairman, Accreditation Board at the address below:

c/o Ministry of Education
Planning Division
Lockhart Street
P O Box 333
BASSETERRE
St Kitts

Table 1 Suggested Chapter Divisions of a Self-evaluation Report.

Introduction Executing the self-evaluation Organization structure of institution and course **1. Philosophy of education and objectives** 1.1 Philosophy of education 1.2 Objectives of the course	**7. The Graduates:** 7.1 Where do graduates end up? 7.2 Unemployment among graduates 7.3 Contact with graduates **8. The Staff** 8.1 Times-spent on teaching

1.3 Translation of objectives in the program

2. The Program
2.1 Evaluation of the program
2.2 Description of the course
2.3 Instruction formats
2.4 Testing

3. Final paper/Final project and practical training
3.1 Place of final paper/final project
3.2 Place of practical training during the course

4. Students
4.1 Intake
4.2 Output
4.3 Average duration of the course

5. Study
5.1 Study load
5.2 Student counselling and educational guidance
5.3 Factors obstructing study

6. Facilities/infrastructure
6.1 Education accommodation
6.2 Educational tools

8.2 Teacher training opportunties
8.3 Personnel management

9. Internal quality assurance
9.1 Boards involved
9.2 Monitoring system
9.3 Evaluation system
9.4 Involvement of students
9.5 Education innovation

10. International contacts

11. Strong/weak-analysis
11.1 Summary of strong points: points the institution is proud of
11.2 Summary of weak points - points which the institution consider weak and need improvement; also indicate what the institution plans to do about it.

APPENDIX

REVIEW AND SITE VISIT

Adapted from document: ***"Eastern Caribbean States: Establishment of a National Accreditation Body. Analyses and Recommendations".*** Prepared for the CARICOM Secretariat by Marie Levens. December 1999.

Institutions applying for accreditation will be subjected to a site visit by a Review Committee, either as part of the initial application or as part of a follow-up review. The review committee may include at least one (1) person from an external (regional or international) accredited institution.

Prior to a site visit, the institutional self-study should be made available to the Accreditation Board. The review and site visit will seek answers to questions under the following headings:

1. Philosophy of Education and Objectives
2. . The Programme
3. . Final Papers, Final Project, practical training
4. . The student and his/her education
5. . Study load and counseling
6. . Facilities
7. . The Graduates
8. . The Staff
9. . Internal Quality Assurance

The following phases will be evident in the work of the review committee involved in a site visit.

1. Preparation for the meeting to be held before the site visit(s).
(a) Studying the self-evaluation; (b) Evaluating final papers).

2. The meeting of the Review Committee.

3. The visit of the Review Committee (introduction to the board, program of visit - interviews with board, staff, coordinators, student panel, consultations, formulating the oral and written reports).

Note: The programme for the visit is finalized in consultation with the Administration of the Institution.

4. The Review Report

Departmental Report for the Accreditation Board
(Optional) A confidential management letter for the board of the institution

Issues relating to the information that should be made public would be addressed.

Extract from ***The Saint Christopher and Nevis Accreditation of Institutions Act. 1999***

INSTITUTIONS ELIGIBLE FOR ACCREDITATION

7. (1) Any institution that is capable of offering or intends to offer tertiary education and such institution wishes to be accredited by the Government of Saint Christopher and` Nevis and offer courses on the basis of that accreditation shall apply to the Board in the prescribed form.

(2) Any institution which is accredited by a recognized accreditation body may, at its option, seek local accreditation except that if it does not opt for local accreditation then it shall enter into an agreement with the Government.

(3) Any institution which is not accredited anywhere and does not wish to be accredited by the Government shall operate in accordance with existing laws relating to educational institutions.

(4) Any tertiary institution that entered into an agreement with the Government of Saint Christopher and Nevis on the basis of which such institution was accredited by the Government of Saint Christopher and Nevis to offer certain degrees or courses prior to the coming into force of this Act shall be deemed to have been accredited under the provisions of this Act, except that such institution shall continue to comply with the terms of its agreement, this Act and the regulations made thereunder for the purpose of maintaining the required academic standards.

(5) For the purposes of this section "tertiary education" means education offered by a college or university following secondary education.

8. (1) Any institution which offers degree programmes or courses shall, before submitting its application for accreditation to the Board, take into account the provisions of subsection (2) of this section when describing any programme the institution offers or intends to offer.

(2) The institution shall, in pursuance of the provisions of subsection (1) of this section, when describing any programme or courses give the following information:-

(a) the degree title and areas of study available;

(b) type or level of previous education required for admission to the programme;

(c) Academic Credit policy for prior learning or with experience;

(d) Academic Credit policy regarding standardized achievement tests;

(e) the number of semesters, terms or quarter hours required to receive a degree;

(f) the minimum on-campus time for study in order to complete the programme

(g) type of instructions for off-campus learning;

(h) student support services provided;

(i) information materials such as programme catalogues;

(j) the grading system used to evaluate students' work while enrolled in the programme;

(k) projected enrolment;

(l) the number of degrees conferred per annum or to be conferred;

(m) commencement of academic programme;

(n) the institution's policy on admission of local, regional and international students;

(o) proposed mechanisms or available mechanism to enable continued self-improvement at the institution.

9. (1) Any application for accreditation submitted to the Board in accordance with the provisions of this Act shall be considered by the Board in accordance with the provisions of this section.

(2) For the purpose of streamlining the consideration of applications referred to in subsection (1) of this section, the Board shall appoint committees to be known as Review Committees.

(3) A Review Committee appointed under subsection (2) of this section shall be responsible for reviewing any proposal accompanying an application submitted to the Board by any institution.

(4) For the purposes of subsection (2) of this section, the Medical Board shall be the Review Committee responsible for reviewing any proposal submitted by any institution that intends to offer medical courses in Saint Christopher and Nevis in accordance with the provisions of this Act.

(5) The chairman of a Review Committee shall be a member of the Board.

(6) A Review Committee shall, in reviewing any proposal referred to it by the Board, mainly deal with the academic and professional aspects of the proposal

(7) A Review Committee shall review a proposal within a period specified by the Board and shall upon completion of the review submit a report to the Board.

(8) The Board shall, upon receipt of the report of the Review Committee and when considering the application, take into account the provisions of section 10 of this Act.

10. The Board shall, in considering an application submitted to it under the provisions of section 7 of this Act, take into account the following matters:-

(a) the mission of the institution and any specialised programme the institution intends to offer or offers;

(b) clearly defined and educationally appropriate goals and objectives of the institution or programme;

(c) conditions under which the goals and objectives are to be achieved;

(d) expected standards and how such standards are to be maintained;

(e) list of programmes or courses to be offered and policies regarding course credits;

(f) links with other accredited institutions;

(g) a student registry, and the admissions policy which shall be in conformity with the objectives set out in the paragraphs of this section;

(h) maintenance of student records;

(i) student counselling services and the procedure for monitoring student performance;

(j) in case of recruitment of students into a faculty:

(i) the recruitment procedures,

(ii) curriculum vitae for the staff,

(iii) the general productivity measures relating to staff performance;

(k) examination regulations and procedures with particular emphasis on:

(i) how written exams are set, marked, and how student appeals are dealt with,

(ii) how oral exams such as research proposals are conducted,

(iii) the grading systems as a basis of evaluating students' performance;

(l) procedure for selecting approved external examiners and how such examiners function;

(m) library and research facilities with particular emphasis on:

(i) the adequacy of such facilities, and

(ii) their linkages with other libraries in Universities and other tertiary institutions in the Caribbean and outside the Caribbean;

(n) The proposed local physical location of the campus with particular emphasis on:

(i) projections regarding student enrolment and staff size,

(ii) provisions for classrooms, laboratories (types, equipment) offices, student residency;

(o) proposals relating to the financing and management of the institution with particular emphasis on:

(i) the charter of the institution,

(ii) the governing body of the institution, and

(iii) costs and efficiency of the institution;

(p) benefits which are to accrue to the local economy.

THE SAINT CHRISTOPHER AND NEVIS ACCREDITATION OF INSTITUTIONS (AMENDMENT)ACT, 2001

SAINT CHRISTOPHER AND NEVIS No. 9 of 2001

AN ACT to amend the Saint Christopher and Nevis Accreditation Act No. 21 of 1999.

BE IT ENACTED by the Queen's most Excellency Majesty by an with the advice and consent of the National Assembly of Saint Christopher and Nevis, and by the authority of the same as follows:

1. This Act may be cited as the Saint Christopher and Nevis Accreditation of Institutions (Amendment) Act, 2001.

2. In this Act, unless the context otherwise requires, "Act" means the Saint Christopher and Nevis Accreditation of Institutions Act, 1999, herein referred to as the principal Act.

3. The principal Act is amended

(a) In section 6(1) by repealing and substituting for paragraph (a) thereof the following:

"(a) Full accreditation reviewable after every five years";

(b) In section 7 by repealing and substitution for subsection (3) thereof the following:

"(3) No institution shall operate in Saint Christopher and Nevis unless it is accredited by the Accreditation Board in accordance with the provisions of this Act";

(c) In section 8 by inserting immediate after paragraph (b) paragraph (c) as follows:

"(c) self-study programme and supporting documentation"; and by renumbering the other subparagraphs

TRADE AND INVESTMENT INCENTIVES

TRADE AGREEMENTS

Saint Kitts and Nevis is a beneficiary of the Caribbean Basin Initiative, CARIBCAN, and Lome agreements qualifying it for trade concessions with the United States, Canada and the European Union.

Saint Kitts and Nevis was admitted to the General Agreement on Trade and Tariffs, (GATT) in 1994 as its 199'" member. It subsequently became a member of the new World Trade Organization (WTO), which became effective from February 1995.

INDUSTRIAL SITES

There are three fully developed industrial sites where production facilities can be constructed to specification and leased at nominal rates. The provision for factory space is forecasted to increase annually by 15,000 square feet in Saint Kitts and 5,000 square feet in Nevis. They are managed and serviced on behalf of the Government by the Saint kitts-Nevis Development Bank.

INVESTMENT INCENTIVES

* **Generous tax holiday of up to fifteen years**
* **Additional tax rebates of up to five years**
* **Exemption from custom duties on material and equipment deemed necessary to establish or update an enterprise**
* **Repatriation of profits, dividends, royalties and imported capital by arrangement with the Ministry of Finance.**
* **Protection of investment through government agreement between Saint Kitts and Nevis and the United States, and;**
* **No personal income tax**

HOTEL AIDS ORDINANCE

The Hotel Aids Ordinance provides duty-free concessions (relief from customs duties and pier dues) on items for use in the construction, extension and equipping of a hotel of not less than ten bedrooms.

In addition, the Income Tax Ordinance provides special tax relief benefits for a hotel proprietor who has been granted a license under the Hotel Aids Ordinance:

... ... the gains or profits of a hotel of more than 30 bedrooms are exempt from income lax for a period of 10 years; for hotels with less than 30 bedrooms, the gains and profits are exempt from income tax for a period of 5 years.

IMPORT DUTY EXEMPTION

Companies which qualify for tax holidays are allowed to import into Saint Kitts and Nevis, duty-free all equipment, machinery, spare parts and raw materials used in production.

TAXATION

Corporate Income Tax;
Corporations are taxed on income at the rate of 40%. Many businesses, however may qualify for development and tax concessions under the Fiscal Incentives Act.

Capital gains Tax;
There is no Capital Gains Tax

Land Tax;
The following is the land tax schedule for Saint Kitts and Nevis (showing the tax rate as US Dollars per acre);

... ...All cultivated land on the Island of Saint Kitts is subject to the rate of $1.48 per acre.

... ...All uncultivated land on the Island of Saint mitts is subject to the rale of $0.37 per acre.

... ...All cultivated and uncultivated land on the Island of Nevis is subject to the rate of $.37 per acre.

HOUSE TAX

The tax is equivalent to 5% of the annual gross rental value for residencies of Saint Kitts or Nevis

NEVIS OFFSHORE BUSINESS

Nevis offer a wide range of offshore business attractions, and its financial services sector has flourished, firmly anchored on the Island's stability, financial integrity, well-planned modern legislation and the implementation of protective regulations.

Relevant legislation includes the Nevis Limited Liability Company (LLC) Ordinance (1995), the Nevis International Exempt Trust Ordinance (1994), and the Nevis Business Corporation Ordinance (1984). For detailed information on the offshore financial sector in Nevis, contact:
The Registrar,
Offshore Companies,
Springate Building,
Government Road,
Charlestown,
Nevis,
W.I,
Telephone; (869) 469-1469
Fax; (869) 469-1081

WAGE RATES

There are minimum wage laws covering domestic servants and employees in stores only. The following are average wage rates in some industries;

... ...garments; US$0.89 p/hr

... ... elecIronics; US$0.98 p/hr

... ... data entry; US$1.26 p/hr

FINANCIAL SERVICES

CENTRAL BANK

Eastern Caribbean Central Bank (ECCB);
P.O Box 89,
Basseterre,
Telephone; (869) 465-2537
Fax; (869) 465-1051

BANKS

Bank of Nevis (Charlestown)
Bank of Nova Scotia (Basseterre and Charlestown)
Barclays Bank (Basseterre and Charlestown)
Development Bank of Saint Kitts-Nevis (Basseterre and Charlestown)
Nevis Cooperative Bank (Charlestown)
Royal Bank of Canada (Basseterre)
Saint Kitts-Nevis National Bank Ltd. (Basseterre and Charlestown)

INFRASTRUCTURE

TRANSPORTATION

Railroads;
57 kilometers (35.4 miles) narrow gauge on Saint Kitts solely for sugar cane..

Highways;
300 kilometers, (186 miles) total; 126.4 kilometers (78.5 miles) paved; 125 kilometers (77.6 miles) unpaved; 50 kilometers, (31 miles) unimproved earth.

Airports;
Saints Kitts; The Robert Llewelyn Bradshaw International Airport is located about two miles from Basseterre.
Nevis; The Newcastle Airport is located about 6 miles from Charlestown

Airlines;
To Robert Llewelyn Bradshaw; American Eagle, BWIA, Crusin Air, LIAT, WinAir

To Newcastle; Air Saint Kilts/Nevis, Carib Aviation, Coastal Air, LIAT and WinAir International access to Nevis' Newcastle Airport can be made through Saint Kitts, Antigua and Saint Maarten

Flight Times;
Miami, 3-5 hours; New York,4-5 hours; San Juan, 1 hour

Air Cargo;
AmeriJet Service, Tel; (869) 465-8861
American Airlines, Tel; (869) 465-8490
Borinquen Air, Tel; (869) 465-2092
BWIA, Tel; (869)465-8444
Evelyn 's Travel, Tel; (869) 469-9333 (To Nevis)
Four,star Cargo, Tel; (869) 465-8861
Liat Air Services, Tel; (869) 465-8489
Regal Air Services, Tel; (869) 465-8861
TDC Air Cargo, Tel; (869) 465-8489

Ports;
There is a deep water port at Basseterre (Saint Kitts). Charlestown (Nevis) has a 368ft. by 26.25ft. pier with a draft of 15 feet at the head. As part of the town expansion program underway in Saint Kitts, a deep water cruise ship facility is being constructed in the heart of Basseterre, capable of accommodating the largest megaships. Work is underway on the development of a port facility at Long Point (Nevis), to handle cargo and provide berthing for mini-cruise ships.

Main Shipping Lines
To Saint Kitts; Bernuth Lines, CGM-Interlines, Crowley American Transport, Geest Lines, Harrison, Navieras, tropical Shipping.

To Nevis; Bernuth and Tropical Shipping. Other cargo for Nevis is trans-shipped mainly in Saint Kitts and Miami.

Main NVOCCs;
Antilles Freight, International Container Line.

Shipping Agents;
A & M Enterprises, Tel/Fax; (869)469-5996
Barker dc Kelly Ltd., Tel; (869) 465-2075
Delisle Walwyn & Co. Ltd., Tel; (869) 465-2631
(Crowley American Transport)
Flemming & Sons, Tel; (869) 465-2592
John Gumbs Ltd., Tel; (869) 465-2370
Nevis Express,Services., Tel; (869) 469-5051
S.I. Horsford & Co. Ltd., Tel; (869) 465-2616
I.D.C Shipping, Nevis, Tel; (869) 465-2511
Tony's Ltd., Nevis, Tel; (869) 465-5413
Tropical Container Services, Tel; (869) 4654-4149
Williams & illiams Enterprises, Tel; (869) 465-4798

COMMUNICATIONS

Newspapers
There are three newspapers. The Democrat and The Observer are published weekly, and the Labour Spokesman is published biweekly.

The Democrat, Tel; (869) 465-2091
The Observer, Charlestown, Nevis, Tel; (869) 469-5907
The Labour Spokesman, Tel; (869) 465-2229

Radio and Television
There are three AM radio stations, and 2 TV stations. Cable Television is also available.

Radio Paradise,
Tel; (869) 465-5043 (Saint Kitts)
Tel; (869) 469-1994 (Nevis)
Voice of Nevis, Nevis,
Tel; (869) 469-1616
Fax; (869) 469-5329
ZIZ Radio and Television (Saint Kitts),
Tel; (869) 465-2622
Fax; (869) 465-5624
Trinity Broadcasting of Nevis,
Tel; (869) 469-0285
Fax; (869) 469-1723

TELECOMMUNICATIONS

Saint Kitts and Nevis Telecommunications Ltd. (SKANTEL) was formed in October 1985 as a joint venture between Cable & Wireless and the Government. Following the sale of shares in 1990, and again in 1992, the respective share holdings are Cable & Wireless (65%), Government (17%) and the Public (18%)

SKANTEL provides all domestic and international telecommunications services to the islands, with digitalization using fiber optic cables. Internet services are provided by the telephone company as well. SKANTEL has approximately 13,000 customers.

Saint Kitts and Nevis BOATPHONE Ltd. Provides cellular phone service. Visitors can pre-register from the United States by calling 1-800-BOATFON from the USA, 1- 800-567-8366 from Canada, or 1 869-480-2628 from elsewhere; or they can dial '0' & 'SND' from their AMPS compatible cellphone and register with an operator upon arrival in Saint Kitts and Nevis. Saint Kitts and Nevis BOATPHONE works on the 'A' cellular system.

International Dialing Instructions;
To call Saint Kitts and Nevis from the US, dial the access code (1), plus the area code (869), plus the city codes (Basseterre 465/466; Charlestown 469), then the four digit local number.

ELECTRICITY

Electricity is supplied at 230 volts, 60 cycles. Contact;
The Electric Department,
Ministry of Communication, Works, Public Utilities and Posts,
Tel; (869) 465 2000 (Saint Kitts)
Tel; (869) 469-5521 (Nevis)

BUSINESS HOURS

COMMERCIAL

8.00am- 12.00noon; 1pm- 4.00/ 4.30pm
Monday- Friday

GOVERNMENT

8.00am- 12.00noon; 1.00pm- 4.00/ 4.30pm
Monday- Friday

NATIONAL HOLIDAYS

New Years Day- January 1
Carnival Day- January 2
Good Friday- March 28
Easter Monday- March 31
Labour Day- May 5
August Monday- August 4
Independence Day- September 19
Christmas Day- December 25
Boxing Day- December 26

POPULATION BY AGE GROUP

	1990	1991	1992	1993	1994	1995	1996	1997	1998
Age									
0-4	4,730	4,680	4,600	4,540	4,450	4,440	4,280	4,190	4,180
5-9	4,500	4,780	4,640	4,560	4,540	4,520	4,350	4,080	3,900
10-14	4,400	4,640	4,670	4,620	4,600	4,470	4,390	4,100	3,880
15-19	3,980	3,940	4,130	4,140	4,150	4,310	4,240	4,010	3,850
20-24	3,600	3,680	3,810	3,900	3,680	3,690	3,660	3,630	3,570
25-29	3,120	3,530	3,690	3,880	3,640	3,480	3,290	3,230	3,230
30-34	2,970	3,270	3,500	3,670	3,490	3,530	3,350	3,190	3,190
35-39	2,750	2,580	2,950	3,140	3,050	3,090	2,920	2,840	2,820
40-44	2,180	1,490	1,950	2,210	2,350	2,490	2,490	2,420	2,470
45-49	1,550	1,170	1,340	1,490	1,640	1,820	1,810	1,860	1,920
50-54	1,390	1,100	1,170	1,170	1,260	1,310	1,330	1,360	1,380
55-59	1,310	1,030	1,060	1,060	1,100	1,180	1,140	1,110	1,080
60-64	1,330	1,170	1,160	1,110	1,120	1,130	1,060	990	970

65-69	1,260	1,210	1,190	1,170	1,130	1,140	1,090	990	940
70-74	1,130	1,050	1,030	1,060	1,040	1,060	1,020	930	880
75-79	820	820	870	850	830	800	770	760	730
80-84	470	550	550	560	540	530	500	460	500
85+	380	310	360	390	440	540	590	590	640
Total	41,870	41,000	42,670	43,520	43,050	43,530	42,280	40,740	40,130

INFORMATION FOR GRANT OF WORK PERMIT

The requirements include the filling out of two forms:

1. An application for Work Permit.

Persons requesting the information should apply to:
The Chief Secretary
Ministry of National Security
Government Headquarters
Basseterre, St. Kitts.
I hereby apply for work permit to employ the undermentioned person. The following details are submitted in support of my application:
Name of Employer

Address

Phone Number

Nature of Business

Social Security Number

Business License Number

No. of Persons Currently Employed:

Locals		Non Locals	
Male	Female	Male	Female

Name of Person to be employed

Occupation

Duties

Period of Employment

Work Experience

Did you contact the Employment Agency of the Labour Department?

Did you advertise the position locally?
If yes, (a) Provide evidence of advertisement
(b) Indicate the # of Nationals who applied
(c) Give reason (s) for the refusal to employ any of the nationals who applied

____

Employers Signature

____

Date of Application

1. Questionnaire for use by persons seeking Employment and/or Residence

a. Surname at present and any other surname used at any time
b. Full Christian Names
c. Present Address
d. Permanent Address (if different from present address)
e. Date of Birth
f. Place of Birth
g. Nationality- Now and at Birth- date of any change and place at which such charge was recorded
h. Description: Height, build, colour of eyes, distinguishing marks
i. Schools attended with date of attendance
j. Languages spoken
k. Dates of marriage of applicant and if divorce, dates of such divorce and place where granted

l. (1) Present occupation and place of occupation
(2) Other occupations since leaving school

m. Proposed source of income while resident in the Federation
n. Particulars of income (give approximate figure per annum)
o. Qualifications
p. Dependants (please list names of children and elderly persons who depend on you for survival)
q. Name, Address, Nationality and Occupation of mother, father, sisters and brothers, wife or husband. If deceased, give date of death
r. All countries where applicant resided with dates of entering and leaving
s. Last date of entry into the Federation of St. Kitts & Nevis
t. Full passport particulars
u. Whether accompanied by or associating with any other person also visiting
v. Details of previous visits to the Federation
w. Intended place of residence whilst here and duration of visit
x. Full details of persons with whom subject will be staying or conducting business
y. Details of aircraft Flight number or method of travel to the Federation

z. Reason for desiring residence in the Federation

Signature of Applicant

Date

N.B. The following documents or Certified Photocopies shall be submitted along with the application-

a. Birth Certificate
b. Passport (pages 1-7 photocopied)
c. A Police Certificate or Affidavit (from country where applicant lived for the last six months)
d. Marriage Certificate (if applicable)
e. Divorce Decree (if applicable)
f. Military Record (if applicable)
g. Affidavit of Support
h. Evidence of own assests
i. One Passport SIZE photograph
j. Birth Certificate of Spouse
k. Birth Certificate of each unmarried child under 18 years
l. Evidence of offer of employment (if applicable)
m. Proof of having pass the HIV Test
n. VDRL
o. X-Ray of Chest

Mantoux for Tuberculosis

REQUIREMENTS FOR GRANT OF VISA

A) Fill Out Form

1. Name
2. Place of Birth
3. Date of Birth
4. Occupation
5. Passport Number
6. Date Passport Issued
7. Date Passport Expires
8. Home Address
9. Name and Address of person you will be staying with in St. Kitts/Nevis
10. Purpose of trip?

B) Three (3) Passport SIZE Photos.

C) $50 E.C. for the application.

D) Bank Statement of at least $3,000 E.C.

E) Job Letter.

CITIZENSHIP

REQUIREMENTS FOR CERTIFICATE OF CITIZENSHIP

A) Through Parents

Parents Birth Certificate
Child Birth Certificate
$120 E.C.
H I V Test
Two (2) Passport SIZE Photos
* if the child is born in England or Canada the long version of the Birth Certificate.

B) Through Grandparents

Grandparents Birth Certificate
Parents Birth Certificate
Child Birth Certificate
$120 E.C.
H I V Test
Two Passport SIZE Photos

C) Through Marriage

Form
If married before 1983 - $250 E.C.
If married after 1983 - $850 E.C.
Birth Certificate of person born in the Federation
Birth Certificate of Applicant
Marriage Certificate
Two (2) Passport SIZE Photos
* all documents should be originals or certified copies by a Justice of the Peace or Notary Public.

D) Through applicant who is a Citizen, but has a child under 18 years of age

Form
$600 E.C.
Certificate of Citizenship of mother/father
H I V Test if person is over 12 years of age
Birth Certificate of Applicant
Two (2) Passport SIZE Photos
Birth Certificate of Citizen

E) Through person residing in Federation for over fourteen (14) years

Form
Two (2) Passport SIZE Photos
H I V Test
Letter of verification as living in the Federation for over fourteen (14) years
Fee - CARICOM Nationals - $1,750 E.C.
- Non CARICOM Nationals - $3,000 E.C.

F) By way of Investment

Form
Birth Certificate
Marriage Certificate (if applicable)
Decree Absolute (if applicable)
Affidavit of support (Bank Statement)
Evidence of own assets (Certificate of Title for house, land or condominium)
One (1) Passport SIZE Photo
Birth Certificate of Spouse (if applicable)
Birth Certificate of each unmarried child under 18 years (if applicable)
Proof of having passed the H I V Test
$100 non-refundable fee for the application for permanent residence
Grant of permanent residence fee - $3,800

CORPORATE ENQUIRIES

Persons seeking to verify the existence of corporate entities can contact the :

Financial Services Department
P.O. Box 898
Basseterre
St. Kitts W.I.
E-mail skanfsd@caribsurf.com or

Financial Services
P.O. Box 689
Charlestown
Nevis W.I.
E-mail nev@caribsurf.com

REQUIREMENTS TO OBTAIN A BETTING AND GAMING LICENCE TO OPERATE AN INTERNET/ON-LINE GAMING ENTERPRISE

The Company must be locally registered at our Financial Services Department.
A proposal outlining the business operation must be submitted to the:

Permanent Secretary
Ministry of Commerce and Consumer Affairs
P.O. Box 132
Basseterre, St. Kitts
Tel: (869) 465-2620 / 4040
Fax: (869) 465-8794

The following should be forwarded with the application:

a) Bank Reference
b) Character Reference
c) Police Records on the shareholders and directors of the company
d) Passport Number
e) A processing fee of US $2,000 per individual must accompany the application

Nationals of St. Kitts/Nevis are not permitted to place bets on the gaming activities.
The Company's Banking Operations, i.e. to receive and settle bets must be carried out through an account with a commercial bank on the island.
Once approval has been granted:-

a) Work Permits must be obtained for non-nationals
b) A registration fee of US $80,000 and an annual licence fee of US $40,000 are payable.

c) Any intended change in the Director (s) or Beneficial Owner (s) of the company must be notified to the Ministry of Commerce and Consumer Affairs so that relevant permits can be sought and obtained, the necessary due diligence done, and relevant fees paid.
d) The Company must consult withthe Ministry of Commerce and Consumer Affairs on the content of any advertisement placed on the Internet.

PRACTICAL INFORMATION FOR CONDUCTING BUSINESS

INVESTMENT AND BUSINESS CLIMATE

OPENNESS TO FOREIGN INVESTMENT

The Government of St. Kitts and Nevis, strongly encourages foreign direct investment, particularly in industries that create jobs, earn foreign currency, and have a positive impact on its citizens. The government has a number of incentive programs in place to attract foreign investment, and is home to the Eastern Caribbean Central Bank, the Eastern Caribbean Securities Exchange and the Eastern Caribbean Regulatory Commission.

The government has instituted a number of investment incentives for businesses considering the possibility of locating in St. Kitts or Nevis, encouraging both domestic and foreign private investment. Government policies provide liberal tax holidays, duty-free import of equipment and materials, and subsidies for training provided to local personnel.

All investment proposals are reviewed by the St. Kitts Investment Promotion Agency (SKIPA) to ensure that the project is consistent with the national interests and provides economic benefits to the country. St. Kitts and Nevis foreign direct investment policy is to attract FDI into the priority sectors as identified under the National Diversification Strategy. These include, Financial Services, Tourism, Agriculture, Information Technology, Education Services, and limited Light Manufacturing. However, investment opportunities also exist in energy and other services. Only qualified projects are granted approval to be established in St. Kitts and Nevis.

While all of these sectors are open to attracting FDI, St. Kitts and Nevis also employs a defensive posture for investments in certain sectors that are reserved for local investors. These include but are not limited to investments and trade in services such as, taxi and tour operators and tour guides. Additionally, potential investors are cautioned that St. Kitts actual level of openness to foreign investment is limited by local expropriation practices, which could put investments at risk.

Trade Agreements

St. Kitts and Nevis is a beneficiary of the Caribbean Basin Initiative, CARIBCAN, and Lomé agreements qualifying it for trade concessions with the United States, Canada, and the European Union. St. Kitts and Nevis is also a member of GATT and WTO.

Industrial Sites

There are four fully developed industrial sites where production facilities can be constructed to specification and leased at nominal rates. Kittitian officials project that factory space will increase annually by 15,000 sq. ft. in St. Kitts and 5,000 sq. ft. in Nevis. The sites are managed and serviced on behalf of the Government by the Development Bank of St. Kitts and Nevis.

Foreign nationals receive the same legal protections as local citizens. The police and court systems are efficient and unbiased in commercial matters, and the government operates in an essentially transparent manner.

Measure	Year	Index/Ranking

TI Corruption Index	N/A	N/A
Heritage Economic Freedom	N/A	N/A
World Bank Doing Business	2011	87
MCC Government Effectiveness	N/A	N/A
MCC Rule of Law	N/A	N/A
MCC Control of Corruption	N/A	N/A
MCC Fiscal Policy	N/A	N/A
MCC Trade Policy	N/A	N/A
MCC Regulatory Quality	N/A	N/A
MCC Business Start Up	N/A	N/A
MCC Land Rights Access	N/A	N/A
MCC Natural Resource Mgmt	N/A	N/A

CONVERSION AND TRANSFER POLICIES

Companies registered in St. Kitts can repatriate all profits, dividends and import capital. There are no exchange controls in Nevis and the invoicing of foreign trade transactions may be made in any currency. Importers are not required to make prior deposits in local funds and export proceeds do not have to be surrendered to Government authorities or to authorized banks. There are no controls on transfers of funds. The Government of Nevis guarantees the free transfers of profits and repatriation of capital.

EXPROPRIATION AND COMPENSATION

St. Kitts and Nevis uses eminent domain laws that allow the government to expropriate private property for the betterment of the public. There are also laws that permit the acquisition of private business, and the government claims such laws are constitutional. The concept of eminent domain and the expropriation of private property is typically governed by laws that require governments to adequately compensate owners of the expropriated property at the time of its expropriation or soon thereafter. The government of St. Kitts and Nevis uses eminent domain to acquire private property, and the law in St. Kitts and Nevis requires the government to compensate owners. In some cases, the procedure for compensation of owners favors the government valuation at the expense of the U.S. owner. In St. Kitts and Nevis in practice, the government has often not paid compensation for private property expropriated under its eminent domain laws. Currently the U.S. Embassy in Bridgetown is aware of five separate cases involving the seizure of private land by the government, and one case involving the seizure of a business by the government. In at least two cases, court rulings favoring the U.S. owner did not deter government action to expropriate the property. There has also been an example of punitive tax laws targeting a U.S. company to push it from the market in favor of local ownership after courts have blocked an attempted expropriation. The U.S. Embassy in Bridgetown therefore recommends caution when investing in real estate or conducting business in St. Kitts and Nevis.

DISPUTE SETTLEMENT

St. Kitts and Nevis bases its legal system on the British common law system. The Attorney General, the Chief Justice, Puisne Judges, and Magistrates administer justice in St. Kitts and Nevis. An appeal may be taken to the organization of Eastern Caribbean States Court of Appeal and the final court of appeal for St. Kitts and Nevis is the Judicial Committee of the Privy Council in the United Kingdom.

The United States and St. Kitts and Nevis are both parties to the World Trade Organization (WTO). The WTO Dispute Settlement Panel and Appellate Body resolve disputes over WTO agreements, while courts of appropriate jurisdiction in both countries resolve private disputes.

St. Kitts and Nevis is also a member of the International Center for the Settlement of Investment Disputes (ICSID), also known as the Washington Convention.

Performance Requirements and Incentives

While there are no formal performance requirements, government officials will more likely approve investments they believe will create jobs and increase exports and foreign exchange earnings. There are no requirements for participation either by nationals or by the Government in foreign investment projects.

There is no requirement that enterprises must purchase a fixed percentage of goods from local sources, but the Government encourages local sourcing.

Fiscal Incentives Act

In an effort to increase investment, St. Kitts and Nevis has implemented a series of investment incentives. The Fiscal Incentives Acts provides a list of incentives including:

Tax holiday of up to 15 years
Additional tax rebates of up to five years
Exemption from custom duties on material and equipment deemed necessary to establish or update an enterprise
Repatriation of profits, dividends, royalties, and imported capital by arrangement with the Ministry of Finance;
Protection of investment through government agreement between St. Kitts and Nevis and the U.S
No personal income tax

Corporate Tax Incentives
Under the Fiscal Incentives Act, four types of enterprises qualify for tax holidays. The length of the tax holiday for the first three depends on the amount of value added in St. Kitts and Nevis. The fourth type, known as enclave industry, must produce goods exclusively for export outside the CARICOM region.

Enterprise	Value Added	Maximum Tax Holiday
Group I	50% or more	15 years
Group II	25% to 50 %	12 years
Group III	10% to 25%	10 years
Enclave	Enclave	15 years

Companies which qualify for tax holidays are allowed to import into St. Kitts and Nevis duty-free all equipment, machinery, spare parts and row materials used in production.

Hotels Aids Act and Taxes

The Hotel Aids Act provides relief from customs duties on items brought into the country for use in construction, extension and equipping of a hotel of not less than 10 bedrooms. In addition, the Income Tax Act provides special tax relief benefits for hotels of more than 30 bedrooms. These hotels are exempt from income tax for 10 years. If the hotel contains less than 30 bedrooms, gains or profits would be exempt from income tax for 5 years.

The hotel and restaurant tax is levied on the total accommodation charges of a hotel or guest house and on the cost of food and beverage sold by a restaurant. The total rate of tax is 9% (with 2% contributing to the Hotel and Accommodation Enhancement Levy). This tax is levied on the total accommodation.

Corporate Income Tax

Additionally, those who invest in St. Kitts and Nevis do not pay a capital gains tax, and have a corporate tax of 35% of net profits. Qualified companies enjoy full exemption from taxes on corporate profits for a period not exceeding 15 years. Corporate tax does not apply to exempt companies or to enterprises that have been granted tax concession.

Individuals and ordinary companies remitting payments to persons outside of St. Kitts and Nevis must deduct 10% withholding tax from the following:

Profits
Administration, management or head office expenses
Technical services fees
Accounting and audit expenses
Royalties
Non-life insurance premiums
Rent

Withholding tax does not apply to profits of an approved enterprise, which is enjoying benefits under the Fiscal Incentives Act. This tax does not apply to exempt trusts, limited partnerships, companies or foundations.

Consumption tax is levied on the gross revenue of services provided by professionals such as Doctors, Lawyers, Dentists, and other specified persons listed in the Schedule to the Consumption Tax Act at a rate of 4%.

Export Allowance

St. Kitts and Nevis provides companies with a further tax concession effective at the end of the tax holiday period. In effect, it is a rebate of a portion of the income tax paid based on export profits as a percentage of total profits.

Exemption from Import Duties

Full exemption from import duties on parts, raw materials, and production machinery is also available.

Citizenship through Investment

Under the Citizenship by Investment Program, foreign individuals can obtain citizenship in accordance with subsection (5) of Section 3 of the Citizenship Act of 1984, which grants the right of citizenship (without voting rights) by investment. The minimum that would entitle an investor to qualify is US$350,000 in real estate. Applicants must also provide a full medical certificate, and evidence of the source of funds.

Right to Private Ownership and Investment

Foreign investors may hold up to 100% of an investment. With one exception, foreign investment in St. Kitts and Nevis is not subject to any restrictions, and foreign investors receive national treatment. The only restriction is the requirement to obtain an Alien Landholders License for foreign investors seeking to purchase property for residential or commercial purposes. The cost of these licenses is 10% of the value of the land or of the interest in the real estate to be purchased. Licenses are granted once properly submitted to Cabinet for consideration and payment of the license fees. Foreign investors do not require a landholding license for the purchase of land in certain parts of the island, such as Frigate Bay or the South East Peninsula.

Protection of Property Rights

Civil law protects physical property and mortgage claims. St. Kitts and Nevis signed the Paris Convention on Intellectual Property Rights (IPR), the Madrid accords, and is a member of the United Nations World Intellectual Property Organization (WIPO). Article 45 of the Protocol Amending the Treaty that established CARICOM commits all 15 members to implement stronger IP protection and enforcement.

The administration of intellectual property laws in St. Kitts and Nevis is under the responsibility of the Attorney General. The registration of patents, trademarks, and service marks is administered by the High Court Registry. The 2000 Act created an Intellectual Property Office responsible for the administration of all laws relating to intellectual property, which began functioning in 2004.

Transparency of Regulatory System

The regulatory system in St. Kitts and Nevis is transparent, and more information regarding the laws governing investment can be provided by contacting the St. Kitts Investment Promotion Agency.

Additionally, the incorporation and registration of companies in the federation differs somewhat on its two constituent islands. In St. Kitts the process is regulated by the Companies Act No. 22 of 1996. The incorporation of companies in Nevis is regulated by the Nevis Island Business Corporation Ordinance No. 3 of 1984. Companies must register in the Companies Registry. There are no nationality restrictions for directors in a company, and in general, national treatment is applied. All registered companies must have a registered office in the Federation of St. Kitts.

The St. Kitts, Nevis and Anguilla National Bank has approximately $2 billion in assets.

Additionally, the Treaty of Chaguaramas provides the competition policy applicable to CARICOM States. Member States are required to establish and maintain a national competition authority for facilitating the implementation of the rules of competition. At the CARICOM level, a regional Competition Commission is established to apply the rules of competition in respect of anti-competitive cross-border business conduct. The CARICOM competition policy addresses anti-competitive business conduct, such as agreements between enterprises, decisions by associations of enterprises, and concerted practices by enterprises that have as their object or effect the prevention, restriction or distortion of competition within the Community; and actions by which an enterprise abuses its dominant position within the Community. No legislation is yet in operation to regulate competition generally. However, sectoral regulation of competition in the telecommunications field is provided for under the Telecommunications Act.

Efficient Capital Markets and Portfolio Investment

St. Kitts and Nevis is a member of the OECS, and as such, it is also a member of the Eastern Caribbean Securities Exchange (ECSE). The ECSE is a regional securities market established by the Eastern Caribbean Central Bank and licensed under the Securities Act of 2001- a uniform regional body of legislation governing securities market activities to facilitate the buying and selling of financial products for the eight member territories. St. Kitts and Nevis is a member of this stock exchange, and is open to portfolio investment.

Competition from State-Owned Enterprises

There is a very limited number of statutory corporations (state-owned enterprises) in St. Kitts and Nevis. Those that exist do not generally post a threat to investors, as they directly support the government in achieving its objectives. For example, the St. Kitts Investment Promotion Agency is a statutory corporation.

Corporate Social Responsibility

Investors in St. Kitts and Nevis are required to recognize the economic and social objects as well as the policies and priorities of the government. They are also equally responsible for maintaining workers rights and safeguarding the environment. While there are no specific health and safety regulations, the Factories Law provides general health and safety guidance to Labor Ministry inspectors. The Labor Commission settles disputes over safety conditions. Workers have the right to report unsafe work environments without jeopardy to continued employment; inspectors then investigate such claims, and workers may leave such locations without jeopardy to their continued employment.

Political Violence

St. Kitts and Nevis does not have a history of political violence.

Corruption

St. Kitts and Nevis does not have a major problem with corruption, although, there have been some allegations against government officials. None of those allegations have been substantiated.

The country is also party to the Inter-American Convention Against Corruption, and recently signed the follow-up mechanism.

Bilateral Investment Agreements

St. Kitts and Nevis has no bilateral investment treaty with the United States. St. Kitts and Nevis has a bilateral investment treaty with Costa Rica (CARICOM), and partial preferential agreements with Columbia and Venezuela. It is a member of the Caribbean Community and Common Market (CARICOM), and also has free trade agreements with Costa Rica and the Dominican Republic. It has double taxation agreements with Denmark, Norway, Sweden, and the United Kingdom.

St. Kitts and Nevis is also party to the following:

Caribbean Community (CARICOM)

The Treaty of Chaguaramas established CARICOM in 1973. Its purpose is to promote economic integration among its fifteen (15) Member States. Investors operating in St. Vincent & the Grenadines are given preferential access to the entire CARICOM market. The Revised Treaty of

Chaguaramas goes further to establish the CARICOM Single Market and Economy (CSME), by permitting the free movement of goods, capital and labor within CARICOM States.

Organisation of Eastern Caribbean States (OECS)

The Treaty of Basseterre establishes the Organisation of Eastern Caribbean States (OECS). The OECS consists of nine Member States of Antigua and Barbuda, Dominica, Grenada, Montserrat, St. Kitts & Nevis, St. Lucia and St. Vincent & the Grenadines with associate members being Anguilla and the British Virgin Islands. The purpose of the Treaty is to promote harmonization among Member States in areas concerning foreign policy, defense and security, and economic affairs.

Economic Partnership Agreement (EPA)

The Economic Partnership Agreement (EPA) was concluded between the CARIFORUM States and the European Community and its Member States. The EPA is designed to replace the now expired transitional trade regime of the Cotonou Agreement. The overarching objectives of the EPA are to alleviate poverty in CARIFORUM, to promote regional integration and economic cooperation and to foster the gradual integration of the CARIFORUM states into the world economy by improving their trade capacity and creating an investment-conducive environment. The Agreement promotes trade related developments in areas such as competition, intellectual property, and public procurement, the environment and protection of personal data.

Caribbean Basin Initiative (CBI)

The objective of the Caribbean Basin Initiative is to promote economic development through private sector initiative in Central America and the Caribbean islands by expanding foreign and domestic investment in non-traditional sectors, diversifying CBI country economies and expanding their exports. It permits duty free entry of products manufactured or assembled in St. Kitts and Nevis into markets of the USA.

Caribbean / Canada Trade Agreement (CARIBCAN)

CARIBCAN is an economic and trade development assistance program for Commonwealth Caribbean countries in which Canada provides duty free access to its national market for the majority of products which originate in Commonwealth Caribbean countries.

OPIC AND OTHER INVESTMENT INSURANCE PROGRAMS

In 1999, the U.S. Government's Overseas Private Investment Corporation (OPIC) signed with Citibank to establish a USD $200 million Investment Facility for the Caribbean and Central America, as one means of encouraging investment and stimulating economic development. The Caribbean Development Bank, which is based in Barbados, administers this program. OPIC provides financing and political risk insurance to viable private sector projects, helps U.S. businesses invest overseas, and fosters economic development in new and emerging markets.

Additionally, in 2004, OPIC approved an additional investment guaranty of up to $100 million to Citibank to establish a lending facility that will enable Citibank to expand its activity in Central America and the Caribbean, including lending to small businesses. Under this facility, Citibank and OPIC share credit risk in loans, and OPIC provides clearances on workers' rights and environmental issues for each downstream loan.

Labor

St. Kitts and Nevis has a labor force of about 25,000 persons, with a literacy rate of 98%. The country's technical and training needs are met largely by local colleges, which offer courses in skilled labor, including, plumbing, electrical engineering, air conditioning and refrigeration, masonry, carpentry, mechanical engineering, motor mechanics, typing and basic hotel skills. There is also a large pool of professionals to draw from, in fields such as law, medicine, business information technology and accounting. Many of the professionals in St. Kitts and Nevis trained in the Caribbean, the United States, Canada and the United Kingdom, where many of them gained work experience before returning to St. Kitts and Nevis.

The island has 3 main labor unions, St. Kitts and Nevis Trades & Labor Union, St. Kitts and Nevis Teachers Union, and the Stevedoring Association. In regards to labor negotiations, the average duration of wage contracts is two years. During contract negotiations, the union with 51% of the workers in that particular industry is recognized by the employer as the worker's representative; however, some unions do not get involved in contract negotiations.

Labor unions are free to organize and to negotiate for better wages and benefits for union members. The law prohibits anti-union discrimination, but does not require employers found guilty of such action to rehire employees who were fired for union activities. However, the employer must pay lost wages and severance pay. There is no legislation governing the organization and representation of workers, and employers are not legally bound to recognize a union, but in practice employers do so if a majority of workers polled wish to organize. Collective bargaining takes place on a workplace-by- workplace basis, not industry wide. The Labor Commissioner mediates all types of disputes between labor and management on an ad hoc basis. However, in practice few disputes actually go to the Commissioner for resolution. If neither the Commissioner nor the Ministry of Labor are able to resolve the dispute, the law allows for a case to be brought before a civil court.

The Constitution forbids slavery and forced labor, and they do not occur in practice. While neither the Constitution nor the law specifically address bonded labor, it has also not been a problem in practice. The 1966 Employment of Children Ordinance outlaws slavery, servitude, and forced labor, and prescribes the minimum legal working age of 16 years old. The Labor Ministry relies heavily on school truant officers and the community affairs division to monitor compliance, which they do effectively. The law mandates compulsory education up to the age of 16.

The minimum wage varies from $56.18 (EC$ 150) per week for full-time domestic workers to $74.91 (EC$ 200) per week for skilled workers. These provide a barely adequate living for a wage earner and family; many workers supplement wages by keeping small animals such as goats and chickens. The Labor Commission undertakes regular wage inspections and special investigations when it receives complaints; it requires employers found in violation to pay back wages. The Government provides unemployment benefits to workers who lose their jobs temporarily or permanently.

The law provides for a 40- to 44-hour workweek, but the common practice is 40 hours in 5 days. Although not required by law, workers receive at least one 24-hour rest period per week. The law provides that workers receive a minimum annual vacation of 14 working days.

Foreign Trade Zones/Free Ports

There are no foreign trade zones or free ports in St. Kitts and Nevis.

FOREIGN DIRECT INVESTMENT STATISTICS

In 2009, according to the St. Kitts and Nevis Federation Statistics Department, FDI inward flow into St. Kitts and Nevis was EC$ 407.23 million (US $150.83 million).

Major U.S. Investors

American Airlines/American Eagle, Amerijet International Inc., Avis Car Rentals, Caribbean Cinemas, Caribbean Cable Communications, Crowley Maritime Corporation, DCK Worldwide, Dominos, Federal Express, Kiawah Partners, Met Life, Pricewaterhouse Coopers, Productions Products Company, Ross University, Stewart Title, Tropical Shipping and Construction Company, UPS, Western Union. Major franchises of U.S. companies include: Ace Hardware, Kentucky Fried Chicken and Marriott Hotels.

An American Chamber of Commerce (AmCham) does not operate in St. Kitts and Nevis.

For further information, please contact the Economic/Commercial Section at the U.S. Embassy.

Gregory Floyd
Commercial Officer
US Embassy, Bridgetown, Barbados
Tel: 246-277-4274
floydga@state.gov

Jonelle M. Watson
Commercial Assistant
US Embassy Bridgetown, Barbados
Tel: 246-277-4052
watsonjm@state.gov

Contacts for Investment Related Inquires
The following are contacts for investment related inquiries:
St. Kitts Investment Promotion Agency (SKIPA)
CAP Southwell Industrial Park
Basseterre, St. Kitts
Tel: 1-869-465-1153
Fax: 1-869-465-1154
Email: info@stkittsipa.org
Website: http://www.stkittsipa.org/

Ministry of Finance
P. O. Box 898, Rams Building, Liverpool Row
Basseterre, St. Kitts
Tel: (869)-466-5048
Fax:(869)-466-5317
Email: skanfed@sisterisles.kn
Website: http://www.skbfinancialservices.com/aboutstkitts.php

St. Kitts and Nevis Chamber of Industry and Commerce
P.O. Box 332
Basseterre, St. Kitts, West Indies
Tel: (869)-465-2980
Fax: (869)-465-4490
Website: www.stkittsnevischamber.org

BUSINESS AND LEGAL CLIMATE & REGULATIONS

INVESTMENT INCENTIVE SCHEMES

Eight industrial and commercial free-trade zones currently operate in St. Kitts and Nevis. They are located at Tacna, Ilo, Mollendo, Tumbes, Trujillo, Paita, Chimbote and Pisco. There are also four fully developed industrial sites where production facilities can be constructed to specification and leased at nominal rates. Projections are that factory space will increase annually by 15,000 sq. ft. in St. Kitts and 5,000 sq. ft. in Nevis. The sites are managed and serviced on behalf of the Government by the Development Bank of St. Kitts and Nevis.

Export processing free zones offer investors exemptions from customs duties for imports and exports, exemption from any St. Kitts and Nevisvian tax for 15 years, temporary labor agreements, and accounting in foreign currency. Special commercial treatment zones are generally located on the jungle frontier. They extend the following benefits to companies operating inside their borders: exemption from value-added taxes; a reduced 10 percent customs duty; and accounting is permitted in foreign currency.

The Hotel Aids Ordinance provides duty-free concessions (relief from customs duties and pier dues) on items for use in the construction, extension and equipping of a hotel of not less than 30 bedrooms. The Income Tax Ordinance provides special tax relief benefits for hotel proprietors granted licenses under the Hotel Aids Ordinance: the gains or profits of a hotel of more than 30 bedrooms are exempt from income tax for a period of 10 years, for hotels with less than 30 bedrooms, the gains and profits are exempt from income tax for a period of 5 years.

Companies which qualify for tax holidays are allowed to import into St. Kitts and Nevis duty-free all equipment, machinery, spare parts and raw materials used in production.
Under the Caribbean Basin Initiative, besides participating in the financial contribution allocated by Washington to the member countries, St. Kitts also qualifies for duty-free entry into the United States of more than 95% of its products, not including sugar. Under the Generalized System of Preferences (GSP), manufactured and semi-manufactured goods are also eligible for duty-free access to United States markets. Virtually all of St. Kitts-produced items and raw materials are eligible for GSP treatment under the list of some 2,800 products eligible for duty-free importation. However, to qualify, the product must have had 35% of its appraised value added in the beneficiary country. Again, this enhances St. Kitts' status as a site for conversion of merchandise because of its skillful and well-trained labor force.

Saint Christopher ("St. Kitts") and Nevis form a twin island federation ("the Federation") located in the northern part of the Lesser Antilles chain of islands in the Eastern Caribbean. St. Kitts, with an area of 69 square miles (168 km2) has a population of 31,880. It is located at 17°15' North latitude and 62°45' West longitude. This places St. Kitts approximately 1,300 miles from Miami (3 hours flight time), 2,000 miles from New York (4 hours flight time), and 4,000 miles from London (8 hours flight time). Nevis, with an area of 36 square miles (93 km2) has a population of 10,080.

The two islands are separated by a channel which is about two miles wide. St. Kitts and Nevis are four hours behind Greenwich Mean Time (GMT-4). Average air temperature is 79°F (26°C) and humidity 71.5% with extremes in temperature and humidity tempered by breezes from the north-east trade winds. The average sea water temperature is 80°F (27°C). Average annual rainfall is 55 inches (1,397 mm).

GOVERNMENT

The Federation is a parliamentary democracy within the Commonwealth of Nations. Her Majesty, Queen Elizabeth II, is head of State and is represented on the islands by a Governor-General.

Basseterre is the capital of St. Kitts and at the same time the administrative capital of the Federation. The capital of Nevis is Charlestown.

LEGAL SYSTEM

The legal system is based upon English Common Law served by a High Court of Justice, a Court of Appeal, and Her Majesty's Privy Council in London.

LANGUAGE

The spoken and official language of the Federation is English. Interpreters are available for other major international languages. The education system has been rated very highly by the World Bank in its report on the Access, Quality and Efficiency in Caribbean Education. With 98%, the Federation has the highest level of literacy in the region and its CXC and GCE results are among the highest in the English speaking Caribbean.

CURRENCY

The currency used in the Federation is the East Caribbean Dollar ("XCD") which is fixed at XCD 2.70 per dollar of the United States of America ("USD").

COMMUNICATION

The Robert L. Bradshaw International Airport on St. Kitts has a runway of 8,000 feet and is equipped to handle large passenger jets. Newcastle Airport on Nevis can accommodate smaller twin-engine aircraft. There are at present no direct scheduled flights from North America or Europe. The islands are using Puerto Rico, St. Maarten and Antigua as their major gateways. Access from and to these gateways is by twin-engine turboprop aircraft operated by regional scheduled airlines on a daily basis and by smaller aircraft operated by local charter companies.

The deep water port in St. Kitts has modern facilities which include roll-on and roll-off docks and easily accommodates large cruise ships and freight carriers.

The islands' telecommunication system is state of the art. Its modern network permitting smooth and prompt telephone, telex, facsimile and Internet connections throughout the world.

St. Kitts enjoys a 39 channel cable TV service which provides 24 hours daily entertainment, sport and news programs from North America and England via satellite.

On average, airmail letters from North America take 10 to 12 days and 7 to 10 days from Europe. Major international courier services are represented by Brinks, D.H.L. Worldwide Express, Federal Express and United Parcel Services.

POLITICAL STABILITY

The Federation has a history of political stability based on the Westminster model of government and continuity of national policy. Since the Federation attained independence from Britain in 1983, it has consistently been adjudged to be among the world's freest nations by Freedom House, an independent and highly respected research organisation in the United States of America.

ECONOMY

Sugar, which was the state's largest export and major income earner, has recently been marginalised as the economic mainstay. The Government's aggressive diversification program has brought tourism, light manufacturing and international financial activities to the fore. The World Bank in a recent report concluded that the Federation achieved the highest rate of growth in per capita income in Latin America and the Caribbean between 1980 and 1991.

The Government of the Federation wishes to promote St. Kitts and Nevis as a regional and international financial centre. Accordingly it actively encourages financial activities and is making a deliberate effort to maintain the Federation's present attractiveness. Financial operations are viewed as a principal economic sector with the Government constantly reviewing new ideas and improving financial legislation.

CONFIDENTIALITY

The Confidential Relationships Act of 1985 prohibits the disclosure of any information obtained in the course of business, and applies to banks and professionals as well as to Government officials.

BANKING

The Eastern Caribbean Central Bank and The Eastern Caribbean Home Mortgage Bank have their headquarters in St. Kitts. Three international banks are represented in St. Kitts and two in Nevis. There is currently no investment banking services. Banks maintain deposits in XCD and USD only. Local foreign currency regulations regarding the conduct of USD current accounts stipulate that an account may not be opened with less than USD 1,000 and if at any time its credit balance falls below that amount such account shall forthwith be closed and shall not again be opened within one year at the same bank.

PROFESSIONAL SERVICES

The legal profession is represented in the Federation by Barristers and Solicitors of the High Court. They alone have the right to practice before the Courts of the Federation, and alone may give advise on local law within the Federation. One of the five major international auditing firms is represented in the Federation.

BUSINESS LICENSES

Certain businesses need licences, and applicants should seek advice locally on each occasion.

SPECIAL INCENTIVES FOR CONDUCTING BUSINESS

FOREIGN COMPANIES

Foreign companies may be domiciled in the Federation under the Companies Act 1996 or the Nevis Business Corporation Ordinance 1984.

CITIZENSHIP BY INVESTMENT

Foreign individuals can obtain citizenship under sub-section (5) of Section 3 of the Citizenship Act 1984 which stipulates that a person is entitled, upon making application to the Minister in the prescribed manner and upon payment of any fee that may be prescribed, to be registered as a citizen of the Federation without any rights of voting save under and in accordance with the provisions of any law governing the qualification of voters, if Cabinet is satisfied that such person has invested substantially in the Federation.

The minimum investment requirement may be satisfied in any of the following ways -

- a minimum of the equivalent in XCD of USD 200,000 in 10-year Treasury Bonds issued and guaranteed by the Federation; or
- a minimum of the equivalent in XCD of USD 250,000 in an investment project approved after March 1996; or
- a minimum of the equivalent in XCD of USD 150,000 in a real estate development approved before March 1996.

Treasury Bonds are issued at their nominal or par value and no interest is paid on them.

The registration fees currently in force are the XCD equivalents of -

- USD 35,000 for head of household (male or female);
- USD 15,000 for spouse;
- USD 15,000 for each child under 18 years of age; and
- USD 35,000 for each adult family member or other adult.

Each citizenship certificate of registration is USD 47 and the cost for each passport is USD 13.

The appropriate citizenship registration fees must be paid to Government at the time of making the application. Funds for the payment of the required investment must be deposited by the applicant with a bank in St. Kitts. If the application is accepted, then the bank will be requested to release the funds to pay for the required investment. If the application is not accepted, the fees paid to the Government and the funds for the payment of the required investment will be returned to the unsuccessful applicant.

Every citizenship application must be made on the prescribed form which must be submitted together with various documents relating to the applicant's identity, civil status, criminal record, financial resources, and health. All documents must be in English or translated into English, and all photocopies of any document submitted must be notarised and properly certified.

A passport is valid for ten years, unless otherwise stated. It remains the property of the Government of the Federation and may be withdrawn at any time. Citizens of the Federation who are also citizens of foreign countries cannot avail themselves of the protection of the representative of the Federation, against the authorities of that foreign country, and are not exempt by reason of possessing the citizenship of the Federation from any obligation (such as military service) to which they may be liable under foreign law. A person having some connection with a Commonwealth or foreign country (e.g. by birth, by descent through either parent, by marriage or by residence) may be a national of that country, in addition to being a national of the Federation. Acquisition of the nationality of the Federation by a foreigner does not necessarily cause the loss of nationality of origin.

A citizen has the right to renew his passport upon its expiration. As at October 1994, no visas were required to travel to the following 56 countries and territories:-

Antigua and Barbuda
Australia (*)
Bahamas
Bangladesh
Barbados
Belize
Botswana
Brunei
Burma
Canada
Cyprus
Denmark
Dominica
Fiji
Gambia
Ghana
Grenada
Guyana
Hong Kong
India
Italy (*)
Jamaica
Kenya
Kiribati
Lesotho
Malawi
Malaysia
Maldives
Malta
Mauritius
Mexico (*)
Nauru
New Zealand
Nigeria
Pakistan
Papua New Guinea
Philippines

Seychelles
Sierra Leone
Singapore
Solomon Islands
South Korea
Sri Lanka
St. Lucia
St. Vincent
Swaziland
Switzerland (*)
Tanzania
Tonga
Trinidad and Tobago
Tuvalu
Uganda
United Kingdom (*)
Vanuatu
Zambia
Zimbabwe
(*) denotes that Entry Clearance is required

Please note that visa requirements are frequently changed and that up-to-date information can be obtained from travel agents and airlines.

INVESTMENT GUARANTEE

The Federation and the United States of America have entered into an Investment Guarantee Agreement.

BUSINESS INCENTIVES

Under the Fiscal Incentives Act, four types of enterprises qualify for a tax holiday. The length of the tax holiday ranges from 10 to 15 years.

The Federation provides companies with a further tax concession effective at the end of the tax holiday period.

Full exemption from import duties on parts, raw materials and production machinery is also available.

Companies registered in the Federation can repatriate all profits, dividends and imported capital.

The Hotel Aids Ordinance provides relief from customs duties and pier duties in items brought into the country for use in the construction, extension and equipment of a hotel of not less than 10 bedrooms. In addition, the Income Tax Ordinance provides special tax relief benefits for a hotel proprietor who has been granted a licence under the Hotel Aids Ordinance. This stipulates that the gains or profits of a hotel are exempt from income tax for 5 years if the hotel has 30 or less bedrooms, and for 10 years if it has more than 30 bedrooms.

The Federation offers trade incentives under US Tariff Schedule 806 and 807, Generalized System of Preferences (GSP), Overseas Private Investment Corporation (OPIC), Caribbean Common Market (CARICOM), Lomé Convention, Business Advisory Services (BAS), Caribbean

Basin Initiative (CBI), Caribican, Puerto Rico income tax credit under Section 936 of its Internal Revenue Code and financing under its Caribbean Development Program (CDP).

FINANCIAL REGULATIONS AND SERVICES

No person is to carry on, or hold himself out as carrying on, any finance business in or from within the Federation unless he is for the time being authorised under the Financial Services (Regulations) Order, 1997 ("the Order").

"finance business" is defined in the Order as being -

- deposit-taking business; *(e.g. bankers, financiers, etc.)*
- investment business; *(e.g. stockbrokers, operators of collective investment schemes, etc.)*
- insurance business; *(e.g. insurers)*
- assurance business; *(e.g. insurance agents, insurance brokers, insurance managers, etc.)*
- trust business; or *(e.g. professional trustees, protectors, etc.)*
- corporate business, *(e.g. nominee shareholders, professional directors, etc.)*

carried on for profit or reward in or from within the Federation.

However, persons carrying on the following finance business (defined as "domestic business" in the Order) are not governed by the Order and must be licensed under the Banking Act or the Insurance Act, as appropriate -

- deposit-taking business conducted exclusively in XCD and any other deposit-taking business when deposits are taken from, or moneys are lent to, persons resident in the Federation;
- investment business conducted exclusively in XCD and any other investment business when the investment represents a claim on persons resident in the Federation;
- insurance business conducted exclusively in XCD and any other insurance business when the contract is in respect of the life, safety, fidelity or insurable interest (other than in respect of property) of a person who at the time of effecting the contract is resident in the Federation, or property that at the time of effecting the contract is in the Federation or, in the case of a vehicle, vessel, aircraft or other movable property, is ordinarily based in the Federation (but does not include re-insurance business);
- assurance business when such business is conducted exclusively on behalf of an insurer who is carrying on domestic business.

This page contains information relevant to finance business, which are not domestic business.

FINANCIAL RESOURCES

No authorisation will be granted under the Order unless the person applying for the authorisation has the following minimum financial resources -

- in the case of deposit-taking business, net assets in the minimum sum of -

☐USD 500,000 or its equivalent in other currencies for an authorisation to undertake unrestricted business and restricted business;

☐USD 50,000 or its equivalent in other currencies for an authorisation to undertake restricted business but not unrestricted business;

☐in the case of investment business, net assets in the minimum sum of -

☐USD 400,000 or its equivalent in other currencies for an authorisation to undertake unrestricted business and restricted business;

☐USD 40,000 or its equivalent in other currencies for an authorisation to undertake restricted business but not unrestricted business;

☐in the case of insurance business, net assets in the minimum sum of -

☐USD 300,000 or its equivalent in other currencies for an authorisation to undertake long-term insurance business and general insurance business;

☐USD 200,000 or its equivalent in other currencies for an authorisation to undertake long-term insurance business but not general insurance business;

☐USD 100,000 or its equivalent in other currencies for an authorisation to undertake general insurance business but not long-term insurance business;

☐in the case of trust business, net assets in the minimum sum of -

☐USD 200,000 or its equivalent in other currencies for an authorisation to undertake unrestricted business and restricted business;

☐USD 20,000 or its equivalent in other currencies for an authorisation to undertake restricted business but not unrestricted business;

☐in the case of any other finance business -

☐net assets in the minimum sum of USD 100,000 or its equivalent in other currencies; or

☐a professional indemnity insurance in respect of the activities of the applicant and extended to include the activities on behalf of the applicant or of his agents, if any, placed with an insurer approved by the Minister of Finance, and for an indemnity in the minimum sum of USD 100,000 or its equivalent in other currencies for any one loss; or

☐a guarantee in the minimum sum of USD 100,000 or its equivalent in other currencies given under seal by a holding company of the applicant approved by the Minister of Finance, provided always, that any guarantee which may be given under this sub-paragraph shall only be effective if it expressly provides that its formal validity, its essential validity, its interpretation and effect and the rights and obligation of the parties to it are governed exclusively by the law of the Federation and that the Court only shall be the forum for these purposes.

"restricted business" is defined in the Order as being deposit-taking business, investment business or trust business undertaken exclusively for persons listed in any undertaking accompanying the application for the relevant authorisation and "unrestricted business" is to be construed accordingly.

OTHER CONDITIONS

Every authorisation is subject to the conditions that the authorised person -

- maintains at all times the minimum financial resources specified in the preceding chapter;

- informs the Minister of Finance by notice in writing of any change, or proposed change, in the information contained in, or supplied in connexion with, the last application for an authorisation;

- carries on business only in accordance with the information referred to in the preceding paragraph and such changes as the Minister of Finance may have approved.

The Minister of Finance may prescribe such conditions as he thinks fit applicable either generally to all authorised persons or to a class of authorised persons and may attach conditions to the authorisation of any particular person and may from time to time vary any general condition, any condition applying to a class of authorised persons or any condition attached to an authorisation or prescribe or attach a new condition.

Every authorisation under the Order will, unless previously revoked, expire on the anniversary date in the next following year of the date on which it takes effect.

DISCLOSURES

An authorised person must within 3 months of the end of each of his financial years -

- prepare annual accounts in accordance with generally accepted accounting principles, audited by an independent auditor;

- deliver to the Director General the annual accounts together with written confirmation from an independent auditor that the annual accounts have been prepared as required under the preceding paragraph and whether or not the auditor's certificate for such accounts is unqualified and if qualified, the nature of the qualification;

- deliver to the Director General a certificate of compliance issued by an independent auditor that the information set out in the application for an authorisation, as modified by any subsequent notification of change, remains correct and gives an accurate summary of the business of the authorised person; and

- deliver to the Director General such other documents as are mentioned in the Order

SUPERVISION

The supervision of finance business is entrusted to the Director General of the Financial Services Department of the Ministry of Finance.

Except for the purpose of the performance or exercise of his duties or functions under the Order or when lawfully required to do so by the Court or under the provisions of any other law, the Director General or any person appointed to assist him shall not disclose any information relating to any application under the provisions of the Order, or to the affairs of an authorised person or of any client of an authorized person which he has acquired in the performance or exercise of such duties or functions under the Order.

GOVERNMENT FEES

Fees for the authorization to carry on -

☐a deposit-taking business -

☐on filing of first application (not refundable) -

for all applications, USD 1,000

☐on granting or renewal of authorisation for - an unrestricted business, USD 8,000 a restricted business, USD 4,000

☐an investment business -

☐on filing of first application (not refundable) - for all applications, USD 800

☐ on granting or renewal of authorisation for - an unrestricted business, USD 6,000 a restricted business, USD 3,000

☐

☐an insurance business -

☐on filing of first application (not refundable) - for all applications, USD 600

☐ on granting or renewal of authorisation for - an unrestricted business, USD 4,000 a restricted business, USD 2,000

☐an assurance business -

☐on filing of first application (not refundable) -for all applications, USD 400

☐ on granting or renewal of authorisation to -

an insurance agent, USD 100
an insurance broker, USD 1,000
an insurance sub-agent, USD 50
an insurance manager, USD 3,000
a principal insurance representative, USD 300

☐a trust business -
☐on filing of first application (not refundable) - for all applications, USD 200
☐ on granting or renewal of authorisation for - an unrestricted business, USD 2,000 a restricted business, USD 1,000

☐corporate business -

☐on filing of first application (not refundable), USD 50

- on granting or renewal of authorisation, USD 500

ESTABLISHING LEGAL BUSINESS ENTITIES

The usual entities available under British law, e.g. companies, partnerships and trusts are available in the Federation.

PRIVATE COMPANY

Private companies may be limited by shares or by guarantee, and are formed under the Companies Act 1996, which has effect in St. Kitts and Nevis. They have the following characteristics:

A minimum of one shareholder is required and a maximum of 50 are permitted.
Either registered or bearer shares may be issued. Bearer shares must be deposited with a regulated company in St. Kitts. Nominee shareholder service is available for registered shares. Fractional and Treasury shares are permitted, but shares cannot be sold at a discount except for commission payments. Public offers of shares may not be made.
A private company must have at least one director. Every company must have a secretary and may have one or more assistant secretaries who, or each of whom, may be an individual or a body corporate.
Every company must hold an annual general meeting unless all the members of a private company agree in writing not to.
No annual returns required.
Certain words are prohibited in company names and the company's name must end in "Limited," "corporation" or their abbreviations.
All companies must have a registered office in the Federation to which communications and notices may be addressed; however a registered agent is not required.
Every company must keep a register of members.

One or more persons associated for a lawful purpose can form a company by subscribing their names to a Memorandum of Association written in the English language. Incorporators either adopt model Articles or draw up their own Articles of Association. These documents are submitted to the Registrar of Companies along with payment of a 540 East Caribbean dollars ($200) registration fee, after which a certificate is issued. In its Memorandum, a company limited by shares must state the maximum number of shares that the company is authorized to issue and the share value, which can be expressed in any currency but may not be printed on share certificates. A company limited by guarantee must state in its Memorandum the number of members it proposes to register and the amount of the guarantee expressed in any currency. Since the doctrine of ultra vires has been abolished, a company has the capacity, rights, powers and privileges of an individual. Perpetuity options are a limited life-span (with the number of years specified) or an unlimited life-span.

PUBLIC COMPANY

A public company is one that has more than 50 members, and is permitted to make public offerings of its shares. It needs three directors, of whom a least two are not employed by the company or related companies. Assistant secretaries can be individuals or corporations.

Members' meetings can be conducted by electronic means, as long as members can hear each other's voices. Public companies must hold an annual general meeting while members of private companies can agree to dispense with this. The first general meeting must take place within 18 months after incorporation. Shareholders holding one-tenth of shares and members of a company limited by guarantee who hold one-tenth of voting rights can demand that directors call a general meeting. If directors do not comply, those who requisitioned a meeting (or requisitionists of the group holding one-half of voting rights) can call a meeting themselves. A quorum consists of a least two members present in person or by proxy (1) holding at least one-third of value of issued shares with voting rights; or (2) one-third of voting rights of a company limited by guarantee. Special resolutions require a two-thirds vote.

EXEMPT PRIVATE COMPANY

An exempt private company is a private company (as above), which pays no income, capital gains, withholding, or stamp taxes as long as it conducts business exclusively with persons who are not resident in the Federation.

An annual fee of US$200 is payable to the government on filing of the annual return. Although company details are kept on the public register, inspection of the register by persons who are not members or officers of the company is not permitted.

The law makes clear that an exempt company does not lose its tax waivers because of certain activities within the Federation including signing contracts or concluding arrangements for employing residents, purchasing goods and services, and exercising other powers to carry on its business such as holding directors' and members' meetings, transacting banking and reinsurance business, and conducting securities transactions or serving as adviser to Federation residents who enjoy exempt status.

ST. KITTS AND NEVIS INTERNATIONAL BUSINESS COMPANY (NEVIS)

This type of company is formed under the Nevis Business Corporation Ordinance, 1984 as amended, particularly in 2000, and is suitable for use as a holding company or an investment company. The legislation closely follows Delaware law and is useful to those familiar with this legislation. Characteristics of the IBC are as follows:

Nothing required to be maintained in the place of incorporation except the Registered Agent's details.
Total tax exemption is automatically provided by law for IBC companies.
No minimum capital required.
Prior approval required of company name. Some words are sensitive eg Assurance, Bank, Trust etc. Must end 'Limited', 'Corporation', 'Incorporated', 'Societe Anonymne' , Gesellschaft mit beschraenkter Haftung or their abbreviations.
Incorporation takes one or two days.
Shelf companies are available.
Capital duty is US$ 200 based on an authorised share capital of 1,000 shares at no par value or on $100,000 of par value shares.
The minimum number of shareholders is one.
Bearer shares and shares of no par value must be held by a custodian.
The minimum number of directors is three, however, if there are fewer than three shareholders then there may also be fewer than three directors.
A secretary is required who may be a company.
There is no requirement for a registered office, but there must be a registered agent.
Information available publicly consists of the articles of incorporation and the name of the registered agent.
There is no requirement for the production or filing of accounts, and no annual return is required
Annual fees amount to US$200.
IBCs do not have access to St Kitts and Nevis double tax treaties.

LIMITED PARTNERSHIP

At least one general and one limited partner are needed to form a limited partnership, under the Companies Act, 1996. The law allows a corporation to be a general or limited partner and permits one person to be simultaneously a general as well as a limited partner in the same limited partnership.

Registration is a simple process of drawing up a declaration of formation of the limited partnership and delivering the document to the Registrar of Limited Partnerships accompanied by a $200 registration fee. The declaration, signed only by general partners, requires the name of the firm, term (if any) for which it is to exist (or, if for unlimited duration, a statement to that effect) and the general partner's names and addresses. The ongoing annual registration fee is US$100.

Contributions of a limited partnership to the firm may be in money (expressed in any currency), other property, and services. A limited partner is not liable for the firm's debts and obligations unless he participates in the management of the partnership, which is the function of general partners. However limited partners have the right to vote on a number of matters affecting the partnership without losing their limited status. Divestiture of a limited partner's interest in the partnership requires consent of all members.

A limited partnership's name must end with the words "limited partnership" or its abbreviation (LP) and may only contain the name of general partners. The firm must maintain an office in the Federation, where a register of limited partners must be kept. Legal proceedings by or against a limited partnership may only identify a general partner as the instigator or target of the action. Accurate accounts reflecting the partnership's financial position must be kept but auditing is not required. Records can be kept in electronic form. A limited partnership may invite the public to acquire units of the partnership's assets after a prospectus has been approved by the Minister of Finance.

If general partners drop out of the firm for any reason, the firm must be dissolved unless limited partners elect one or more general partners. The firm can be continued under the existing agreement or a subsequent agreement.

EXEMPT LIMITED PARTNERSHIP

A limited partnership can qualify for tax exemption if it refrains from doing business with Federation residents. Partners of an exempt limited partnership are not subject to income, capital gains, and withholding taxes. Furthermore, no estate, inheritance, succession or gift taxes have to be paid by any person regarding property owned by or securities created or issued by an exempt limited partnership. Also, stamp duties are not levied on any person with regard to transactions in securities issued or create in respect of an exempt limited partnership.

The rules for allowing an exempt limited partnership to carry on some onshore activities are the same as for a corporation (see above). The annual registration fee for an exempt limited partnership is US$200.

LIMITED LIABILITY COMPANY

Nevis LLCs are formed under the Nevis Limited Liability Company Ordinance, 1995, whose features include:

No corporate tax, income tax, withholding tax, stamp tax, asset tax, exchange controls or other fees or taxes are levied on assets or income originating outside of Nevis;
Members may be individuals or business entities of any nationality or domicile; there may be a single member;
No annual or other reports are required;

Foreign Limited Liability Companies or other business entities may re-domicile to Nevis; Limited Liability Companies may have limited life.
The name of an LLC must end in one of the following: "Limited Liability Company", "LLC", "L.L.C.", "LC" or "L.C.".
Shelf companies are available immediately; the formation of a company normally takes 2 to 4 working days.

TRUSTS

The Trusts Act 1996 was a replacement for the 1961 Trustee Ordinance modeled after the 1925 English Trusts Act, and contains modern asset protection provisions. Trusts and their beneficiaries receive the same tax waivers as companies, with the similar proviso that all transactions must be confined to non-residents for the trust to enjoy exempt status. Trusts may have a protector but, with the exception of unit, spendthrift and charitable trusts, the protector needs acceptable professional qualifications. Both the settlor and trustees can be beneficiaries of a trust.

St Kitts and Nevis trusts are exempt from income, withholding, capital gains and stamp taxes as long as all transactions are confined to non-residents, and subject to a statutory declaration of exempt status accompanied by an annual registration fee of US$200.

Section XV of the Act makes it clear that beneficiaries do not lose their exemption if trustees are active in the Federation owning or leasing property for an office or residences for beneficiaries, holding meetings, conducting banking, signing employment contracts, and arranging for goods and services.

Every trust must maintain an office in the Federation for service of papers. At least two trustees must be appointed, unless one trustee is a corporation or only one trustee was originally appointed under previous legislation. One trustee must either be a Federation resident or carry on business from an office within the Federation. Trustees' duties include registering the trust with the Registrar of Trusts (who may also be the Registrar of Companies).

Trusts do not have to be audited, unless trust terms call for this. The annual statement filed by trustees need not include any financial information. Strict confidentiality rules for trustees prevail. In response to a written request, trustees may in a "reasonable time" provide information about the trust's financial situation and management to the Eastern Caribbean Supreme Court, Government inspectors, and, subject to the terms of the trust, the settlor, protector, a beneficiary, and a charitable beneficiary.

Every non-charitable trust is restricted to a 100-year life span. No restriction is imposed on charitable trusts. Trust terms should specify how long the trust might accumulate income. Asset protection provisions, covered in Part V of the Act dealing with a settlor's rights and responsibilities and applicable to all trust, shield the settlor against forced heirship, compulsory division of matrimonial property, and creditors' suits. A creditor who wants to bring a court action against trust property must first purchase a 25,000 East Caribbean dollars ($9,250) bond from a Federation financial institution and deposit it with the Minister of Finance to cover all costs should the action prove unsuccessful.

The proper law of the trust is the law of the jurisdiction expressed by the trust's terms as the proper law; or, failing that, implied from the trust's terms; or failing either, the jurisdiction with which the trust at the time it was created had the closest connection.

INTERNATIONAL EXEMPT TRUST

These trusts are formed under the Nevis International Exempt Trust Ordinance of 1994, as amended to September 2000. The Trust Ordinance includes special provisions to enhance the use of Nevis as a preferred jurisdiction for the establishment of Asset Protection Trusts. Highlights of the Trust Ordinance include:

Exemption from all forms of Nevis taxation and exchange controls provided that transactions take place only with non-residents;
The trustee may be either a trust company licensed to do business in Nevis or a company incorporated under the Corporation Ordinance;
The proper law may be the law of Nevis or the law of another jurisdiction;
The rule against perpetuities does not apply;
Forced heirship rules are specifically excluded;
Spendthrift and charitable trusts are permitted;
There is a US$25,000 bond requirement prior to the commencement of an action or proceeding against trust property;
There is no registration requirement other than for the Trust's name, name of Trustee and the registered office address;
Settlor and Beneficiary must be non-residents and may be the same person;
One trustee must be a Nevis offshore company or a trust licensed company;
Protectors are allowed for and may be the same person as the Settlor and Beneficiary of the Trust;
An IET is valid and enforceable notwithstanding that it may be invalid according to the law of the Settlor's domicile or residence or place of current incorporation;
The Trust is not considered fraudulent if settled up to 2 years after the date of the creditor's cause of action;
The creditor must prove the intent of the debtor to defraud with "clear and convincing" evidence;
The Statute of Queen Elizabeth is excluded.

MULTIFORM FOUNDATIONS ORDINANCE

The Multiform Foundations Ordinance came into force on October 1st 2005. It introduces a flexible hybrid multiform of foundation into the Nevis international financial services regime.
The Nevis Multiform Foundation is a legal entity shell into which a subscriber can self-design the form of the Foundation, subject to given rules that define it. Therefore, each Nevis Foundation will have a stated multiform, meaning that the constitution of the foundation will state how it is to be treated: whether as a trust, a company, a partnership or an ordinary foundation.
Through the multiform concept the stated identity of the Foundation can be changed during its lifetime, thus allowing for greater flexibility in its use and application.

The Ordinance provides for other entities to be converted or transformed, continued or consolidated or merged into a Nevis Multiform Foundation. Therefore, an entity incorporated outside of Nevis can be transformed into a Nevis Foundation; an existing Nevis entity can be converted into a Nevis Foundation; and any two or more entities from outside or within Nevis can merge into a Nevis Multiform Foundation.

The Ordinance provides for a balance between privacy and transparency and also provides for healthy corporate governance. In light of this, the Ordinance anticipates that Nevis Multiform Foundations will be used for estate planning, charity, financing and special investment holding arrangements.

The Ordinance has a section on forced heirship, making it clear that any Multiform Foundation governed by the laws of Nevis cannot be made void, voidable or liable to be set aside, or defective in any manner by reference to the law of a foreign jurisdiction.

The Ordinance provides that a Foundation can become tax resident in Nevis, subject to an annual fee of $1,000. The Multiform will then be subject to Corporation Tax at a rate of 1% of net income (net profits) with a minimum tax payable of US$1,000 per annum. This is particularly important for some jurisdictions, and again enhances the flexibility of these entities.

FORMATION AND REGISTRATION

REGISTRATION REQUIREMENTS

Procedure 1.	Deposit required amount in a bank and obtain deposit evidence		
Time to complete:	1 day	Cost to complete:	no charge
Procedure 2.	Search and reserve company name		
Time to complete:	1 day	Cost to complete:	XCD 5
Procedure 3.	Prepare and notarize company statutes		
Time to complete:	1 day	Cost to complete:	XCD 2500 (lawyer's fees) + 150 (notarization cost)
Procedure 4.	Procurement of directors' criminal record		
Time to complete:	1 day	Cost to complete:	XCD 375
Procedure 5.	Register with Commercial Registry and obtain Certificate of Incorporation		
Time to complete:	7 days	Cost to complete:	XCD 770
Procedure 6.	Purchase Company Stamp		
Time to complete:	10 days	Cost to complete:	XCD 50
Procedure 7*.	Obtain business License and tax identification number		
Time to complete:	35 days (simultaneous with procedure 6)	Cost to complete:	XCD 2000
Procedure 8*.	Register firm as an employer with the Social Security Office		

Time to complete:	21 days	Cost to complete:	no charge

Note: Procedures sometimes take place simultaneously. Instances of this are marked with an asterisk (*).

COMPANIES

There are two laws governing companies in the Federation, namely:-

The Companies Act 1996, which has effect in St. Kitts and Nevis; and

The Nevis Business Corporation Ordinance 1984, which has effect only in Nevis.

Information in respect of companies governed by the Companies Act 1996 are given on this page.

Any one or more persons associated for a lawful purpose may by subscribing their names to a memorandum of association form a company the liability of the members of which may, according to the memorandum, be limited either to the amount, if any, unpaid on the shares respectively held by them (i.e. a company limited by shares), or to such amount as the members may respectively undertake by the memorandum to contribute to the assets of the company in the event of it being wound up (i.e. a company limited by guarantee).

Any of the subscribers to the memorandum of association of a company, or a person acting on their behalf, may on delivering the memorandum to the Registrar of Companies and on payment of the prescribed registration fee apply for the registration of an incorporated company with limited liability. There must also be delivered to the Registrar of Companies articles of association if they differ from the model articles.

A company limited by shares must state in its memorandum of association the maximum number of shares that the company is authorised to issue and the minimum amount per share (which may be expressed in any currency or currencies) to be received by the company for shares issued by it (i.e. the stated value of a share). No subscriber to the memorandum of a company limited by shares may take less than one share.

A company limited by guarantee must state in its memorandum of association the number of members with which the company proposes to register and the amount of the guarantee (which may be expressed in any currency or currencies) that each member is required to contribute to cover the debts and liabilities of the company in the case of it being wound up.

Companies may limit their period of existence.

NAMES OF COMPANIES

The name of a company must end with the word "Limited" (or the abbreviation "Ltd."), "Corporation" (or the abbreviation "Corp.") or "Incorporated" (or the abbreviation "Inc.").

A company can use any name provided that the name chosen is not considered misleading or otherwise undesirable by the Registrar of Companies.

PRIVATE AND PUBLIC COMPANIES

A company which has 51 or more members is deemed to be a public company.

A private company is a company which is not a public company but if it should make an invitation to thc public to acquire or apply for any shares and debentures issued by it, or interest in any such shares or debenture, or rights to acquire any of the foregoing, it will become a public company even if it has fewer than 51 members unless such an invitation is addressed exclusively to a restricted circle of persons.

CORPORATE CAPACITY AND TRANSACTIONS

The doctrine of *ultra vires* in its application to companies is abolished and accordingly a company has the capacity and, subject to certain other provisions of the Companies Act, the same rights, powers and privileges as an individual.

Where a transaction purports to be entered into by a company, or by a person as agent for a company, at a time when the company has not been formed, then, unless otherwise agreed by the parties to the transaction, the transaction has effect as one entered into by the person purporting to act for the company or as agent for it, and he will be personally bound by the transaction and entitled to its benefits.

No person is deemed to have notice of any record by reason only that they are made available by the Registrar of Companies, or by a company, for inspection.

REGISTER OF MEMBERS AND SHARE CERTIFICATES

Every company must keep a register of members but inspection of the register by persons who are not members or officers of the company is not permitted in the case of a private company which is an exempt company (i.e. a company which is exempt from all taxes under the Companies Act).

Subject as otherwise provided in the Companies Act, every company must issue share certificates in respect of shares allotted by it.

A private company which is an exempt company may issue bearer certificates in respect of fully paid-up shares.

No share certificate issued by a company shall in any manner whatsoever bear any indication of the stated value of the shares comprised in it.

ADMINISTRATION

All companies must have a registered office in the Federation to which communications and notices may be addressed.

A private company must have at least one director and a public company must have at least three directors of whom at least two are not employed by the company or any of its related companies.

A body corporate may not be a director.

Every company must have a secretary and may have one or more assistant secretaries who, or each of whom, may be an individual or a body corporate.

MEETINGS

Every company must hold an annual general meeting but if all the members of a private company agree in writing that an annual general meeting should be dispensed with, then so long as that agreement has effect, that company is dispensed from holding an annual general meeting.

In the case of an equality of votes the chairman of a meeting (whether it is a meeting of the members of the company or of its directors) has a second or casting vote in addition to any vote which he may have.

Where a company has only one member or, if all the shares of a particular class of shares are held by only one member, that member present in person or by proxy constitutes a meeting. If a private company has only one director, that director present in person constitutes a meeting.

ACCOUNTS

All companies must keep accounting records and prepare annual accounts.

Where a company is a public company; or the articles of the company so require; or a resolution of the company in general meeting so directs, then that company must appoint auditors to audit its annual accounts.

A public company must deliver to the Registrar of Companies a copy of its audited annual accounts. A private company which is an ordinary company (i.e. a company which is not an exempt company) must deliver to the Registrar of Companies either a copy of its audited annual accounts or a certificate of solvency.

WINDING-UP AND DISSOLUTION OF COMPANIES

A company may be wound-up and dissolved either by a summary winding-up if the company is solvent, a winding up by the Court if the Court is of the opinion that it is just and equitable that the company should be wound up, or by a creditor's winding up if the company is insolvent.

A company will be dissolved without formal winding up if the Registrar of Companies strikes off the company's name from the register of companies, but the liability of every director and member of the company continues and may be enforced as if it had not been dissolved.

TAX AND OTHER EXEMPTIONS

Companies are exempt from all taxes as long as they conduct their business exclusively with person who are not resident in the Federation.

A company is called an exempt company if it qualifies for the tax exemption mentioned above. An ordinary company is a company which is not an exempt company.

Ordinary companies will not pay income tax on dividends, interest and royalties received from a qualifying participating interest in another body corporate.

No estate, inheritance, succession or gift tax, rate, duty, levy or other charge is payable by any person with regard to any property owned by, or securities issued or created by or in respect of, an exempt company.

No stamp duty or other tax is payable by any person with regard to any transaction in any securities issued or created by or in respect of an exempt company.

GOVERNMENT FEES

Registration and annual filing fees for companies are as follows:-

- ☐Ordinary private company USD 100
- ☐Exempt private company USD 200
- ☐Ordinary public company USD 400
- ☐Exempt public company USD 600

LIMITED PARTNERSHIPS

FORMATION AND ESTABLISHMENT OF LIMITED PARTNERSHIPS

Any two or more persons can form a limited partnership, but a limited partnership must consist of one or more persons who are general partners and one or more persons who are limited partners.

A body corporate may be a general or a limited partner and a person may be a general partner as well as a limited partner at the same time in the same limited partnership.

Any of the general partners of a limited partnership or a person acting on their behalf may on delivering to the Registrar of Limited Partnerships a declaration of the formation of the limited partnership and on payment of the prescribed registration fee apply for the registration of the declaration.

An association of persons will not be a limited partnership until the Registrar of Limited Partnerships has issued a certificate in respect of the above mentioned declaration.

NAMES OF LIMITED PARTNERSHIPS

The name of a limited partnership must end with the words "Limited Partnership" or the abbreviation "L.P."

A limited partnership may use any name provided that the name chosen is not considered misleading or otherwise undesirable by the Registrar of Limited Partnerships and does not contain the name of any limited partner who is not also a general partner.

ADMINISTRATION

Every limited partnership must have an office for service in the Federation.

Except as otherwise provided in the Limited Partnerships Act, legal proceedings by or against a limited partnership may only be instituted by or against any one or more of the general partners and no limited partner may be a party to or named in such proceedings.

ACCOUNTS

The general partners of every limited partnership must keep accounting records which are sufficient to show and explain their transactions in respect of the limited partnership and are such as to disclose with reasonable accuracy at any time the financial position of the limited partnership.

Unless the partnership agreement otherwise provides, it is not necessary for the general partners of a limited partnership to appoint an auditor to audit their accounts in respect of the limited partnership.

DISSOLUTION OF LIMITED PARTNERSHIPS

A limited partnership can not be dissolved by an act of the partners until a statement of dissolution signed by one of them has been delivered to the Registrar of Limited Partnerships.

A limited partnership must be dissolved if there are no general partners, but if the limited partners elect one or more general partners, then its activities may be taken over and continued as provided for in the partnership agreement or a subsequent agreement.

The Court has the power to order the dissolution of a limited partnership if the Court is of the opinion that it is just and equitable that the limited partnership should be dissolved.

In the event of the dissolution of a limited partnership its affairs are wound up by the general partners or, if there are no general partners, in such manner as the Court may direct.

TAX AND OTHER EXEMPTIONS

A limited partnership is not itself a subject for assessment to any tax in the Federation and the partners of a limited partnership are exempt from all income, capital gains and withholding taxes which may arise out of their interest in the limited partnership if the general partners of the limited partnership are in respect of it effecting transactions exclusively with persons who are not resident in the Federation.

A limited partnership is called an exempt limited partnership if its partners qualify for the tax exemption mentioned above. An ordinary limited partnership is a limited partnership which is not an exempt limited partnership.

No estate, inheritance, succession or gift tax, rate, duty, levy or other charge is payable by any person with regard to any property owned by, or securities issued or created in respect of, an exempt limited partnership.

No stamp duties are payable by any person with regard to any transaction in securities issued or created in respect of an exempt limited partnership.

Government Fees

Fees for the registration of the declaration of a limited partnership and for filing of its annual statement are as follows:-

- Ordinary limited partnership USD 100
- Exempt limited partnership USD 200

TRUSTS

There are two laws governing trusts in the Federation, namely:-

- The Trusts Act 1996, which has effect in St. Kitts and Nevis; and
- The Nevis International Exempt Trust Ordinance 1994, which has effect only in Nevis.

Information in respect of trusts governed by the Trusts Act 1996 are given on this page.

Creation and Establishment of Trusts

Any person may create a trust, but a trust must have at least one trustee who ordinarily resides within the Federation or carries on business from an office or other fixed place within the Federation.

A body corporate may be the settlor or a trustee or a beneficiary of a trust and the settlor or a trustee of a trust may be a beneficiary at the same time of the same trust.

Any of the trustees of a trust or a person acting on their behalf may on delivering to the Registrar of Trusts an attestation of the existence of the trust and on payment of the prescribed registration fee apply for the registration of the attestation.

No trust will be recognised under the laws of the Federation as valid and enforceable until the Registrar of Trusts has issued a certificate in respect of the above mentioned attestation.

Types of Trusts

A trust under which the income or capital or the income and capital of the trust property is applied for a purpose regarded as charitable, is a charitable trust.

A trust under which the interest of a beneficiary is subject to restriction, diminution or termination, is a spendthrift or protective trust.

A trust established for the purpose, or having the effect, of providing, for persons having funds available for investment, facilities for the participation by them as beneficiaries under the trust, in any profits or income arising from the acquisition of any property whatsoever, is a unit trust.

A trust which is not a charitable trust, or a spendthrift or protective trust, or a unit trust, is a common trust.

A common trust may be created for a purpose which is not a charitable purpose, provided that the trust must vest in natural persons within the perpetuity period applying or expressed to apply to the trust. Any trust so created must be enforceable by the settlor or his personal representative or by a person named in the terms of the trust as the person appointed to enforce the trust and the trust must be enforceable at the instance of the person so named notwithstanding that such person may not be a beneficiary under the trust

PROPER LAW

The proper law of a trust is the law of the jurisdiction expressed by the terms of the trust as the proper law; or failing that, implied from the terms of the trust; or failing either, with which the trust at the time it was created had the closest connexion.

The term of a trust may provide for the proper law of the trust or the law governing a severable aspect of the trust to be changed from the law of one jurisdiction to the law of another jurisdiction.

DURATION OF TRUSTS

A trust which is not a charitable trust may continue until the one-hundredth anniversary of the date on which it came into existence.

ASSET PROTECTION PROVISIONS

The asset protection provisions of the Act deal with the capacity of a settlor to transfer or dispose property to a trust, the retention of control and benefits by a settlor, the bankruptcy of a settlor and the prevention of fraud on a settlor's creditors.

ADMINISTRATION

Subject to the terms of the trust, the number of trustees must not be less than two, unless only one trustee was originally appointed or the sole trustee is a corporate trustee.

Every trust must have an office for service in the Federation.

Except as otherwise provided in the Trusts Act, legal proceedings by or against a trust can only be instituted by or against any one or more of the trustees.

ACCOUNTS

The trustees of every trust must keep accounting records which are sufficient to show and explain their transactions in respect of the trust and are such as to disclose with reasonable accuracy at any time the financial position of the trust.

Unless the terms of a trust otherwise provides, the trustees of a trust need not appoint an auditor to audit their accounts in respect of the trust.

TERMINATION OF TRUST

A trust can not be terminated by an act of its trustees until a statement of termination signed by one of them is delivered to the Registrar of Trusts.

Where all the beneficiaries of a trust are in agreement so to do, they may require the trustee to terminate the trust.

The Court has the power to order the termination of a trust if the Court is of the opinion that it is just and equitable that the trust should be terminated.

On the termination of a trust the trust property will be distributed by the trustee in accordance with the terms of the trust to the persons entitled thereto.

TAX AND OTHER EXEMPTIONS

A trust is not itself a subject for assessment to any tax in the Federation and the beneficiaries of a trust are exempt from all income, capital gains and withholding taxes which may arise out of their interest in the trust if the trustees of the trust are in respect of it effecting transactions exclusively with persons who are not resident in the Federation.

A trust is called an exempt trust if its beneficiaries qualify for the tax exemption mentioned above. An ordinary trust is a trust which is not an exempt trust.

No estate, inheritance, succession or gift tax, rate, duty, levy or other charge is payable by any person with regard to any property held in, or securities issued or created in respect of, an exempt trust.

No stamp duties are payable by any person with regard to any transaction in securities issued or created in respect of an exempt trust.

GOVERNMENT FEES

Fees for the registration of the attestation of a trust and for filing of its annual statement are as follows:-

- ☐Ordinary trusts USD 100
- ☐Exempt trusts USD 200

TAXATION

TREATIES

The Federation is party to double taxation treaties with Denmark, Norway, Sweden, the United Kingdom and the United States of America (limited to social security benefits).

There are no Mutual Legal Assistance Treaties in effect.

INCOME TAX

There is no personal income tax in St. Kitts or Nevis.

Ordinary companies are liable to a 38% tax on profits.

This tax does not apply to trusts, limited partnerships and exempt companies or to enterprises which have been granted a tax concession.

WITHHOLDING TAX

Individuals and ordinary companies remitting payments to persons outside of the Federation must deduct 10% withholding tax from profits, administration, management or head office expenses, technical service fees, accounting and audit expenses, royalties, non-life insurance premiums and rent.

This tax does not apply to trusts, limited partnerships and exempt companies or to enterprises which have been granted a tax concession.

CAPITAL GAINS TAX

There is a capital gains tax of 20% on profits or gains derived from a transaction relating to assets located in the Federation which are disposed of within one year of the date of their acquisition. This tax does not apply to trusts, limited partnerships and exempt companies or to enterprises which have been granted a tax concession.

LAND AND HOUSE TAXES

There is a tax on land located in the Federation, this tax is charged at various rates depending on the size and nature of the land concerned. In Special Development Areas, such as the South East Peninsula on St. Kitts, there is a tax of 0.5% of the assessed market value of the land, or land and improvements.

A house tax is charged at the rate of 5% of the annual gross rental value for residences in St. Kitts or Nevis with a 25% rebate for properties that are occupied by their owner solely as residence. The minimum annual rental value is XCD 600 (USD 222) in St. Kitts and XCD 48 (USD 18) in Nevis.

OTHER TAXES

There is no net worth tax, gift tax, sales tax, turnover tax, or estate duty.

ST. KITTS AND NEVIS: OFFSHORE BUSINESS SECTORS

St.Kitts and Nevis offshore legislation, which applies on both islands, includes the Companies Act 1996 and the Trusts Act 1996. A Merchant Shipping Act and Foundation Act were added in 2002 and 2003.

St Kitts and Nevis has however aimed primarily at attracting industrial and tourist investment with very tax-friendly incentive legislation under the Fiscal Incentives Act 1974 and the Hotel Aids Ordinance.

Nevis emerged as an offshore jurisdiction after enacting its Nevis Business Corporation Ordinance in 1984, based upon American corporate law of the state of Delaware. Trusts are created under the Nevis International Exempt Trust Ordinance of 1994, as amended to September 2000. Limited Liability Companies (LLCs) which have emerged as Nevis's star product, are formed under the Nevis Limited Liability Company Ordinance, 1995.

All offshore finance businesses in the Federation need authorisation under the Financial Services (Regulations) Order, 1997. This includes deposit-taking business, investment business, insurance business, trust business and corporate service provision.

St Kitts and Nevis maintains a high level of confidentiality for offshore entities under the Confidential Relationships Act of 1985. The Confidentiality Act safeguards investors by prohibiting disclosure of any information obtained in the course of business. The law is considered to provide the most rigid secrecy in the Caribbean region as it applies to banks and professionals as well as Government officials.

FORMS OF OFFSHORE OPERATION

Offshore operations may take place within the following forms:

Exempt Private Company (St Kitts and Nevis)
International Business Company (Nevis)
Exempt Limited Partnership (St Kitts and Nevis)
Limited Liability Company (Nevis)
Trust (St Kitts and Nevis)
International Exempt Trust (Nevis)
Multiform Foundations Ordinance (Nevis)

In addition, there are free zones whose occupants don't have to have offshore status as such, but which offer benefits broadly similar to those available to offshore companies;

BANKING

Domestic banking is regulated by the Banking Act 1991 and non-domestic banking falls under the Financial Servicers (Regulations) Order 1997. Nevis has its own Offshore Banking Ordinance 1996.

Two types of banking licenses are granted under the Federation's 1997 Financial Services (Regulations) Order. 'Unrestricted' licenses require minimum financial resources of 1,350,000 East Caribbean dollars ($500,000), while for 'restricted' licenses the level is only 135,000 East Caribbean dollars ($50,000).

The Confidential Relationship Act, 1985 for St. Kitts-Nevis offers complete confidentiality should foreign authorities seek private banking and financial records. Prison terms are mandatory for violation of the statute.

The banking system consists of the Government owned St Kitts-Nevis National Bank, the Development Bank of St Kitts and Nevis, the privately-owned Bank of Nevis and the Bank of Nevis International, First Caribbean International, Royal Bank of Canada, Bank of Nova Scotia, RBTT Bank, the Nevis Co-operative Credit Union, the St Kitts Co-operative Credit Union and the Foundation for National Development.

In 2002, the assets of commercial banks increased by $181.5 million or 10.2% to total just under 2 billion at year end. The National Bank, which is the largest commercial bank in the Eastern Caribbean Currency Union has assets in excess of a billion dollars. By mid-2005 the assets of commercial banks had reached $3 bn. The Nevis Offshore Banking Ordinance 1996 defines offshore banking as follows:

> Receiving of foreign funds through the acceptance of foreign money, deposits payable upon receipt demand or after a fixed period or after notice;
> The sale or placement of foreign bonds certifcates, notes or other debt obligations or other securities, or
> Any other similar activities involving foreign money or foreign securities, and
> Either in whole or in part using foreign funds so acquired for loans, advances and investments whether in Nevis or elsewhere.

Licences under the Banking Ordinance are issued to eligible companies or qualified foreign banks. An eligible company must be a wholly owned subsidiary of a local bank regulated by the Eastern Caribbean Central Bank that is licensed under the Banking Act to do business in Nevis. A qualified foreign bank is a foreign bank that is licensed under the Banking Act, or is foreign bank with minimum capitalization and assets, as prescribed by the Minister, that is not licensed under the Banking Act but is licensed to do domestic banking in its jurisdiction of incorporation.

An eligible company must be incorporated under the Companies Act as a company limited by shares, and must have objects or business activity restricted to offshore banking from within Nevis. It must have at least one director who is a citizen of St. Kitts and Nevis with a residence in Nevis. The minimum Authorised Capital must be at least ECD2 Million, of which not less than ECD1 Million has been Subscribed and Paid Up in cash, such cash being deposited in an account maintained by the Permanent Secretary at the Eastern Caribbean Central Bank.

Not later than four months after the close of its financial year, a licensee must forward to the Permanent Secretary copies of its balance sheet and profit and loss account and the full and correct names of the directors of the licensee. The balance sheet and the profit and loss account must bear on its face the certificate of an auditor.

REGULATION OF BANKING

Offshore banking falls under the Financial Services (Regulations) Order 1997. Nevis has its own Offshore Banking Ordinance 1996.

Two types of banking licenses are granted under the Federation's 1997 Financial Services (Regulations) Order. 'Unrestricted' licenses require minimum financial resources of 1,350,000 East Caribbean dollars ($500,000), while for 'restricted' licenses the level is only 135,000 East Caribbean dollars ($50,000).

Fees for a banking license are: on filing of first application (not refundable) - for all applications, USD 1,000; on granting or renewal of authorisation for an unrestricted business, USD 8,000, and for a restricted business, USD 4,000.
The Nevis Offshore Banking Ordinance 1996 defines offshore banking as follows:

> Receiving of foreign funds through the acceptance of foreign money, deposits payable upon receipt demand or after a fixed period or after notice;
> The sale or placement of foreign bonds certifcates, notes or other debt obligations or other securities, or
> Any other similar activities involving foreign money or foreign securities, and
> Either in whole or in part using foreign funds so acquired for loans, advances and investments whether in Nevis or elsewhere.

Licences under the Banking Ordinance are issued to eligible companies or qualified foreign banks. An eligible company must be a wholly owned subsidiary of a local bank regulated by the Eastern Caribbean Central Bank that is licensed under the Banking Act to do business in Nevis. A qualified foreign bank is a foreign bank that is licensed under the Banking Act, or is foreign bank with minimum capitalization and assets, as prescribed by the Minister, that is not licensed under the Banking Act but is licensed to do domestic banking in its jurisdiction of incorporation.

An eligible company must be incorporated under the Companies Act as a company limited by shares, and must have objects or business activity restricted to offshore banking from within Nevis. It must have at least one director who is a citizen of St. Kitts and Nevis with a residence in Nevis. The minimum Authorised Capital must be at least ECD2 Million, of which not less than ECD1 Million has been Subscribed and Paid Up in cash, such cash being deposited in an account maintained by the Permanent Secretary at the Eastern Caribbean Central Bank.

Not later than four months after the close of its financial year, a licensee must forward to the Permanent Secretary copies of its balance sheet and profit and loss account and the full and correct names of the directors of the licensee. The balance sheet and the profit and loss account must bear on its face the certificate of an auditor.
Nevis offshore banks pay tax as follows:

> 2½% on all profits and gains up to ten million dollars;
> 2% on all profits and gains in amounts exceeding ten million dollars but not exceeding twenty million dollars;
> 1½% on all profits and gains in amounts exceeding twenty million dollars but not exceeding thirty million dollars; and
> 1% on all profits and gains in amounts exceeding thirty million dollars.

However, a licensee and the Minister may enter into an agreement determining the amount to be paid as income tax in lieu of other taxes on income by the licensee in respect of the business it does from within Nevis.
The Minister may by order exempt a licensee in respect of its business from all or so much of any duty payable under the Customs Act in respect of any goods imported by the licensee in respect of its business as the Minister deems expedient, if the licensee in respect of its business satisfies the Minister that the goods concerned are not being made or manufactured in Nevis, are essential as equipment or fixtures for doing business from within Nevis and are not merely goods that will be used up or expended in the ordinary course of business.
Where the Minister is satisfied that a licensee must use the services of specially qualified persons in order to do its business effectively from within Nevis and that it is unable to acquire those services in Nevis, and it is unable to retain or hire those services from outside Nevis without special tax benefits being made available, the Minister may authorise an offshore benefit

provision for the employment of those specially qualified persons, whereby a prescribed percentage of an employee's or contractor's salary or fees from a licensee:

is exempt from any duty or tax in Nevis;
may be paid in a foreign currency;
may be paid in some other prescribed manner in another currency or otherwise.

Fees charged by the Nevisvian government in respect of an Offshore Banking Business are as follows:

Government License Fee USD 15,000;
Government Due Diligence Fee 600;

Incorporation Fee 1,400.

INSURANCE

See Offshore Business Review – Insurance for a more general treatment of captive insurance companies.
Non-domestic insurance and assurance businesses must be licensed under the Insurance Act. The Federation's 1997 Financial Services (Regulations) Order set the following minimum net assets for applicants wishing to engage in insurance business: long-term and general insurance business, 810,000 East Caribbean dollars ($300,000), reduced to 540,000 East Caribbean dollars ($200,000) for long-term but not general insurance, and further lowered to 270,000 East Caribbean dollars ($100,000) for general but not long-term insurance.
In July, 2004, the Nevis Ministry of Finance and Development in Nevis announced the passage of the Nevis International Insurance Ordinance. The Ordinance is divided into six sections, and provides for the licensing and regulation of general insurance, captive insurance and reinsurance companies. It is compulsory for insurance companies to have a physical presence in Nevis, whether via a resident manager or a fully trained registered agent, with adequate knowledge and experience of the insurance industry.

BACK TO TOP

TRUSTS

Trust management has become an important business for St Kitts and Nevis.
Like all offshore finance businesses in the Federation, trust management companies need authorisation under the Financial Services (Regulations) Order, 1997. Under the Order, applicants wishing to establish a trust business handling both unrestricted and restricted business must have net assets of 540,000 east Caribbean dollars ($200,000) or its equivalent in other currencies, reduced to 54,000 east Caribbean dollars ($20,000) for restricted business.

Nevis trusts are formed under the Nevis International Exempt Trust Ordinance of 1994, as amended to September 2000. The Trust Ordinance includes special provisions to enhance the use of Nevis as a preferred jurisdiction for the establishment of Asset Protection Trusts.
The St Kitts and Nevis Trusts Act 1996 was a replacement for the 1961 Trustee Ordinance modeled after the 1925 English Trusts Act, and also contains modern asset protection provisions.

REGULATION OF TRUSTS

Like all offshore finance businesses in the Federation, trust management companies need authorisation under the Financial Services (Regulations) Order, 1997. Under the Order, applicants wishing to establish a trust business handling both unrestricted and restricted business must have net assets of 540,000 east Caribbean dollars ($200,000) or its equivalent in other currencies, reduced to 54,000 east Caribbean dollars ($20,000) for restricted business.

The St Kitts and Nevis Trusts Act 1996 was a replacement for the 1961 Trustee Ordinance modeled after the 1925 English Trusts Act, and also contains modern asset protection provisions. Nevis trusts are formed under the Nevis International Exempt Trust Ordinance of 1994, as amended to September 2000. The Trust Ordinance includes special provisions to enhance the use of Nevis as a preferred jurisdiction for the establishment of Asset Protection Trusts.

Nevis trusts are exempt from all forms of taxation and exchange controls provided that transactions take place only with non-residents. The trustee may be either a trust company licensed to do business in Nevis or a company incorporated under the Corporation Ordinance (ie an International Business Company). There is no registration requirement other than for the Trust's name, name of the Trustee and the registered office address.
There is a US$25,000 bond requirement prior to the commencement of an action or proceeding against trust property.

TAX TREATMENT OF OFFSHORE OPERATIONS

Whether under Federation legislation or Nevisvian legislation, offshore entities in St Kitts and Nevis are exempt from Corporate Income Tax, Withholding Tax and Capital Gains Tax, as long as they carry on business only with non-residents of the Federation. However, the various laws make it clear that an exempt entity does not lose its tax waivers because of certain activities within the Federation including signing contracts or concluding arrangements for employing residents, purchasing goods and services, and exercising other powers to carry on its business such as holding directors' and members' meetings, transacting banking and reinsurance business, and conducting securities transactions or serving as adviser to Federation residents who enjoy exempt status.

An **Exempt Private Company (St Kitts and Nevis)** pays an annual fee of US$200 to the government on filing of the annual return.

An **International Business Company (Nevis)** pays an annual fee of US$200 to the government (no annual return is required). Capital duty is US$200 based on an authorised share capital of 1,000 shares at no par value or on $100,000 of par value shares.

An **Exempt Limited Partnership (St Kitts and Nevis)** pays an annual registration fee of US$200 to the government.

A **Limited Liability Company (Nevis)** pays an annual registration fee of US$220 to the government.

A **Trust (St Kitts and Nevis)** pays an annual fee of US$200 to the government along with a statutory declaration of exempt status.

An **International Exempt Trust (Nevis)** pays an annual registration fee of US$220 to the government.

TAXATION OF FOREIGN EMPLOYEES OF OFFSHORE OPERATIONS

There is no personal income tax in St Kitts and Nevis but foreign nationals working in the country are required to obtain a work permit for which there is an annual charge of 1,500 East Caribbean dollars ($635). Persons or companies remitting payments to persons or companies outside of the nation must deduct a 10% withholding tax on profits, administration or management and head office expenses, technical service fees, accounting and audit expenses, royalties, non-life insurance premiums and rents.

There is no capital gains tax other than on short-term investments, but the St. Kitts and Nevis house tax of 5%, payable in two installments a year, applies on annual rental value of a property, with a 25% rebate on residential property. The controversial Alien Landowners Tax places a 14% levy paid by buyers and 4% by sellers on residences. Although it also applies to commercial land, it is subject to negotiations on a case-by-case basis. A 1% sales tax on gross sales, a hotel tax of 5% and a 2% tax on foreign currency transfers are in effect.

EMPLOYMENT & RESIDENCE

Work permits are granted on application by employers, provided that no local worker is available, and involve the production of a number of documents, including health certificates.
The Nevisian Banking Ordinance gives discretion to the responsible Minister to reduce taxes and other conditions for the foreign employees of an enterprise which has had trouble sourcing suitable labour locally.

NATIONAL INFORMATION AND COMMUNICATIONS TECHNOLOGY (ICT) STRATEGIC PLAN AND INVESTMENT OPORTUNITIES

STRATEGIC INFORMATION

St. Kitts and Nevis is an independent Federation with a parliamentary democracy based on the British model with Queen Elizabeth II of the United Kingdom as the Head of State. It is the only Federation in the Caribbean. The Sugar Industry, which was once a major employer and contributor to the economy, has come to an end. Additionally, the September 11 terrorist attacks reverberated widely throughout the Caribbean, resulting in a major downturn during its high tourist season with St Kitts and Nevis being particularly hard hit. The country has met these challenges by rebuilding its tourism facilities and diversifying into other industries ranging from financial services, light manufacturing, specialized agriculture to electronics and informatics. As part of this economic diversification strategy, the Government of St Kitts and Nevis (GSTK&N) has also made a serious commitment to provide the framework whereby Information and Communication Technology (ICT) can become a lead sector of the economy of St Kitts and Nevis.

It is the goal of the GSTK&N that within St Kitts and Nevis, Information and Communication Technologies would be used to the widest possible extent by all segments of society with a view to fostering, accelerating and sustaining the long-term social, cultural and economic development of the country.

ICT IN ST KITTS AND NEVIS

The GSTK&N, private sector and other stakeholders in the nation's development share a common belief that ICT can provide the foundation whereby a society can be built with equitable distribution of opportunity and knowledge. They also believe that it is a key determinant of the competitive advantage of nations. The *National Strategic Plan* seeks to present the composite ICT initiative and also to set out a national ICT roadmap which is comprehensive and overarching. The *National ICT Strategic Plan* if carefully followed and implemented will allow the GSTK&N to achieve its aforementioned goal of cementing ICT as one of the leading sectors of the economy. It is an outgrowth and consolidation of several preliminary assessments that were prepared by international organizations as well as a series of consultations with the major stakeholders and desk research into several prior reports. Feedback from attendees at the Project Launch has also contributed to this report.

After a careful review of all of the information that was gathered in this manner it was determined that the five major branches of the *National ICT Strategy* would be as shown below:

x building the information infrastructure

x enabling the policy and legal environment

x developing ICT human resources and building capacity (information society)

x modernizing government and delivering citizen services electronically

x leveraging ICT for economic and social development through public-private partnerships.

BUILDING INFORMATION INFRASTRUCTURE

Infrastructure is necessary to deliver ICT services such as e-government, e-learning, and e-health to the citizens of St Kitts and Nevis and to facilitate e-commerce among its people and businesses. A landmark 1996 study by the World Bank identified the high price of communications as a barrier to the development of services export in the Caribbean Since then, nearly all countries have put new legal and regulatory structures in place and have established independent regulators. Yet, in spite of this the benefits of reform still elude most Caribbean islands, this being particularly true in St Kitts as Nevis where residents continue to pay high prices and where the unavailability of good affordable telecommunications services continues to be a barrier to the development and growth of the ICT sector

- x St Kitts and Nevis enjoys a relatively high teledensity and growth in telephone lines. This stands at 51.76%1 .
- x A mobile penetration rate of 70% currently exists.
- x Internet Accounts are relatively low at 8%, which is probably due to the high cost.
- x There are currently 21 fibre optic submarine cable systems in the Caribbean. Of these, two land in St Kitts Nevis, the ECFS and GCN cable system.
- x Cable & Wireless [St. Kitts and Nevis] Ltd. has deployed a double fibre ring around St. Kitts and a fibre link to its international gateway switch. The islands of St. Kitts and Nevis are connected via microwave. The Cable, C&W's licensed fixed wire competitor, also has deployed a fibre ring plus fibre strands to high-density business sites.

The current infrastructure is definitely adequate. But almost without exception business people, public officials, and residential customers alike complain about high prices and network reliability. The lack of choice and high prices of leased circuit capacity are important barriers to investment and development of ICT in St Kitts and Nevis. The main ICT businesses that the Government wishes to attract are information-based industries including data entry, data manipulation, data conversion, information processing, and information management, and these require fairly inexpensive broadband connection in order to flourish.

The EU faced with a similar situation in 1992 banded together to apply harmonization measures to conditions for leasing circuit capacity, procedures and conditions of licensing, use of frequencies, etc. This effort by EU members led to a fall in prices that St Kitts and Nevis may similarly achieve through regional cooperation on the matter.

POLICY AND LEGAL ENVIRONMENT

St Kitts and Nevis needs to update laws to accommodate the emergence of online commerce and communications so as to provide the enabling environment. The four main areas that are being urgently addressed are: *Electronic Transactions, ICT Crimes, Data Protection,* and *Intellectual*

Property Rights.

Electronic Transactions Legislation

This project component would ensure the preparation of an Act of Parliament for the facilitation and recognition of electronic contracts, the creation and exchange of electronic communication, the establishment of a Certification Authority and the accreditation of Certification Service

Providers and the facilitation of the recognition of electronic filing by Government departments.
This project component also envisages institutional and capacity building in Government for the accreditation of Service Providers under the proposed Act of Parliament and the development of legal standards with UNCITRAL Secretariat as well as assisting in the formulation of appropriate regulations.

ICT Crimes Unit (ICTCU)

– The ICTCU would function as the convenor in a review of the Computer Crimes Bill. This project component would

a. o Examine the criminal implications of spamming and e-surveillance
b. o Facilitate the establishment of a specialized Digital Forensic Lab in the Police Department for the enforcement of Computer Crimes
c. o Create the framework for the analysis of forensic evidence.
d. o Build capacity of enforcement officials
e. o Establish linkages with foreign enforcement agencies.

Data Protection

- The aim here is to develop and implement legislative or other measures to ensure that St Kitts and Nevis meets the adequacy levels required by the EU Directive on Data Protection (and other important standards), and promote institutional development for data protection and privacy issues.
- This would help to ensure that St Kitts and Nevis complies with required international legal standards for the development of the IT Enabled Services sector and the Business Process Outsourcing sector

Intellectual Property Rights (IPRs)

- This Project component would ensure the appropriate development of legal standards with UNCITRAL Secretariat as well as assist in the formulation of appropriate regulations to ensure that IPRs are protected as per international standards.
- The OECS Legal Drafting Unit as well as ECTEL would play a significant role in assisting St Kitts Nevis to draft these laws.

The establishment of an appropriate legal framework for ICT development would facilitate the growth of ICT in St Kitts and Nevis, including e-business and e-government related activities, and create the environment for ICT related foreign direct investment.

DEVELOPING ICT HUMAN RESOURCES

Of absolute priority is the continuing struggle towards a smarter society. The widespread deployment and utilization of ICTs is directly dependent upon the ability of a population to become ICT proficient. To that end one should first seek the widest possible level of ICT literacy through inclusion of ICT in formal and informal education and the training of teachers and instructors.

• To that end Government should

-Call for and support vocational training (e.g. with a professional education levy or incentive, subsidies, study loans, etc.) with a view to upgrading the ICT skills of the present workforce.

-Call for and support learning and information-oriented lifelong education programmes to be initiated through community access points (CAPs).

- Expand on-going computer literacy efforts in primary and secondary schools into information literacy and culture in the formal education system through appropriate curriculum and pedagogic changes.

E-GOVERNMENT

The credibility of any ICT policy is to a large extent dependent on the government sector's own efforts toward an effective deployment and use of these technologies. To accomplish E-Government, the Government should undertake the following steps

Design and implement a stepwise programme for installing computer networks in public administration agencies and related training of all civil servants with a view to supporting the deployment of Government-to-Government and Government-to-Public systems, including E-procurement, and electronic transactions through Intranets, Extranets and Internet sites. Priority may be given to transactions between businesses and public administration.

Set up web-based resources providing basic official information for the citizens of OECS countries, especially information related to main circumstances of life.

Set up web-based services and other appropriate electronic resources (e.g. CD Rom versions of the web sites) providing practical information and advice on natural disaster preparedness and emergency situations in conjunction with alert and rescue programmes.

Establish a country portal providing basic information about the country, its administrative organisation, investment and migration regulations and procedures, etc, targeted at economic partners and customers in other countries.

Establish a phased programme with a view to allowing for electronic payment to the public administration.

PUBLIC-PRIVATE PARTNERSHIPS

Ultimately, it is the private sector that must generate the business activity that establishes and maintains economic growth and improves the living standards of the citizens. In view of the extensive transformation that ICT use calls for, the market structure and enterprises' size may present obstacles until ICTs have become commonplace. Since the objective is to be among the early adopters rather than laggards, targeted support is required. To that end Government should

x Establish a scheme for encouraging firms to invest in ICT and train their staff, e.g. through low rate loans to be administered by commercial banks with a consolidation or guarantee from the government. Such schemes should apply to existing companies as well as new investors.

x Support the participation of enterprises of the tourism sector and tourism authorities in portals that can provide a variety of information and inquiry services as well as on-line reservations and auctions.

x Support the creation and/or development of agri-business portals that can provide to the farmers and enterprises of the sector, with their active participation, when appropriate, directly or through their organisations, a variety of technical, commercial and administrative information and inquiry services as well as support co-operative commercial services.

- x Develop IT parks that can offer state of the art wired premises, call centres, industrial and warehousing space, training facilities, incubator facilities, business development support, accommodation, catering, and entertainment facilities that can attract and host external investors and host temporary events (such as staff training and leisure packages, professional meetings, etc.)
- x Encourage and support the introduction of electronic banking, including Internet banking, and electronic payment technologies for domestic, international and inter-bank transactions.

KEY STRATEGIC STEPS FOR IMPLEMENTING THE ICT INITIATIVE

As mentioned before, to ensure that the *National ICT Strategic Plan* comes to fruition, a long-term commitment must be made. A thorough re-engineering of existing processes and a cultural change must also take place.

A number of key strategic steps are essential to the overall success of the plan and these are outlined below:

- x The first step would be the official endorsement of the overall policy and strategy. The National ICT Strategic Plan must first be publicly accepted by the Prime Minister and Cabinet as the roadmap to take St Kitts and Nevis to the ICT empowered society that has long been envisioned.
- x No less critical is the creation of an enabling environment for E-Business in particular through adaptation or adoption and continuing adjustment of appropriate legal and regulatory frameworks. It should become top priority to pass the laws that are necessary to create this environment within as short a timeframe as possible.
- x Within the central government administration, a senior officer should be appointed as co ordinator of ICT programmes. He/She should be attached directly to the Cabinet Minister in charge of ICT policy and programmes.
- x A specific Information and Communications Technology Unit (ICTU) should be formed and staffed, within the ministry of the Cabinet Minister responsible for ICT policy and programmes. This unit would be headed by the senior officer that was placed in charge of these ICT programmes. This unit would be responsible for ensuring the implementation of the National ICT Strategic Plan.
- x ICT officers should be appointed in each entity of the central government, that is within each Ministry. These officers would be responsible for interacting with the ICTU regarding all ICT related matters for each of these ministries. As a result, in the public administration a network of ICT officers in all entities would work under a national co ordinator toward the implementation of the related activities.
- x The ICTU would be responsible for initiating a long term effort toward ICT and information literacy and fostering an innovation and learning culture among all segments

of the population. This would be both a requirement and an ultimate goal.

- x A long-term view must be taken as to bring about the necessary change. A time-frame of five years is deemed to be appropriate.

INTRODUCTION AND OVERVIEW:

ST. KITTS AND NEVIS

St. Kitts and Nevis is an independent Federation with a parliamentary democracy based on the British model with Queen Elizabeth II of the United Kingdom as the head of state. It is the only Federation in the Caribbean. Nevis has its own island assembly which consists of five members, a Premier, and a Deputy Governor General. St Kitts and Nevis became independent from Britain in 1983. The population is estimated to total 45,000, of which 34,000 reside on St. Kitts and 11,000 on Nevis. St. Kitts and Nevis occupy areas of 168 square kilometers and 93 square kilometers respectively.

The Sugar Industry, which was once a major employer and contributor to the economy, has come to an end. Additionally, the September 11 terrorist attacks reverberated widely throughout the Caribbean, resulting in a major downturn during its high tourist season with St Kitts and Nevis being particularly hard hit. The country has met these challenges by rebuilding its tourism facilities and diversifying into other industries ranging from financial services, light manufacturing, specialized agriculture to electronics and informatics. This is a direct outcome of the Government of St Kitts and Nevis (GSTK&N) offering generous incentives to investors, such as corporate tax holidays, export allowances, and exemption from import duties on many items. Industry-specific incentives are also available for investments in tourism and financial services. As part of these economic diversification strategies, the GSTK&N has also made a serious commitment to provide the framework whereby Information and Communications Technology (ICT) can become a lead sector of the economy of St Kitts and Nevis.

It is the goal of the GSTK&N that within St Kitts and Nevis, Information and Communication Technologies would be used to the widest possible extent by all segments of society with a view to fostering, accelerating and sustaining the long-term social, cultural and economic development of the country.

The GSTK&N is fully aware that for ICT to become such a major player within St Kitts and

Nevis the following factors are essential:

- x A long-term permanent commitment
- x A thorough re-engineering of existing processes
- x A cultural change

ICT IN ST KITTS AND NEVIS

The GSTK&N, private sector and other stakeholders in the nation's development share a common belief that ICT can provide the foundation whereby a society can be built with equitable distribution of opportunity and knowledge. They also believe that it is a key determinant of the competitive advantage of nations. This belief has resulted in a shared vision for St Kitts and Nevis and has produced an initiative that will use Information and Communications Technology to further develop the economy of Saint Kitts and Nevis.

This paper seeks to present the composite ICT initiative and also to set out a national ICT roadmap which is comprehensive and overarching. This *National ICT Strategic Plan* if carefully followed and implemented will allow the GSTK&N to achieve its aforementioned goal of cementing ICT as one of the leading sectors of the economy. It is an outgrowth of several preliminary assessments that were prepared by international organizations as well as a series of consultations with the major stakeholders. The process that was utilized is as follows:

a) Desk research into several prior reports that are listed below:

x *St Kitts and Nevis ICT Assessment* by the CARANA Corporation 17-22 March 2002

x *A Rainbow Technology for a Rainbow People: E-Business Capacity Development for the CARICOM,* Alwyn Didar Singh, for the Commonwealth Fund for Technical Cooperation, September 2001 (Includes all member states of the OECS)

x *GOPA Final Report ICT Policy and Strategic Plan* Member States of the Organisation of Eastern Caribbean States (OECS) Grenada, St Vincent & The Grenadines, St Lucia, Dominica, St Kitts & Nevis, Antigua & Barbuda, Montserrat, Anguilla and the British Virgin Islands Telecommunication Reform & Modernisation Project Consulting Services in Information & Communication Technology IBRD Loans No 4334-DOM, 4335-GRD, 4336-SC, 4337-SLU, 4338-SV IDA Credit No. 3086-DOM, 3087-GRD, 3088-SLU, 3089-SV, June 2002

x *Draft ICT Strategy for Government of St. Kitts & Nevis, Version 7,* Burchelle Crooke

x *Readiness for the Networked World A Guide for Developing Countries,* Information Technologies Group Center for International Development at Harvard University

x *Promoting Investment in Information and Communication Technologies in St Kitts and Nevis,* Peter A Stern, Inter-American Development Bank, May 2006

x *The National Strategic Plan of Barbados 2005-2025*

x *e-Sri-Lanka http://www.icta.lk/insidepages/e-srilanka/e-srilanka.asp*

x *Draft Policy on IT in Education (Jamaica)*

b) Feedback from attendees at Project Launch.

c) A series of consultative meetings with major stakeholders.

After a careful review of all of the information that was gathered in this manner it was determined that by following a five-pronged programme strategy the GSTK&N would certainly be able to fulfill its vision of using Information and Communications Technologies (ICT) as a means of developing the economy of St Kitts and Nevis, reducing poverty and improving the quality of life of the people. The five major branches of this *National ICT Strategy* would be as shown below:

x building the information infrastructure

x enabling the policy and legal environment

x developing ICT human resources and building capacity (information society)

x modernizing government and delivering citizen services electronically x leveraging ICT for economic and social development, through public-private partnerships.

The 2004-2005 *Global Information Technology Report* highlights the policy, institutional, and structural obstacles that prevent countries from fully capturing the benefits of ICT. It analyzes a country's networked readiness based on three so-called pillars.

(i) the environment for ICT development, such as the regulatory regime and the legal framework for ICT, the available infrastructure, and other technological development factors;

(ii) the actual levels of networked readiness of individuals, businesses, and governments; and

(iii) the actual levels of usage of ICT by individuals, businesses, and governments.

(iv) The five areas that have been identified as being of national imperative would cover these all-important pillars

KEY STRATEGIC STEPS FOR IMPLEMENTING THE ICT INITIATIVE

As mentioned before to ensure that the *National ICT Strategic Plan* comes to fruition, a long-term permanent commitment must be made. A thorough re-engineering of existing processes and a cultural change must also take place.

A number of key strategic steps are essential to the overall success of the plan and these are outlined below:

x The first step would be the official endorsement of the overall policy and strategy. The *National ICT Strategic Plan* must first be publicly accepted by the Prime Minister and Cabinet as the roadmap to take St Kitts and Nevis to the ICT empowered society that has long been envisioned.

x No less critical is the creation of an enabling environment for E-Business in particular through adaptation or adoption and continuing adjustment of appropriate legal and regulatory frameworks. It should become top priority to pass the laws that are necessary to create this environment within as short a timeframe as possible.

x Within the central government administration, a senior officer should be appointed as coordinator of ICT programmes. He/She should be attached directly to the Cabinet Minister in charge of ICT policy and programmes.

x A specific Information and Communications Technology Unit (ICTU) should be formed and staffed, within the ministry of the Cabinet Minister responsible for ICT policy and programmes. This unit would be headed by the senior officer that was placed in charge of these ICT programmes. This unit would be responsible for ensuring the implementation of the *National ICT Strategic Plan*.

x ICT officers should be appointed in each entity of the central government, that is within each Ministry. These officers would be responsible for interacting with the ICTU regarding all ICT-related matters for each of these ministries. As a result, in the public administration a network of ICT officers in all entities would work under a national coordinator toward the implementation of the related activities.

x The ICTU would be responsible for initiating a long term effort toward ICT and information literacy and for fostering an innovation and learning culture among all segments of the population. This would be both a requirement and an ultimate goal.

x The ICTU would also attempt to widen the effects of the telecommunications divestiture by enforcing interconnectivity, expanding universal service and catering for competition. This ground work would facilitate the implementation of further policies geared at encouraging business competitiveness and development through ICT investments in all sectors and the development of ICT industries.

x The financial services should themselves fully incorporate electronic transactions in their operations as well as adjust their loans practices to the nature of digital economy.

x Furthermore, ICTs should be harnessed with a view to promoting national cultures and identities, expanding citizenship and democratic participation and supporting the enhancement of the quality of life, especially for disabled persons.

x For the governance and management of these endeavours at the local, national and regional levels, it is recommended that regular round table discussions be held, where all stakeholders could meet to co-operate in observing and analysing the situation and needs, making propositions, joining forces in their implementation and assessing the results.

x A long-term view must be taken as to bring about the necessary change. A time-frame of five years is deemed to be appropriate.

THE NATIONAL ICT STRATEGIC PLAN

This paper seeks to outline the *National ICT Strategic Plan* and how it can take St Kitts and Nevis on the path to an ICT empowered society. A long term view is essential as the re-engineering and cultural change that are essential aspects of this plan will not happen overnight or easily. Rather they will be the result of continuous/ongoing tasks that are diligently and painstakingly pursued.

The plan takes a look at each of the major areas that have been identified as being part and parcel of the initiative. In so doing it looks at where St Kitts and Nevis currently stands, where the country would like to be and what can and must be done to achieve the desired state.

SAINT KITTS AND NEVIS

St Kitts and Nevis is a premier small island developing state as is evidenced by its successful record of economic performance and social development. An analysis of St Kitts and Nevis' situation from the geopolitical, social, economic and structural perspectives showcases the odds of the country achieving greater long-term sustainable economic growth and development over the strategic planning period 2007 to 2012.

St Kitts and Nevis is one of 12 Small Island Developing States (SIDS) in the Caribbean Basin. The islands have no known mineral resources. Despite its small size, St Kitts and Nevis has a relatively high per capita income of approximately US $8,800 making it a middle-income developing country. Since independence from Britain in 1983, successive governments have sought to diversify the production base of the economy. Given its soil, topography and rainfall patterns, sugar - manufactured from sugar cane - has traditionally been the island's most significant export product. However, manufacturing and tourism emerged as major foreign exchange earners during the 1990s. St Kitts and Nevis' beautiful beaches and its social stability have been important factors in attracting an increasing number of tourists since the late 1980s. In addition, a relatively stable economic climate has provided an attractive environment for foreign investment and a growing offshore services industry.

St Kitts and Nevis is a member of the major international organisations such as the United Nations (UN), World Health Organisation (WHO), World Bank (IBRD), International Monetary Fund (IMF), Inter American Development Bank (IDB), International Labour Organisation (ILO) and the World Trade Organization (WTO).

In 1968 several Caribbean countries formed the Caribbean Free Trade Association (CARIFTA), which was successful to the extent that it solidified trade among its members. In an effort to deepen regional integration and to expand cooperation in other areas of development, members of CARIFTA signed the Treaty of Chaguaramas in July 1973 to create the Caribbean Community (CARICOM). St Kitts and Nevis is a member of CARICOM. Currently, countries in the CARICOM region are taking steps to further deepen the integration movement through the creation of a CARICOM Single Market and Economy (CSME).

In the creation and pursuit of the vision for St Kitts and Nevis, it is important that we harness our strengths, exploit all opportunities, minimize our weaknesses and mitigate the impact of threats emanating from the internal and external environment.

STRENGTHS

1. Political stability: This stability is reflected in the uninterrupted practice of representative government since 1983, upon which post-colonial Kittitians and Nevisians have built a remarkable and cohesive democratic system, which compares favourably with world-class standards.
2. Justice and legal system: St Kitts and Nevis has a well-developed, judicial and legal system in which fundamental human rights, civil liberties and respect for the rule of law are strongly upheld.
3. Social cohesion: A very high level of social cohesiveness characterises the two island's populations. There is in place a network of social organisations (sports clubs, community clubs, interest groups and churches) that fosters this cohesiveness.
4. Social safety net: St Kitts and Nevis has a relatively comprehensive social safety net which caters to its citizens from birth to death. There are several agencies that execute this important work.
5. Education: St Kitts and Nevis, with a literacy rate over 90 per cent, possesses one of the most comprehensive educational systems in the developing world. Education is compulsory to age sixteen and free at the primary and secondary levels. Educational opportunities range from preschool to university education, and include vocational and technical training, as well as special schools for the mentally and physically challenged.
6. Macroeconomic stability: St Kitts and Nevis has an enviable record of macroeconomic stability as a result of prudent fiscal, and monetary policies. The EC Dollar dollar has maintained a fixed parity with the US dollar since 1975. There has also been a low and stable rate of inflation, relatively low unemployment and a reasonably equitable distribution of income.
7. Infrastructure: St Kitts and Nevis has a relatively well-developed infrastructure of public buildings, airport, seaport, road network, telecommunications, water, solid waste management, and electricity.

8. Competitive investment incentive regime: St Kitts and Nevis possesses a competitive regime for the attraction of foreign investment, especially in the area of international business services.
9. Ambiance: An excellent tropical climate, clean white, golden and black beaches, blue water, developed coral reefs and a friendly population make St Kitts and Nevis particularly attractive to tourists.

OPPORTUNITIES

1. New export opportunities through increased access to global markets: Trade liberalisation provides St Kitts and Nevis with new market opportunities in a wide range of services and products for which we have a competitive advantage, particularly in the Americas and within CARICOM.
2. Increased access to investment resources: Globalisation and liberalisation of trade and finance provide new and increased access to both portfolio and foreign direct investment.
3. Strengthening of intersectoral linkages: Domestic sectors can strengthen their productive capacities through intersectoral linkages.
4. Agricultural diversification: Opportunities lie in the production of high-valued products, such as white potatoes, peppers and tomatoes.
5. Benefits from market unification: Market unification offers opportunities for economies of scale and scope, thereby facilitating greater efficiency, growth and profitability to Kittitian and Nevisian businesses, lower prices to its consumers and increased consumer welfare. The unification of regional capital markets provides the opportunity for increased market capitalisation thereby allowing the Eastern Caribbean Stock Exchange to realise significant expansion. This would enhance capital market efficiency by channeling investment to the areas of greatest return.
    1. Reduced transaction cost of business: Globalisation, which has led to the enhancement of
    2. information technology and e-commerce, offers greater opportunities to Kittitian and Nevisian businesses and consumers through reductions in transaction costs and prices.
6. Business innovation: The increasing diversity of market requirements presents new opportunities for business innovation and an expansion in production capacity.
7. Access to employment overseas: Globalisation, trade liberalization and the formation of the CARICOM Single Market and Economy will create greater opportunities for Kittitians and Nevisians nationals to access employment overseas.
8. Enhanced capacity to accelerate St Kitts and Nevis' human resource development thrust: A greater opportunity exists to use diplomatic and economic relations to develop St Kitts and Nevis' human resources. There is also the opportunity to develop the human resources through the enhanced capacity to use highly developed telecommunication networks and information technology to access and encourage distance or home-based learning/training.

WEAKNESSES

1. Vulnerability: The Kittitan and Nevisian economy possesses the defining characteristics of Small Island Developing States (SIDS), which make it especially vulnerable to external events. These special and peculiar structural and institutional characteristics impact on our macroeconomic fundamentals, economic sectors and individual units in the society. These characteristics also impact structurally on the process of economic growth, constrain our ability to compete and limit our capacity and speed to undertake adjustment and transformation in the structure of the economy. The most serious vulnerabilities for St Kitts and Nevis are:

(a) Exposure to hurricanes.

(b) Limited land and natural resource base.

(c) A fragile marine ecosystem.

(d) Limited economic diversification and a high degree of economic openness, with foreign trade accounting for more than two-thirds of GDP.

(e) High cost of infrastructural services relative to the population and the tax base.

(f) The rising cost of fuel

1. Lack of economies of scale and scope: Our small size has made it difficult to realise economies of scale and scope especially in industry and agriculture. Relatively high labour and operating costs also act as a constraint on doing business in St Kitts and Nevis.
2. Market imperfection: There is a high incidence of monopolistic and oligopolistic behaviour in our domestic markets. Financial markets, in particular, are narrow and shallow and, as such, limited in their capacity to absorb domestic and external shocks. These market imperfections suppress efficiency and competitiveness, leading to higher production costs and prices, suboptimal quality of service delivery and reduced consumer welfare.
3. Public Sector bureaucracy: the Public Sector is characterised by over-centralisation and over-dependence on rigid regulations.
4. Limited capacity in the Public Sector: The St Kitts and Nevis Public Sector is operating within the same modalities as it has for over the last 30 years while the economy has grown significantly and society has become infinitely more complex. In addition, this has contributed to general tardiness in the implementation processes.
5. Weak entrepreneurial culture: There is a low level of entrepreneurship, with Kittitians and Nevisians generally disinclined to take business risks and to turn innovative ideas into enterprises. In addition, there is limited institutional capacity.
6. Paucity of research, development and innovation: There is a general lack of intensity and continuity in research and development in the areas of enterprise development, product development and ideas development.
7. Weak management tradition: Managerial practice and technology lag behind international standards in the private and public sector.
8. Loss of competitiveness: There is increasing evidence of loss of international competitiveness, especially in the manufacturing and agricultural sectors.
9. Lack of food security: As a physically small developing country with limited capacity for producing food to satisfy domestic demand, St Kitts and Nevis is categorised as a Net Food Importing Developing Country.
10. Demographic trends: St Kitts and Nevis has an ageing population with almost zero growth. This means that the work force will be required to support an increasing number of retired persons. Our ageing population therefore makes for a large dependency ratio.

THREATS

1. Trade liberalisation: This poses a number of competitive challenges to St Kitts and Nevis, especially in the sectors of manufacturing and agriculture because of the availability of cheaper imports.
2. Financial and capital market liberalisation: This presents a challenge to St Kitts and Nevis' fixed exchange rate regime and the degree of monetary autonomy. In addition, it provides greater avenues for money laundering and other financial crimes.
3. Global degradation of the environment: Greenhouse gas emissions contribute to global warming which has a very negative effect on our climate. The rise in sea levels is a

distinct possibility with frightening adverse impacts for small island states such as St Kitts and Nevis. St Kitts and Nevis' marine ecosystem is also threatened by the passage of radioactive materials through the Caribbean Sea.

4. HIV/AIDS, chronic non-communicable diseases, crime and drug abuse: These pose a serious challenge to the development of social capital, the linchpin of further economic growth. HIV/AIDS, although appearing in about 1% of the population is undoubtedly a critical health issue facing St Kitts and Nevis. This pandemic poses a serious threat to our youth, to the most productive elements of our labour force, and to our established social capital formation. Noncommunicable diseases such as cancer and diabetes pose serious threats to the health of the productive segment of the population and can place enormous strain on the health system.

The foregoing analysis has substantially informed the formulation of the strategies presented in this *National ICT Strategic Plan.*

BUILDING THE INFORMATION INFRASTRUCTURE

TELECOMMUNICATIONS IN ST KITTS AND NEVIS

St Kitts and Nevis was for many years dependent on the Sugar Industry. This industry has now come to an end and St Kitts and Nevis is actively seeking to diversify. One of the main areas that we have been looking to develop, are information-based industries including data entry, data manipulation, data conversion, information processing, and information management. St Kitts and Nevis has many advantages which would support the development of such activities including a strong affinity to North America, a common language and time zone, relatively easy and quick access from the USA and Canada, a basic core of highly skilled professionals, wages which may be high with respect to other centers of outsourcing but are nevertheless lower than those in the USA and Canada, and some experience already gained in information based industries. In addition, there is an important Kittitan and Nevisian Diaspora, living mainly in the USA, Canada, the United Kingdom and to a lesser extent in France and the Netherlands which has the skills and the wealth, which can be tapped to support the development of dynamic Information and Communication Technologies (ICT) in the country.

This section of the report focuses on the infrastructure necessary to deliver ICT services such as e-government, e-learning, and e-health to the citizens of St Kitts and Nevis and to facilitate e-commerce among its people and businesses. The high prices that users have to pay for international calling, Internet use, and leased lines have been the single most important obstacle to developing an information-based industry in St Kitts and Nevis. This impacts not only the traditional industries such as tourism and agriculture which depend on communications to market and sell their services and goods but also the new information-based sectors where high costs affect Caribbean firms' ability to compete effectively internationally. There is a large potential for developing a variety of information-based services in St Kitts and Nevis from the fairly basic (mainly outbound calling) through the more sophisticated (customer care and technical support) call centre services to the more highly specialized network services. For these, however, the costs of communication to and from and within St Kitts and Nevis including the cost of leased lines and the conditions attached to their use remain a significant barrier to further developing such activities.

A landmark 1996 study by the World Bank identified the high price of communications as a barrier to the development of services exports in the Caribbean. At the time all but one country (Dominican Republic) had monopoly suppliers of telecommunications networks and services. The Organization of Eastern Caribbean States (OECS) and the Dominican Republic began the process of reform and sought financial support from the World Bank. Others such as Trinidad &

Tobago, Haiti, Jamaica, and Guyana got support from other funding institutions including the Inter-American Development Bank (IADB), International Telecommunications Union (ITU), the World Bank, the Canadian International Development Agency (CIDA) and the United States Agency for International Development (USAID). Nine years after the conclusion of the WTO's negotiations on basic telecommunications in February 1997 the process of sector reform has advanced in the whole region. Nearly all countries have put new legal and regulatory structures in place and have established independent regulators. Some have yet to complete the process. In spite of this the full benefits of reform still elude most Caribbean islands, this being particularly true in St Kitts as Nevis where residents continue to pay high prices and the unavailability of highly affordable telecommunications services continues to be a barrier to the development and growth of the ICT sector.

FIXED AND MOBILE LINES

The figures below show fixed and mobile telephone penetration in CARICOM and how St Kitts and Nevis compares.

CARICOM Member State	Population 2004	per capita GNP (2004)	Penetration rates % (2004)	
			Main Line	Mobile
Antigua and Barbuda	77,000	$11,000 *	49.4	70.1
Bahamas	317,000	$17,700	44.1	58.7
Barbados	271,000	$16,400	50.1	73.9
Belize	261,000	$6,500	12.9	37.5
Dominica	71,000	$5,500 **	29.5	58.9
Grenada	103,000	$5,000 *	31.8	42.1
Guyana	767,000	$3,800	13.4	18.8
Haiti	8,437,000	$1,500	1.7	4.7
Jamaica	2,676,000	$4,100	18.7	82.2
Montserrat	9,300	$3,400 *		
Saint Kitts and Nevis	50,000	$8,800 *	50.0	20.0
Saint Lucia	150,000	$5,400 *	32.2	62.0
St. Vincent and the Grenadines	121,000	$2,900 *	15.7	47.1
Suriname	439,000	$4,300	18.5	48.5
Trinidad and Tobago	1,307,000	$10,500	24.6	49.6
Total	**15,056,300**			
Average			**10.8**	**29.0**

Source: ITU WTI 2005 * 2002 ** 2003

However, more recent work places the penetration of mobile phones in St Kitts and Nevis at 70%.

In St. Kitts and Nevis there is one fixed line provider (C&W), two ISP's (C&W and The Cable), and three mobile providers (UTS-CariGlobe, Digicel and C&W).

Cable & Wireless (St. Kitts and Nevis) Ltd. has deployed a double fibre ring around St. Kitts and a fibre link to its international gateway switch. The islands of St. Kitts and Nevis are connected via microwave. The Cable, C&W's licensed fixed wire competitor, also has deployed a fibre ring plus fibre strands to high-density business sites. Its traditional cable subscribers are served over a hybrid fibre coaxial (HFC) network.

Three service providers have been licensed to compete against C&W - The Cable in fixed services, including high-speed Internet access, and CariGlobe and Digicel in mobile wireless. With two fibre rings, St. Kitts is better provisioned with modern transmission facilities than Nevis. The principal reason for this disparity is that C&W faces vigorous competition from The Cable, whose operations are limited to St. Kitts, where its serves roughly 10,000 households, more than 95% of the potential market. The Cable claims that it has deployed more fibre than C&W. It plans to connect customers who need high bandwidth connections directly to its fibre ring using fibre. Residential customers who order high speed Internet access will be served with a cable modem over the existing hybrid fibre coaxial (HFC) plant. Finally, it will compete head-to-head against C&W with its planned packetized voice service.

St Kitts and Nevis enjoys a relatively high teledensity and growth in telephone lines. Relative to the world average for Upper-Middle income countries, St Kitts and Nevis has a higher than average teledensity at 51.76%. as per the CARANA report (page 19)

INTERNET AND PCS IN ST KITTS AND NEVIS

The number of Internet hosts in St Kitts and Nevis is considerably below the averages for similar income countries. The average for Upper-Middle income countries is 37 hosts per 10,000 population. SKN has 2.06 hosts per 10,000 inhabitants.

The number of Internet users in St Kitts and Nevis in 1999 was above the average for Upper-Middle income countries, that being 461 per 10,000 population. SKN had 516 users per 10,000 population.

There is a high percentage of PCs per 100 population compared to other countries of similar income levels (5.8 per 100 population for Upper-Middle income countries). SKN stands at 15.48 PCs per 100 population.

There are also some 3,000 Internet accounts in the country, which is relatively high for an emerging economy with high Internet-access prices.

The relatively high availability of PCs and the comparatively low use of the Internet is likely a direct result of limited access and costs.

CARANA Report (page50)

FIBRE OPTIC BACKBONE NETWORKS

There are currently 21 fibre optic submarine cable systems in the Caribbean. Of these, thirteen primarily serve the region. The other six serve other regions (mainly South America) but have landing points in the Caribbean. (See Figure 25 and Table 26). The combined total capacity of the thirteen "Caribbean" cables at the time of their construction was about 70 Gbps. Their combined potential capacity, however, is nearly 3 Terabits/second (Tbps) due largely to the huge potential capacity of ARCOS cable system.

Of these fibre optic backbone networks, two land in St. Kitts and Nevis: The ECFS as can be seen from the table below. The other, *Global Caribbean Network (GCN),* was landed early in 2006.

Country/Territory	No. of cables	Cable systems landing in country or territory
Anguila	1	ECFS
Antigua & Barbuda	1	ECFS
Aruba	2	Pan American, Alfonso de Ojeda
Bahamas	3	Arcos-1, Bahamas II, Bahamas Internet Cable System (BICS)
Barbados	1	ECFS
Belize	1	Arcos-1
British Virgin Islands (Tortola) - BOT	2	CARAC, Taino
Cayman Islands (BOT)	2	CJFS, MAC
Curacao (incl. Bonaire)	3	Amerigo Vespucci, Americas-2, Alfonso de Quejeda
Dominican Republic	4	Antillas-1, Arcos-1, TCS-1, FibraLink
French Guyana	1	Americas-2
Grenada (OECS)	1	ECFS
Guyana	1	Americas-2 via French Guyana and Suriname
Jamaica	3	CJFS, TCS-1, FibraLink
Martinique/Guadeloupe	2	Americas-2, ECFS
Montserrat (BOT)	1	ECFS
Puerto Rico	7	Americas-2, Antillas-1, Arcos-1, Emergia, Taino, TCS-1, SMITCOMS
St. Kitts & Nevis	1	ECFS
St. Lucia (OECS)	1	ECFS
St. Martin/St. Maarten	3	ECFS, SMPR-1, SMITCOMS
St. Vincent (OECS)	1	ECFS
Suriname	1	Americas-2 via French Guyana
Trinidad & Tobago	3	Americas-1, Americas-2, ECFS
Turcs & Caicos (BOT)	1	Arcos-1
US Virgin Islands (St. Croix, St. Thomas)	7	Americas-1, Americas-2, Pan American, PAC, MAC, SAC-1, Taino

CARIBBEAN FIBRE OPTIC CABLE SYSTEM

Global Caribbean Network (GCN), (http://www.globalcaribbean.net/index.htm) is an initiative of The Guadeloupe Region, the regional government of Guadeloupe, and some private investors.

The northern section of the 1 Tbps GCN cable is has recently (February – March 2006) finished construction. It connects Guadeloupe with St. Croix and Puerto Rico and lands in St. Kitts (branch) and St. Martin (See Fig. 29). The St. Croix – Puerto Rico segment is being built by Centennial, one of the partners in the project. A planned southern section will connect Martinique, Dominica (branch) and eventually Trinidad & Tobago. The € 21.9 million project is 75% publicly funded with € 7 million coming from the Region Guadeloupe, €9.4 million from the European Union (FEDER) and the rest from the private sector partners which include Groupe Loret, AT&T, Alcatel, Centennial and Global Crossing.

Business people, public officials, and residential customers alike complain about C&W's high prices and, secondarily, about its network reliability. The increased competition that should result from the GCN cable landing in St Kitts may result in the price of telephone services declining and becoming more affordable for most customers. Market forces may result in universal improved service and pricing without governmental intervention.

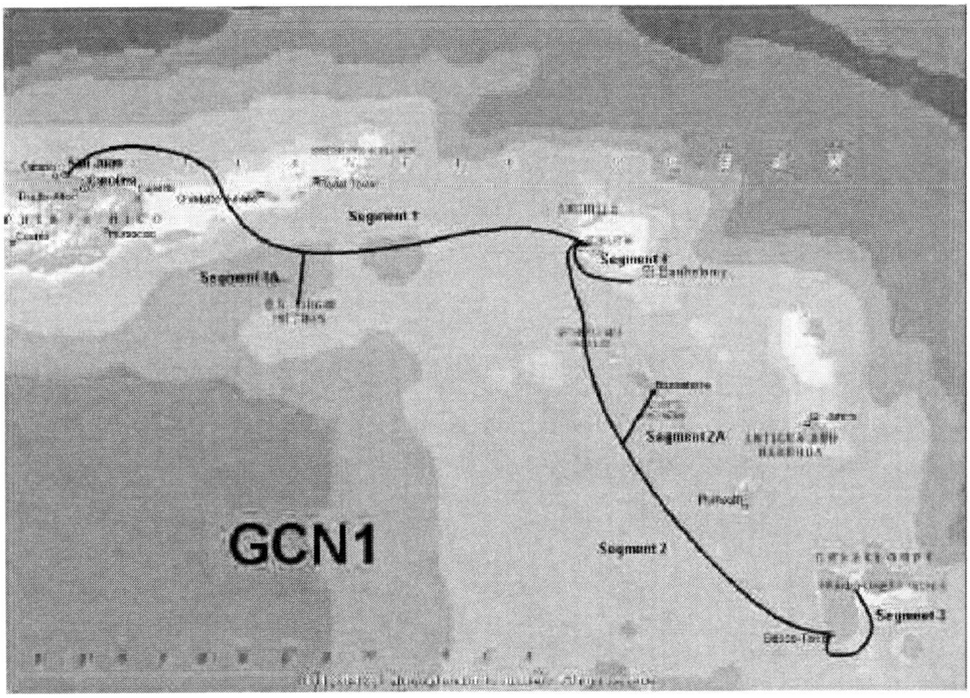

Northern Section of Global Caribbean Network (GCN)

SUMMARY

Earlier we showed that the lack of choice and high prices of leased circuit capacity were important barriers to investment and development of ICT in St Kitts and Nevis. Faced with a similar situation the European Commission in 1992 issued a directive to harmonize conditions – tariffs (which must be cost-oriented and transparent), technical characteristics, supply and usage conditions, and licensing requirements) - for the provisions of leased lines in the then twelve member states of the European Union. EU harmonization directives were part of a wider policy of establishing a single market for goods and services which along with competition directives have, inter alia, resulted in bringing down prices for circuit leases as was shown earlier. Whether such harmonization measures are applied to promoting economic integration or simply to promote regional cooperation there are lessons to be learned from the European experience. By mutually agreeing to apply harmonization measures to conditions for leasing circuit capacity, procedures and conditions of licensing, use of frequencies, regulation of dominant suppliers and other measures, regulators, policymakers and citizens of St Kitts and Nevis can benefit through their impact on the development of ICT in the region. It would be essential to employ mechanisms to promote harmonization such as establishing a regional forum of policymakers and regulators to harmonize policies, laws, regulations, procedures and standards.

STRATEGIC STEPS TOWARDS BUILDING INFRASTRUCTURE

Additionally in order to ensure that infrastructure is built, certain key steps should be taken. The goal would be to enforce affordable universal access and interconnectivity, reliability and technological neutrality

Important steps have already been taken through the Telecommunications Acts to achieve affordable and universal access to telecommunications facilities. Steady efforts towards their actual implementation and improvement by the Government should boost market forces and compensate for their imperfections in order for all citizens and organisations, irrespective of their location, to have access to state of the art ICT facilities at an affordable cost. In addition it is essential for effective competition to bear fruits and to guarantee the reliability, innovation, and technological neutrality of the ICT infrastructure.

Related strategic moves include:

x Rural, isolated or ill-favoured communities which commercial operators are not willing to offer high quality services to within the year following their introduction into the more densely populated and easily accessible areas should be granted the right to use any suitable alternative for local and wide area networking and obtain for themselves or their providers all required licenses.

x An annual audit of the implementation of the deregulation of the telecommunications sector should be conducted in conjunction with the National Round Tables, its results made public and appropriate adaptations brought into the Telecommunications Act and related policy positions.

x Ongoing evaluation should be conducted on the need to issue new telecommunications licenses to respond to demand and to improve the competitive environment.

x Government should enforce regulations that allow for providing services adjudged essential at a socially acceptable cost e.g. by compensating users for price differences resulting from localization constraints or abuse of dominant situations.

x Government should pursue the efforts underway with a view to reclaiming the administration of the Internet Top Level Domain Names for the OECS countries and establish suitable and effective registry operations.

x Government should develop plans by which all citizens can obtain a free electronic mail address and organisations a domain name address at an appropriate cost under the countries top level domain name, with a view to expand the visibility of OECS countries on the Internet.

x The combined use of open source software and proprietary software should be pursued and open source software systematically applied whenever appropriate, especially in the public sector.

x

The current legislation should be revised in order to exempt certain value added and not-for-profit services from the need to obtain telecommunications licenses. For example opening a small Internet Café of less than ten computers is a very involved and costly process. Streamlining this could possibly help facilitate the creation of more of these type of services.

x

The regulatory authorities should be required to constantly review the range of services that are available or could become available under normal economic conditions in the countries with a view to updating the definition of those services included under universal service and ensure that access to high quality services is not restricted de facto to certain categories of citizens and organisations.

ENABLING THE POLICY AND LEGAL ENVIRONMENT

In his 2000 survey of e-readiness and capacity for e-business of various Caribbean countries, Alwyn D. Singh found that little had been done by St Kitts and Nevis to update laws to accommodate the emergence of online commerce and communications. E-commerce affects a vast array of subjects and issues and entails an enormous commitment of resources. E-business and online activities are requiring countries to examine subjects that range from the general to very specific e-commerce issues and policies. Laws dealing specifically with cybercrime are non-existent. Laws to facilitate online transactions and communications, such as digital signature and electronic transaction laws, are also absent but are currently being worked on urgently. Other statutes, such as those dealing with intellectual property rights (IPR), need to be updated for the online environment. Consumer protection, child protection, and privacy laws that are important to the new ICT environment are also needed so that users feel more confident when they go online to surf the Net or to conduct business.

These legal/regulatory gaps are important and must be addressed. Jurisdiction over online activities must also be addressed. Some countries take an expansive view of their courts' legal jurisdiction, while other countries accept only a limited jurisdiction of other countries' courts. At present, St. Kitts and Nevis as well as other Eastern Caribbean nations are lagging in the development of their legal/regulatory frameworks to accommodate the widespread utilization and deployment of ICTs. It is important that a legal analysis be undertaken to identify gaps in the legal framework and where new laws are needed. This must be done, however, in harmony with the developing global legal framework.

Furthermore, the SKN Government needs to identify operational policies and practices that will be substantially affected as a result of increased usage of ICTs and an online environment. This includes requirements for authentication, certification, network availability and reliability, and combating cybercrime. For example, all enterprise networks (which include Government networks) now face the threat of attack or unauthorized intrusion. The administrators of SKN's Government network must be prepared to handle security breaches and restore systems. SKN law enforcement officials need to be trained in how to conduct cybercrime investigations and cooperate on an international level, and forensic scientists need to develop skills in handling electronic evidence. At a minimum, this means establishing round-the-clock contacts and obtaining assistance from the U.S., EU, and other governments and donor organizations. The area of cybercrime is but one example of how the SKN Government must anticipate problems that are caused or exacerbated by an interconnected global network. The OECS Legal Drafting Unit and ECTEL have some important experience in this matter and can be counted on to provide ongoing assistance to St Kitts and Nevis in this area.

As has been noted elsewhere, five (5) multinational institutions will also have an impact on ICT deployment and e-readiness. Chief among these are the WTO (World Trade Organization) and WIPO (World Intellectual Property Organization). The WTO at one time commenced a new round of trade negotiations entitled the Doha Round that would have had, as a major component, a focus on e-commerce to fall under the General Agreement on Trade in Services (GATS). The Doha round has since stalled. Since trade negotiations are still evolving, no firm trade-related ICT policies are required at this time. However, governments need to be aware of the negotiations and the relevant issues and to educate themselves about the evolution of the debate so that they can fully participate and not be blindsided when decisions are made during the negotiations. The St Kitts Nevis Government will be working mainly through CARICOM.

IPR is another e-commerce-related area of which SKN must be aware. In 1996, the WIPO concluded a new treaty on copyrights that seeks to limit the copying that is legally permissible in the digital electronic environment. For example, it specifically limits the copying that can occur during transmission via electronic means, including a PC. It requires its members to adopt laws consistent with the treaty and to enforce its provisions. The treaty has gone into force, and WIPO is encouraging members to become signatories. If St Kitts and Nevis signs the treaty, it will be obliged to impose limits on personal and enterprise behavior, which will have to be reflected in its other e-commerce laws.

LEGAL AND REGULATORY FRAMEWORK FOR E-COMMERCE

ICTs have led to new electronic markets that extend customer choice while resulting in significant benefits in efficiency. This new environment, however, requires new policies and laws and amendments to existing legal frameworks. For e-commerce to flourish in SKN and become a significant economic factor, market participants must have confidence that transactions will follow predictable guidelines and that the rule of law will protect all stakeholders. A basic legal framework must cover an extensive list of issues and policies, beginning with electronic transactions, digital signatures, privacy and protection of data, cybercrime, consumer rights, quality of service, dispute resolution, and jurisdiction of courts to hear disputes, to name a few. The absence of a comprehensive legal/regulatory framework does not preclude online commerce but it will limit the value and growth potential of electronic markets. The task of reforming or adopting new laws will be time consuming and St Kitts Nevis should consider regional initiatives and mechanisms to share information to facilitate the process. The task of identifying laws implicated in e-commerce requires the active participation of both the private and public sectors and the dedicated assistance of local attorneys and experienced consultants who know the global legal framework and the issues under discussion.

KEEPING LEGISLATION ATTUNED TO ICT AND ICT USE

St Kittts and Nevis needs to ensure that legal rules and procedures are adapted and kept up-todate so that individuals and organisations can use ICT to the fullest possible extent. This effort is a fundamental requirement for all other policies to come into effect. However a number of E-business activities can and in fact have begun before the new legislation has been passed. Due attention ought also to be paid to securing the fullest possible compatibility with internationally accepted standards and regulations (e.g. UNCITRAL model laws) as well as those of major partner countries. Major topics requiring attention are the legal force of electronic documents and contracts, authentication of parties, protection of intellectual property and privacy, definition of the legal responsibilities of participants in electronic communications, prevention of new forms of crime, and protection of pluralism and democracy.

STRATEGIC STEPS TO PRODUCE LEGISLATORY ENABLING ENVIRONMENT

x A thorough inventory of all existing legislation and regulations related to the use of ICT should be conducted with a view to identifying inadequacies and gaps and to draw a programme for legislative revision and drafting. An annual review of all ICT-related legislation should be conducted.

x Existing legislation should be revised with a view to ensuring that electronic record or documentation would not be denied legal effect, validity, admissibility or enforceability, that a legal requirement for "writing", or a description of something as being "in writing", and that the requirement for information to be presented or retained under "original form" is satisfied by an electronic record if the integrity of the information can be reliably assured.

x Legislation should be put in place with a view to authorizing certification service providers to issue accredited certificates that confirm the veracity of an electronic signature and ensure authentication of issuers of electronic documents or Internet users when required by administrative or legal provision. A regional electronic signature and authentication agency, with due control of all governments and private sector (e.g. financial institutions) should be put in place as soon as possible. This legislation should be technology neutral.

x Legislation should be adapted or established in order to define the conditions of the formation of contracts and provision of contractual documents in electronic form, including the protection of the legitimate interests of vendors and buyers and the provision of legal evidence to the administration and jurisdictions. Provisions should be made in order to give legal force to agreements between partners in business-to business electronic commerce regarding the appropriate technological and business methods of authentication.

x Legislation should be established for the protection of privacy and personal data in all forms of electronic transactions in the private and public sectors. This includes the establishment of an independent agency, led by representatives of the public sector, private sector and civil society organisations with powers to take quick action in order to correct infringements. St Kitts and Nevis may further wish to follow the specifications that may help turn the region into a *"safe harbour"* in North American and European Union terms.

x Legislation should be established in order to allow for the lawful acquisition, use, import and export of encryption programs or other encryption methods with due provision for national security and justice prerogatives.

x Legislation should determine the taxation rules applying to the various forms of electronic commerce. These rules should to the extent possible be harmonised across the OECS if not the CARICOM countries.

x Legislation should make provision for clear definition of the liabilities of Internet Service Providers, owners of Internet-based resources, providers of Internet-based services and Internet users at large, for information transmitted or transactions carried out over the Internet. It should adapt existing basic democratic, social and human rights to the new environment. It should put in place a regulatory and arbitration body representing all categories of stakeholders, that can take immediate action in order to correct a situation pending final judiciary decision, when appropriate.

x Legislation needs to be developed with a view to reducing and punishing the new forms of crime that global ICT networks facilitate. This "cybercrime" legislation would better be harmonised if not unified among OECS member countries. It should further seek to be aligned as appropriate with comparable legislation in other countries. Since this is a domain in continuing transformation, a regional commission should be entrusted with its monitoring and proposing required adaptations. ECTEL presents itself as the best possible facilitator of such a need.

x Existing legislation regarding intellectual property rights should be revised and adapted to the globalised ICT environment. Due account should be taken of the similar developments in other countries as well as of the need for protecting the natural and cultural heritage of the Caribbean nations. Appropriate provisions should be made for all materials essential for the citizens or produced with public funding to be made accessible in open archive systems.

x Legislation would need to be devised with a view to facilitate the establishment and activities of virtual companies operating mainly from physical installations in an OECS country and/or owned by a majority of individuals or companies of these countries, or owned by foreign interest, as well as those operating mainly from physical installations outside of the OECS countries but having a domain name from these countries.

x Standards and regulatory bodies representing all categories of stakeholders, including civil society organisations, should be put in place with a view to supporting pluralism and preventing over-concentration in the ICT sector generally, and digital media specifically.

OBJECTIVE

The four main areas of legislation that need to be urgently addressed are *Electronic Transactions, ICT Crimes, Data Protection,* and *Intellectual Property Rights.* It would become the top priority of the GSTK&N to create the enabling legal environment for the development of ICTs including the enactment of required Laws by Parliament to facilitate e-government, e-business as well as attract ICT-related foreign direct investment. Keeping abreast of the developments on the WSIS, WTO, UNCITRAL, WIPO and other important international organizations and acceding to related treaties are critical to having an up-to-date legal framework.

ELECTRONIC TRANSACTIONS LEGISLATION

This strategic component would ensure the preparation of an Act of Parliament for the facilitation and recognition of electronic contracts, the creation and exchange of electronic communication, the establishment of a Certification Authority and the accreditation of Certification Service Providers and facilitate the recognition of electronic filing by Government departments.

This project also envisages institutional capacity building in Government for the accreditation of Service Providers under the proposed Act of Parliament and the development of legal standards with UNCITRAL Secretariat as well as assisting in the formulation of appropriate regulations.

ICT CRIMES

The ICTU would function as the convenor in a review of the Computer Crimes Bill. This project component would examine criminal implications of spamming and e-surveillance, and facilitate the establishment of a specialized Computer Crime Forensics Unit (CCFU) in the Police Department for the enforcement of Computer Crimes and also create the framework for the analysis of forensic evidence. Further, capacity building for law enforcement officials would be undertaken under this project as well as developing linkages with foreign law enforcement agencies. To exploit existing synergies across the government, the CCFU may be integrated with the Financial Crimes Unit in the Police Force.

DATA PROTECTION

The aim here is to develop and implement legislative or other measures to ensure that St Kitts and Nevis meets the adequacy levels required by the EU Directive on Data Protection, and promote institutional development for data protection and privacy issues. This would help to ensure that St Kitts and Nevis complies with required legal standards for the development of the IT Enabled Services sector and the BPO sector.

INTELLECTUAL PROPERTY RIGHTS

This strategic component would ensure the development of appropriate legal standards with the UNCITRAL Secretariat as well as assist in the formulation of appropriate regulations to ensure that IPRs are protected as per international standards.

TARGET GROUP

The target groups would be Ministries, Government Departments, Legal and Judicial, Commercial, Banking, Shipping and corporate sector.

EXPECTED RESULTS

x The formulation of proposals for e-Transactions Legislation and finalised legislation through the Legal Department

x The establishment of a Unit for the Accreditation of service providers at the Ministry of Technology

x The development of appropriate regulations under the e-Transactions Legislation in conjunction with UNCITRAL.

x Establishment of an integrated Computer Crimes Forensic Unit and Financial Crimes Unit in the Police Force

x Preparation of a Code of Practice on Data Protection

BENEFITS

The establishment of an appropriate Legal framework for ICT development would help facilitate the growth of ICT in St Kitts and Nevis, including e-business and e-government related activities, and create the environment for ICT-related foreign direct investment.

Developing ICT Human Resources and Building Capacity

INFORMATION SOCIETY

The widespread deployment and utilization of ICTs is directly dependent upon the opportunity of a population to become ICT proficient. Whereas the public sector can set ICT strategy and policy, and the private sector can bring together opportunities and needed financial resources, both are dependent upon the intellectual capital of a nation and the ability of its people to provide the requisite skills and human capabilities. In the end, the ultimate change agent is a nation's citizens.

This section explores the intellectual resources of the people of St. Kitts/Nevis, their educational background, their capabilities and potential from an ICT-related perspective, and their desire and willingness to use ICTs and help develop the ICT sector. There are a few countries that serve as development models of success and useful case studies for countries to emulate. Ireland and India are two of the more prominent. Ireland used about a third of its EU infusion money to develop education and human resources that in turn developed knowledge industries, like IT.

One of the major constraints to the growth of the ICT sector in SKN has been the lack of a skilled labor force. The availability of appropriate skills is a major concern of the Government, SMEs, and educational institutions. The Government of SKN has launched a number of initiatives to address this issue, but time lags may mean that the shortage of trained labor will act as a constraint to growth and productivity improvements in the short to medium term. It has been reported that firms encounter myriad difficulties, ranging from getting IT service professionals to trouble-shooting basic PC problems to finding and retaining systems administrators. For educators, retaining good IT faculty and identifying the appropriate ICT curriculum components are difficult because of the demand for qualified professionals in this field. This shortage of ICT personnel is exacerbated by limited public sector funding.

SKN's labor sector competitiveness has been eroded somewhat in the last few years as wages have risen faster than in most countries in the region. The labor force numbers about 22,000 workers. As for ICT professionals, a SKN private sector manager estimates that salaries for ICT network professionals are roughly half of the U.S. level. The SKN Government is the main provider of basic education. It has invested significant resources into outfitting primary and secondary schools with computers and Internet connectivity.

STRATEGIC STEPS TO DEVELOP ICT HUMAN RESOURCES

BEYOND ICT LITERACY - SHAPING AN INFORMATION AND LEARNING CULTURE

Of absolute necessity is the continuing struggle towards a smarter society. To that end one should first seek the widest possible level of ICT literacy through inclusion of ICT in formal and informal education and the training of teachers and instructors. One should further seek that all citizens are given the chance to achieve the highest possible level of education, develop their skills and talents throughout their lives, have their innovative and creative capabilities encouraged to be in a position to actively contribute to the production of local content for the electronic resources. This requires deep changes in curricula, teaching methods, operation and management of formal and informal educational programmes and institutions, provision of teaching and learning materials as well as supporting lifelong learning through a combination of traditional classroom (face to face), distance and open education methods.

Related strategic steps are to:

x Develop a sensitisation and training programme about the opportunities and challenges of the effective use of ICT in organizations and society targeted at senior and middle managers, and decision-makers in all sectors.

x Call for and support vocational training (e.g. with a professional education levy or incentive, subsidies, study loans, etc.) with a view to upgrading the ICT skills of the present workforce. Special attention must be paid to the unskilled workforce and women.

x Call for and support learning and information-oriented lifelong education programmes to be coordinated by community-based organizations and other NGOs.

x Expand on-going computer literacy efforts in primary and secondary schools into information literacy and cultural improvement programmes through appropriate curricular and pedagogic changes.

x Train teachers in the use the computer as a tool for teaching Reading, Writing, Mathematics, Art, and other core subjects, and working with the Curriculum Development Unit (CDU) and the Education Planning Division.

x Support the establishment of an Education Management Information System (EMIS) for the management of education at the school and Ministry levels. The monitoring and evaluation of the teaching-learning process with the involvement of parents and parent-teacher associations (PTAs) should be a central feature of the EMIS.

x Initiate the building of training and support capacity in the use and customization of open source software in order to sustain generalised use of open source software in parallel with proprietary ones. The new Saddlers High School can be a test bed for the use of open source application and system software.

x Support the creation of a national or regional consortium for education that can negotiate licenses for access to learning material and courses, serve as a hub for the distribution of these materials, facilitate sharing of efforts in the use of Internet-based distance education modalities, and support the development of a national and regional inter-library loan system. Support the creation and use of digital libraries. Give strong support to educational institutions including the CFB College and the University of the West Indies for the use of ICTs in the delivery of education and the possible emergence of an open university. The concept of the Caribbean Knowledge Learning Network (CKLN) or CaribNet must also be strongly supported.

COMMUNITY ACCESS POINTS

Community Access Points (CAPs) are community or public buildings where computers, colour printers and scanners are installed for persons in the community to use either free of charge or for relatively low costs. It is hoped that all the computers would have broadband connection to the Internet. Currently in St Kitts and Nevis the Community Centres have been designated to fulfill this role. These centres have been newly built with grant support from the Taiwanese government.

The CAPs are intended to help rural and disadvantaged communities finance and implement projects aimed at improving their daily lives through the use of ICT. It is hoped that these CAPs would be characterized as being demand-driven development programme where decisions are taken by the communities themselves and funds are allocated according to priorities decided on by the community. Furthermore these CAP seek to build capacity of communities by enhancing existing skills and facilitating the acquisition of new skills. To ensure the success of these initiatives, the rollout of CAPs should be done alongside an awareness campaign in target communities on the role of ICT as a tool for development and empowerment.

Local Community Access Point would generally be able to do the following:

x access government information and services
x surf the Net
x send and receive e-mails
x shop online
x follow on-line training courses
x review job adverts
x book plane tickets
x trace ancestors or long lost friends
x scan photographs or other pictures
x write a letter or resume

x play games x receive beginner to intermediate training courses

PROMOTE THE SYSTEMATIC USE OF ICT BY ORGANISATIONS OF THE CULTURAL SECTOR

Projecting cultural activities of St Kitts and Nevis on the Internet will enhance the image of the region as an ICT savvy one. It will also contribute to a balanced long term cultural transformation by ensuring the preservation and visibility of national cultures. In the short term, many cultural activities are also likely to contribute to income generation. By creating a critical mass of ICT-savvy actors in the various cultural associations and activities, and by supporting the development of cultural products using ICT, a dynamic process of expansion of the use of ICTs will be created.

Related strategic steps:

x Design a program for training a nucleus of members of local musical and other artistic groups in the use of ICT for production, marketing and distribution of musical recording and other artistic works.

x Design and implement a program to demonstrate electronic publishing and E-book techniques; train an initial nucleus of instructors or resource persons and build a demonstration collection of original literature from St Kitts and Nevis.

x Support the electronic creation of literary works, particularly on local history and culture, through the institutionalization of an award (monetary) system for such works.

x Design and implement a program for the training in St Kitts and Nevis of a nucleus of specialists that can assist the cultural associations and local artists in producing quality web sites to be hosted on the co-operative cultural web site.

x Initiate a program for the systematic recording and presentation on quality web sites of our historical, cultural and natural heritage (e.g. museums, places of interest, etc.)

x Ensure web streaming and if possible live diffusion on the Internet of major cultural events in the region.

HARNESSING ICT FOR MAKING EVERYDAY LIFE EASIER

Segments of society or certain societal issues require special attention and measures to which the application of ICT can bring more effective solutions. In the mean time ICT application should, from the inception, cater for the particular requirements of persons with disabilities.

The provision of practical information and guidance or special services to cope with the particular situations such as gender and age discrimination, incidence of disease (morbidity), disabilities, Diasporic relations, etc. in conjunction with related civil society organisations are among the contemplated activities.

Related strategic moves are to:

x Promote compliance of electronic resources with internationally recognised standards for accessibility by persons with disabilities.

x Establish or expand public information and advice resources with related Internet-based resources for women in particular (e.g. about health, social benefits, child care, prevention of abuse, self-employment, geriatric care, etc.).

x Liberalise the use of Internet telephony by individuals and its provision by all Internet Service Providers, at a reasonable cost, with a view to strengthening the interaction among families and social groups with members and affiliates abroad.

x Establish or expand public information and advice resources with related Internet-based resources on common public health and other issues.

x Establish a regional / international tele-medicine network among hospitals, health centres and practitioners for exchange of information, access to medical information resources world-wide, preliminary diagnosis and assistance for treatment. At one point the JNF General Hospital had a relationship with Dalhousie University in Canada and that is certainly a relationship that we can look to build upon.

x Establish or expand public information with related Internet-based resources for persons with disabilities and train personnel from the organisations of civil society that are supporting particular groups of disabled persons to act as intermediaries in the gathering and diffusion of electronic information.

ICT IN SCHOOLS

Research has shown that ICT can provide stakeholders and administrators with new tools for increased communication for management efficiencies, and teachers and learners with improved learning opportunities by:

x empowering citizens, managers and other stakeholders by enabling online teamwork for increased participation, collaboration and information sharing through the use of email, the Web-logs and other remote collaboration tools.

x enabling the rapid creation and inexpensive distribution of educational information and knowledge x encouraging professional development, in-service-training, remote support and mentoring

for lifelong learning for teachers, managers and other citizens x facilitating fast and easy access to information and expertise around the world. x increasing motivation through the use of multimedia (sound, video, graphics, animation

and text.) x allowing each student to learn at his/her level and speed thereby giving pupils greater control over their own learning.

x enhancing the development of the abilities of mentally and physically challenged students.

x promoting active rather than passive learning.

x engaging students in research, data analysis and problem solving, thereby facilitating higher-order thinking processes such as synthesising , interpreting and hypothesising.

OBJECTIVES OF ICT IN EDUCATION

x promote equitable access to educational resources through the strategic application of ICT.

x make all school-leavers computer literate thereby providing them with the requisite ICT skills as a platform for imminent employment and/or entry to specialised training for the information economy

x create a teaching force in which all practitioners possess the critical requisite skills and competencies required to use ICT as a tool in enhancing the teaching/learning process and a cadre of ICT teacher specialists.

x improve the efficiency and effectiveness of educational administration through the promotion of the use of appropriate school management information systems

x exploit the interactive potential of Information and Communications Technology in the provision of lifelong learning, anytime, anywhere via distance education programmes x create smart partnerships for a sustainable ICT programmes through collaboration with

between the public, private and community sectors, x establish a schools network system for the collaborative sharing of educational resources and stakeholder participation. x employ the new ICT tools for increased online communication, stakeholder participation and improved management of the sector

FACTORS WHICH WILL IMPACT ON ICT IN EDUCATION

x Equity of access to the technology for all students x Preparation of teachers to optimize the use of ICT in the teaching/learning process. The process of preparing teachers in training as well as the upskilling of those now in the classroom

x Provision of technicians to support the work of teachers and administrators in the schools

x Security of hardware and software in schools

x Health and safety issues .

x Cultural relevance and suitability of courseware .

x Sustainability of programmes considering the high rate of obsolescence of equipment and the high cost of replacement relative to the country's resources

x Capacity of the central Ministry to manage the partnership process for development and to monitor the implementation of the policy at the institutional level

x The Ministry of Technology websites will be developed, together with an INTRANET for the school system using content prepared by the various units of the Ministry of Technology and the Ministry of Education as well as individuals and groups within the sector. The Intranet will be of help to teachers, administrators, students, parents and other stakeholders.

STRATEGIC CONCERNS AND EXPECTATIONS

Equity of access is an overriding consideration. The Ministry of Technology will therefore work collaboratively with educational institutions to make available facilities, equipment and personnel to permit access to ICT for all students.

x Schools will be expected to use the most effective configuration - classroom, type of equipment, networking, software - to optimize both access and quality.

x Accountability for all ICT resources, as with all other school property and facilities rests with the school's administration.

x Students completing primary education should have had some exposure to ICT, and possess some awareness of its applications.

x Students leaving Fifth Form after five years of secondary education must be computer literate defined as being able to use a computer safely to do the following

1. o compose a document using word processing functions, being able to copy, cut,
2. paste, save and print

b. o prepare a simple spreadsheet
c. o send and receive an electronic mail message
d. o access sites desired on the internet

x ICT at the institutional level will serve multiple purposes, all of which contribute to the creation of a knowledge-based, information-oriented, system driven by modern society. These include primarily

a. o supporting individual mastery of literacy and numeracy skills at the primary level
b. o improving the general quality of learning throughout the curriculum
c. o providing strong support for technical/vocational programmes in the upper levels of the secondary system
d. o remediation where needed
e. o increasing professional development opportunities for teachers and other staff
f. o improving the efficiency of the school's administration, including student record keeping, and evaluation of academic and non-academic progress
g. o facilitating the accurate and timely flow of data and information between institutions and the Ministry of Education
h. o building the creative capacity and the expertise of ICT users and sharing the products with others

x The Ministry of Technology will have the responsibility of ensuring the most efficient use of all resources involved. It will expand its existing courseware evaluation committee to include a broader representation from the stakeholder community to perform a number of functions. The ICT Standards Committee will perform the following:

a. o advising on the appropriateness of hardware
b. o determining approved software for educational/curriculum purposes
c. o determining management systems to ensure compatibility with the national system

x The Ministry of Technology will actively encourage collaborative partnerships in furtherance of the national development objectives. To this end, it will

a. o work with public, private, local and foreign training institutions to expand the number of teachers equipped to work in an ICT mode within the schools
b. o develop guidelines for schools to work directly with providers of goods and services required by the ICT programme in their institutions
c. o remain responsive to the needs of corporations, small business enterprises and individuals in respect of ICT skills and the relevant curricula
d. o encourage the sharing of skills between the schools and the workplace so that curricula can be adapted to suit skills required for the workplace

e. o provide information to the private sector on partnership opportunities with individual educational institutions, not excluding the extent of tax incentives for benefactions.

x The Ministry of Finance, Sustainable Development, Information and Technology and the Government in general will work to make maximum use of the opportunities available through the Telecommunications Policy arrangements to ensure that access to the relevant services is available to the entire student population at the best possible cost.

x The staffing arrangements in the schools and the recurrent costs for approved programmes will be reviewed and modified from time to time by the Ministry of Technology to ensure that the efficiency of the operations is supported.

x Financing of ICT within the education sector will remain as a partnership exercise. The partners will include:

a. o The Government of Saint Kitts and Nevis
b. o Public Corporations and Statutory Bodies
c. o Private Enterprise
d. o Local and International Foundations
e. o Bilateral and Multilateral Organisations
f. o Community Organisations
g. o The educational institutions through income-generating activities
h. o Parents through the cost-sharing mechanisms in secondary and tertiary institutions

All policies and provisions in respect of copyright, professional conduct, confidentiality, rights and responsibilities of lecturers, teachers, instructors, trainees and students will apply to the conduct of ICT programmes.

Issues regarding ICT in Education

Several issues have been considered in order for the country to make optimal use of ICT in the teaching/learning process. With the rapid changes in the technology itself and its applications, these issues and others will have to be constantly reviewed to ensure that policies are kept relevant and current.

Relevant considerations and policy objectives include:

x The Ministry of Technology's institutional capacity to utilize information management tools and to ensure the implementation and support of ICT programmes in the nation's schools.

x The revised policy instruments, including incentives, guidelines and performance evaluation instruments as appropriate to management in the information age.

x The supply of hardware and relevant software to allow students equitable access to the technology.

x The equipping and retooling of the Teacher Training College to prepare teachers in the integration of ICT in the curriculum.

x The country's capacity to develop software and courseware, which support the curriculum and reflect Kittitian and Nevisian culture.

x The capacity of suppliers to maintain hardware and software supplied to the school system.

x The funding required for the introduction, maintenance and review of ICT programmes.

x The development of ICT curricula for the primary and lower secondary levels of the education system.

MODERNIZING GOVERNMENT AND DELIVERING CITIZEN SERVICES

ICT USE BY GOVERNMENT AND E-GOVERNMENT INITIATIVES.

The SKN Government is fully committed to deploying information and communications technologies more widely throughout Government. For the most part, ICTs are currently used for point-to-point communications, rather than to deliver services and to make government information more readily available or to enable citizens to communicate with their Government. Some Government information is available online, but there is no consistent, uniform policy pertaining to information disclosure and publication. The Honourable Prime Minister has recently met personally with private sector consultants abroad to discuss successful e-government programs and the development of integrated consistent policies to guide future initiatives of the GSKN . One aspect of e-government that must be thoroughly addressed is how to improve program design and organizational structures to accommodate the new online environment. Few, if any, programs were originally designed with ICTs specifically in mind. The Prime Minister's personal interest gives this sector the necessary impetus, leadership, and political urgency, and he has access to experienced IT consultants who can help SKN develop a national plan and strategy to advance ICTs. As each country has its idiosyncrasies, ordinary citizens and industry must be part of the process of designing and rolling out e-services to ensure their appeal to and use by local citizens.

EXPANDING SKN'S INTERNET PRESENCE.

The lack of an Internet presence by the Government is largely due to the under-utilization of the Web by Government agencies for basic services such as posting information, much less hosting services and applications. Once control over the ".kn" domain name is regained, there should be more Web sites with the country's domain name. The Government may wish to encourage a shift to the ".kn" domain. More importantly, the Government and the private sector should consider the value of a content-rich national portal with an anchor in interactive e-government services. Simultaneously, the Government should engage its neighbors in discussions regarding the establishment of a regional portal to enable Caribbean enterprises to more effectively market their goods and benefit from the synergies, and strengths of one another.

GOVERNMENT AS A CATALYST AND EXAMPLE OF BEST PRACTICES

The credibility of any ICT policy is to a large extent dependent on the government sector's own efforts toward an effective deployment and use of these technologies. As a major employer, service provider and consumer the government is also in the best position to initiate and sustain the spread of ICT applications in the other sectors and the subsequent growth of ICT industries. This requires the application of ICT in all administrative procedures and the related reengineering of the latter with a view to making them more cost-effective and more customer-oriented, overcoming when necessary existing boundaries and prerogatives. A significant training and retraining effort should be undertaken. The definition and actual construction of a public information domain accessible to all citizens now and in the future is also an important aspect of this effort. The introduction of knowledge management practices is furthermore a natural complement to the above endeavours.

Related strategic moves are to:

x Undertake a stepwise and thorough revision of all procedures (in order of priority) involving direct transactions between the public, individual and corporate, in any area, on the one hand and government offices on the other hand, with a view to simplifying and streamlining them and installing these new procedures on E-government sites.

x Design and implement a stepwise program for installing computer networks in public administration agencies and related training of all civil servants with a view to supporting the deployment of Government-to-Government and Government-to-Public, including E-procurement, electronic transactions through Intranets, Extranets and Internet sites. Priority may be given to transactions between businesses and public administration.

x Determine what documents and transactions form part of the public domain and should remain available to the general public at zero or nominal cost.

x Set up Web based resources providing basic official information for the citizens of OECS countries, especially information related to main circumstances of life.

x Set up Web based services and other appropriate electronic resources (e.g. CDRom versions of the web sites) providing practical information and advice on natural disaster preparedness and emergency situations in conjunction with alert and rescue programmes.

x Establish a country portal providing basic information about the country, its administrative organisation, investment and migration regulations and procedures, etc. targeted at economic partners and customers in other countries.

x Establish fixed and/or mobile administrative service points that will allow the public to accomplish administrative formalities related to basic social and economic events at single points. While using ICT-based transactions these points should cater for the needs of the persons who cannot use ICT as well as provide the required advisory services.

x Establish a phased program with a view to allowing for electronic payment to the public administration.

x Establish a phased programme aimed at making the public sector as a whole an example of best practices in ICT applications, knowledge management and learning.

GOVERNMENT ICT POLICY

The Policy is to be a guide for the Government sector in using ICTs to achieve overall development within agencies and in delivery of services. It will assist in benchmarking each organization's activities against the Policy, which will enable agencies to identify the areas which need attention and where interventions need to be carried out. It will also ensure consistency and synergy in ICT activities. The Policy articulates the minimum requirements expected of Government organizations, and Government organizations could add to this and create their own organizational ICT policies, within this policy framework. Thus, the Policy will be a first step towards implementing a standards-based approach in implementing e-Government services. The mission of the Policy is enunciated below:

Mission:

- x Improved efficiency and effectiveness of Government organizations in Saint Kitts and Nevis thereby making each Government organization's budget go farther.
- x Ease and accessibility of Government information and services for citizens, thus creating a citizen-friendly Government.
- x Creating a business-friendly environment by improving the interface between Government and business.
- x Promoting transparency, inclusion and general good governance.
- x Developing ICT competence among Government employees to improve productivity and customer service.

TIME FRAME:

The implementation time frame is to be 5 years, commencing January 2007.

SCOPE:

The ICT Policy is to be implemented by all Government organizations; Ministries and Government Departments. Adoption of the Policy by Government Corporations, Statutory Bodies, and fully government owned companies is recommended.

PROCESS:

The ICTU of Saint Kitts and Nevis will set up an ICT Policy Implementation Committee in December 2006 to formulate the first draft of the ICT Policy Implementation Plan for the Government. The document will be circulated to the members of the ICTU Working Group and Focus Groups, and to members of academia, to obtain their views. The document will be made available on the web in order to ascertain the views of a wider audience. Comments will be received from the Government organizations, private organizations, citizens, associations, health personnel, etc. All comments will be reviewed and the policy amended thereafter incorporating recommendations.

ENABLING LEGAL ENVIRONMENT:

The issue of formulating and incorporating into the country's legal system suitable measures relating to ICT, so as to promote the development of ICT, and to create a facilitating legal environment will be addressed as being top priority by the ICTU. The emphasis will be placed on legislation to facilitate e-transactions and the preparation of a Code of Practice for Data Protection. The drafting of Electronic Transactions legislation will also be regularized.

SALIENT POINTS:

The Government should identify the following factors, which are intrinsic to e-Government, as key principles on which ICT solutions will be implemented. E-Government solutions will contain the attributes listed below.

Accessibility: Providing information and citizen services over the web and ICT channels will make them available to a larger section of the general public. Therefore all possible measures should be taken to make the services accessible to the public without discriminating on ethnicity, religion, gender, disability, or based on geographical locations, time, or on economic levels.

x Transparency: ICT based solutions should improve the transparency by allowing the pubic to monitor the mandate of the organization, functionality, decision making processes, the progress of a process at different stages and clearly informing them of the type and the quality of the services they obtain. The e-government models should always encourage transparency within Government.

x Efficacy: It is important that the services provided by Government organizations using ICTs, meet and exceed the expectation of the citizens. The efficacy at which the services offered should be a key factor that determines the quality of the services provided through using ICTs.

x Efficiency: Services should be available to the public within the minimum possible time. A concept popular in e-government solutions, is *"same day service";* where a service requested by a citizen in the morning should be made available to him/her before the end of the same day. Although it is difficult to expect this level of delivery from every service from the inception, all Government organizations are expected to provide citizen services efficiently so that the public is not made to wait for the services requested. Citizen centric: In providing services, Government organizations should have a holistic approach. Thus, citizens should be able to obtain a service through submitting the minimum necessary supporting documents and visiting a minimum number of organizations.

x Inter-operational: Government organizations should ensure when implementing ICT programs that these are inter-operational - enabling data sharing and data exchange between different systems - throughout all Government organizations, and also with the industry and other key sectors.

x Confidentiality, integrity and availability: All Government organizations should preserve the confidentiality, integrity and availability of the information within their purview. This entails that citizens should have the assurance that Government information is shared only among authorized persons or organizations, that the information is authentic and complete and can be relied on for the purpose for which it is

needed, and also that it is accessible when needed by those who need it.

x Accountability: Government organizations should be accountable towards the citizens and for the services provided, so as to foster confidence in citizens in the use of such services, and in interacting with Government organizations.

x Equity: Information and services should be fairly distributed to citizens to enable them to be benefited on equal terms. It is essential that the marginalized groups and differentlyabled persons be taken into account while devising e-government solutions

LEVERAGING ICT FOR ECONOMIC AND SOCIAL DEVELOPMENT, THROUGH PUBLIC-PRIVATE PARTNERSHIPS

Ultimately, it is the private sector that must generate the business activity that establishes and maintains economic growth and improves the living standards of the citizens. This third area of the ICT Assessment focuses on two key areas relative to leveraging ICTs in St. Kitts and Nevis:

1. Determining and improving the strength and potential of the ICT-related sector in domestic and international markets, and
2. The utilization of ICTs by the local business community in an effort to improve the productivity and efficiency of their operations and, where appropriate, to potentially become more competitive in the regional and global marketplace.

NATIONAL ECONOMY AND PRIVATE SECTOR

Over the past decade, the Federation of St. Kitts and Nevis (SKN) has been reasonably effective at diversifying its economy. SKN has achieved long periods of uninterrupted growth in services (tourism, financial services) and relative prosperity in light manufacturing and assembly. Notwithstanding negative external economic forces and extensive damage caused by two consecutive hurricanes in 1998 and 1999, levels of inflation, employment, and overall GDP continue to be favourable. During the years that followed the hurricanes, a world economic slowdown prevented the islands from achieving a full recovery, only to have conditions exacerbated by the September 11 terrorism attacks and the overall downturn in the tourism industry. GDP growth dropped five percentage points in the first year of the new millennium when compared to pre-hurricane growth but still remained positive. Additionally, the Sugar Industry, which was once a major employer and contributor to the economy, has come to an end.

Economic strengthening is being led by (1) the construction of several large tourism projects and new tourism product development and (2) the redirection of foreign investment strategies towards more near-term and low-risk opportunities in information technology areas. SKN has also realized investment benefits as a result of the legal/regulatory changes that resulted in the country's removal from the OECD Financial Action Task Force (FATF) blacklist. Since its appearance on the OECD's list of uncooperative tax regimes in early 2001 and its subsequent removal in the first quarter of 2002, SKN has demonstrated a commitment to fair banking practices. This led to the creation of the Financial Intelligence Unit to facilitate investigations of suspected tax avoidance as well as to enforce a transparency mechanism, which was recently added to the Companies Act. The imminent launching of a website where offshore companies can register will give tremendous boost to the financial services sector.

The government has emphasized the advantages of ready-to-work commercial infrastructure for targeted ICT FDI, and already development space has been earmarked and a plan of action is being developed for the placement of the infrastructure. The government has stressed the importance of equipping commercial space as part of an overall strategy to attract ICT investment. Called "smart" facilities, they play on the notion that "intelligent" jobs are created there.

BUSINESS COMPETITIVENESS AND DEVELOPMENT - PROMOTING AND SUPPORTING INITIATIVES OF THE ENTERPRISES TOWARDS ICT USE

In view of the extensive transformation that ICT use calls for, the market structure and enterprises' size may be obstacles until ICTs have become commonplace. Since the objective is to be among the early adopters rather than laggards, targeted support is required. It should be directed in the first place at small and medium enterprises, the tourism industry and agribusinesses. The development of e-commerce further requires appropriate logistics to be in place as well as quality of service standards and consumer protection mechanisms.

Related strategic moves will:

x Support the formation of service centres, especially as cooperatives, joint ventures or as part of trade associations, that can provide ICT based services(such as e.g. accounting, clients data bases, customer relationship management (CRM), billing., Internet market places, e-shops, etc.) for the Small and Medium Enterprises, offer training in the use of ICT, support the transfer of these functions into the individual enterprises or trade associations when feasible.

x Include in the programmes for promotion and support of Small and Medium Enterprises incentives and services for training in ICT applications, ICT investments, formation of users groups and appropriate fora for sharing of experience among SMEs managers.

x Establish a scheme for encouraging firms to invest in ICT and train their staff, e.g. through low rate loans to be administered by commercial banks with a consolidation or guarantee from the government. Such schemes should apply to existing companies as well as new investors.

x Establish a consumer information and protection service related to e-business transactions by companies operating in St Kitts and Nevis to be jointly operated by public sector, private sector and civil society organisations. It should offer an arbitration procedure and benefit from fast judicial action procedures.

x Support the participation of enterprises of the tourism sector and tourism authorities in portals that can provide a variety of information and inquiry services as well as on-line reservations and auctions. Also support training for entrepreneurs in digital content development.

x Support the creation and/or development of agri-business portals that can provide to the farmers and enterprises of the sector, with their active participation, a variety of technical, commercial and administrative information and inquiry services as well as support cooperative commercial services.

x Encourage and support efforts geared towards strengthening of logistics (e.g. warehousing facilities, packaging, transportation, courier services, customs clearance, contracting distributors, marketing, contracting intermediaries for payments and transfers, etc.) required by e-Commerce, in the country as well as abroad, including the formation of co-operative or joint ventures.

x Promote the establishment of standards about quality of service by e-commerce providers and put in place appropriate regulation mechanisms to ensure compliance .

x Develop IT parks that can offer state of the art wired premises, call centre, industrial and warehousing space, training facilities, incubator facilities, business development support, accommodation, catering and entertainment facilities that can attract and host external investors and host temporary events (such as staff training and leisure packages, professional meetings, etc.)

x Establish an employment portal to be jointly operated by public sector, private sector and civil society organisations that would compile professional profiles, labour regulations, notices of training opportunities, job offers and demands, etc. The contents shall also be made available to communities in CD-ROM or print format.

x Explicitly include ICT activities in the investment promotion packages and adjust the latter when appropriate.

FINANCIAL SERVICES - SWITCHING PROGRESSIVELY TOWARD ELECTRONIC PAYMENTS AND FINANCIAL TRANSACTIONS

The implementation of e-business rests with adaptations of the financial system so that electronic transactions become a standard feature. The deployment of ICT also requires that the financial sector adjust its practices to an economy that relies upon services and intangible assets with a view to offering attractive packages especially for the creation of new enterprises.

Related strategic moves will:

x Assign priority to ICT investments, including manpower development, and creation of ICT activities by existing or new business in the loans policies of the financial sector and adapt existing regulations and business rules to the particular requirements of this type of business.

x Establish mechanisms for the consolidation or guaranteeing of loans made by banks to ICT investments, enterprises or activities under appropriate conditions e.g. recruitment and training of nationals.

x Establish a package that includes access to study loans, access to incubators and access to employment or business creation loans, with a preferential regime for women. This package would be operated by commercial banks but supported by government incentives (e.g. cofinancing or guarantees).

x Encourage the establishment of micro-finance or credit unions by community organisations that can take advantage of Internet banking to channel remittances of expatriates to their relatives in the home country. These transactions may enjoy reduced rates and charges and at the same time contribute to the funding of community projects through a small percentage received on the transactions.

x Encourage and support the introduction of electronic banking, including Internet banking, and electronic payment technologies for domestic, international and inter-bank transactions.

x Develop an online registering facility for offshore financial services businesses.

CONCLUSION

The National ICT Strategic Plan (NISP) represents a major achievement for the Government of St. Kitts and Nevis. The NISP represents simultaneously both a vision roadmap for ushering in the information society. It provides a basis for engaging our local, regional and international social and economic development partners in a much more focused way in relation to ICT and how it can transform our society. Bearing this in mind, the NISP will go into wide circulation among our development partners.

The achievement of an information society, and therefore the implementation of the NISP, will require the commitment of significant amounts of resources in human and financial terms. Government must commit a considerable fraction of these resources to both lead and demonstrate support for the vision of an ICT-transformed society.

The first order of business emanating from this plan is the drafting of a three-year NISP Implementation Plan that attempts to identify specific activities, maximize synergies and identify specific resources. Undoubtedly, the instituting of the ICT Unit which will itself constitute the framework for the implementation of the plan will be critical to the early success of the plan.

As it is with any important long term plan, the NISP will be reviewed, revised and fine-tuned on a periodic basis to take into consideration emerging ideas and experiences. On an annual basis, audits will be conducted to measure progress on the five major facets of the ICT plan. These audits will attract cross-sectoral involvement and will form the basis for interventions that will be designed to ensure that development targets are achieved.

PRACTICAL INFORMATION FOR BUSINESS AND INVESTMENTS

INVESTING ST. KITTS AND NEVIS BASICS

From the 1620's until 2005 sugar production was the main industry on St. Kitts and the biggest earner of foreign exchange for the country. This industry has been replaced by tourism as the main industry on both islands. Tourism is capital intensive. Given its small local capital base the country is heavily dependant on and positively welcomes direct foreign investment.

The number of nationals of the country who live in North America, the United Kingdom and other Caribbean islands far outnumber the number of residents. Remittances from such nationals also contribute significantly to the economy as do offshore financial services and education services, the latter consisting of medical, veterinary and nursing universities providing education to non-nationals. The direct capital investment to build and manage these facilities and the monies spent by resident students of these universities (which are accredited and regulated by the Government under a statutory system) contribute significantly to the country's economy.

Government agencies devoted to the promotion of foreign investment include the Saint Christopher Tourism Authority, St. Kitts Investment Promotion Authority and Nevis Tourism Authority. Private sector agencies are St. Kitts-Nevis Chamber of Industry & Commerce and the Hotel & Tourism Association.

There are also agencies dedicated to the promotion of investment by nationals including the Development Bank of St. Kitts & Nevis, the Foundation for National Development and the private sector organizations referred to above.

Investors in major projects usually negotiate agreements with Government allowing for the importation of business and industrial materials and some personal belongings free of customs duties.

FINANCIAL OGRANIZATION

EASTERN CARIBBEAN CENTRAL BANK (ECCB)

St. Kitts is the headquarters of the Eastern Caribbean Central Bank which is located at Bird Rock, Basseterre.

The Eastern Caribbean Central Bank (www.eccb-centralbank.org) was established in October 1983. It is the Monetary Authority for a group of eight island economies namely -Anguilla, Antigua and Barbuda, Commonwealth of Dominica, Grenada, Montserrat, St Kitts and Nevis, St Lucia, and St Vincent and the Grenadines.

EASTERN CARIBBEAN CURRENCY UNION (ECCU)

St. Kitts & Nevis and the remaining member states of the ECCB make up the Eastern Caribbean Currency Union. The financial system in the ECCU comprises domestic banks, International Financial Services Sector banks, credit unions, insurance companies, national development foundations, development finance institutions, building and loan associations and finance companies.

FINANCIAL SYSTEM IN ST. KITTS & NEVIS

The financial system in the Federation is bank centric with banks dominating the financial landscape. Commercial banks operating in St. Kitts & Nevis are as follows:

LOCAL BANKS

THE BANK OF NEVIS LIMITED

(www.bankofnevis.com) is locally incorporated and owned and has its headquarters at Main Street, Charlestown Nevis and has been operating since 1985.

RBTT BANK (SKN) LIMITED

(www.rbtt.com) is a locally incorporated foreign subsidiary of RBTT Bank of the Republic of Trinidad & Tobago. Its offices are located at Chapel Street, Charlestown, Nevis.

ST. KITTS-NEVIS-ANGUILLA NATIONAL BANK LIMITED

(www.sknanb.com) is locally incorporated and owned has been in operation in St. Kitts & Nevis since 1971. Its head office is situated on Central Street, Basseterre, St. Kitts with branches at Pelican Mall, Saddlers and Sandy Point, St. Kitts and at Prince William Street, Charlestown, Nevis.

INTERNATIONAL BANKS

THE BANK OF NOVA SCOTIA

(www.stkittsandnevis.scotiabank.com) operates local branches at Fort Street and at Bird Rock, Basseterre, St. Kitts and at Main Street, Charlestown, Nevis. Scotiabank has been doing business in the Federation since 1983.

FIRSTCARIBBEAN INTERNATIONAL BANK (BARBADOS) LIMITED

(www.firstcaribbeanbank.com) is incorporated in Barbados with its head office at Warrens, St. Michael's, Barbados and has branches at Bank Street, Basseterre, St. Kitts and at Main Street, Charlestown, Nevis. FirstCaribbean is the successor to the banking business of Barclays Bank PLC in St. Kitts & Nevis since October 2002. Barclays was the first foreign bank to operate in St. Kitts & Nevis in 1837.

RBTT BANK CARIBBEAN LIMITED

(www.rbtt.com) is a foreign subsidiary of RBTT Bank of the Republic of Trinidad & Tobago. Its offices are located Fort Street, Basseterre, St. Kitts.

ROYAL BANK OF CANADA

(www.rbc.com) operates local branches at The Circus and at Wellington Road, Basseterre, St. Kitts. RBC has been in operation in the country since 1915.

All of the above banks are licensed under and governed by The Banking Act of St. Kitts & Nevis and regulated and supervised by the Eastern Caribbean Central Bank.

The locally incorporated and owned St. Kitts-Nevis Finance Company Limited (FINCO) is also licensed to do financial business which is regulated and supervised by ECCB. FINCO is a subsidiary of St. Kitts-Nevis-Anguilla Trading and Development Company Limited (TDC), a local public company.

In addition to commercial banks, local financial institutions include The Development Bank of St. Kitts and Nevis, a statutory corporation owned and operated by the Government, St. Kitts Co-Operative Credit Union Limited and Nevis Co-Operative Credit Union Limited.

FOREIGN INVESTORS

Foreign investors are not required to maintain a bank account in the Federation. However, if they desire to do so, they can open and operate bank accounts in St. Kitts & Nevis once they satisfy the requirements of the individual financial institutions for the opening of an account to be held by a foreigner. These requirements may include the following:

Two valid pieces of picture identification – passport, driver's licence, country identification card
One character reference from a professional acquaintance (i.e. lawyer, doctor, accountant)
One bank reference from investor's current bank
Document(s) showing that the individual has ties to St. Kitts & Nevis (e.g. owns property here; proof of an authorized project or business being carried out in the country, a work or residency permit)
A copy of corporate documents if the investor is a company; personal information of shareholders of the company (name, address, occupation, date of birth); identification for directors and account signatories
Source of funds and expected activities of the account.

Foreign investors can also (subject to Ministry of Finance approval) obtain bank loans locally once they satisfy the loan application requirements of the individual financial institutions for the granting of loans to foreign individuals or entities. These requirements may include the following in addition to the requirements listed above to open an account:

Verification of income (e.g. the last three years tax returns)
Two copies of public utility bills of investor's current primary residence
Accountant-prepared financial statements
Detailed assets and liabilities statement

EASTERN CARIBBEAN SECURITIES EXCHANGE (ECSE)

St. Kitts is the headquarters of the Eastern Caribbean Securities Exchange which is also located at Bird Rock, Basseterre.

The ECSE (www.ecseonline.com) is a regional securities market established by the Eastern Caribbean Central Bank and licensed under the Securities Act of 2001 and Regulations passed under it - a uniform regional body of legislation governing securities market activities.

The Bank of Nevis Limited and St. Kitts-Nevis-Anguilla National Bank Limited are among the five local public companies which are listed on the Eastern Caribbean Securities Exchange.

EXCHANGE CONTROLS

BUSINESS TRANSACTIONS WITH NATIONALS, RESIDENTS OR NON-RESIDENTS

Citizens are persons born in the Federation, or descended from such persons within criteria set out in the Constitution; or persons registered or naturalized by virtue of the Constitution or the Saint Christopher and Nevis Citizenship Act.

Residents are categorized as permanent residents, annual residents, temporary residents and work permit holder residents under the Immigration Act.

The grant of residency status only does not entitle the holder to work or to do business in St. Kitts & Nevis. All persons who are not citizens require a work permit to engage in any occupation or to accept employment in the country. In addition all citizens and work permit holders who wish to conduct business in the Federation are required to obtain a business licence from the Ministry of Finance under the Licences on Businesses and Occupations Act.

There are no restrictions on an investor's use of a bank account. However account activity may be monitored to ensure that there is no suspicious activity that may trigger a suspicious activity report to the Financial Intelligence Unit for potential money laundering.

INVESTMENT CONTROLS

A foreigner (alien) investor may be required to make application to the federal Government in St. Kitts or to the Nevis Island Administration in Nevis to obtain an alien land holding licence in accordance with the provisions of the Aliens Land Holding Regulation Act to be a director of a company, to hold shares in a company, to exercise votes in a company or to hold title to an interest in real estate in the Federation.

In addition, in order to protect or to promote local investment the Government may restrict or deny foreign investors permission to operate certain industries, particularly those which are over-subscribed and non-capital or technical intensive. See further, "Requirements for the Establishment of Business."

MONEY TRANSFERS

The Eastern Caribbean Central Bank provides exchange rates for foreign currency which all commercial banks use as a guide in setting their foreign currency exchange rates.

There are no direct restrictions on the transfer of money into or out of the country unless the transfer of funds triggers Anti Money Laundering Regulations.

Anti-Money Laundering Regulations require that a regulated person must pay special attention to certain types of transactions e.g. complex, unusual or large business transactions; unusual patterns of transactions; insignificant but periodic transactions which have no apparent economic or lawful purpose.

In addition the Regulations require that upon reasonable suspicion of any the foregoing apparently questionable types of transactions which may constitute or be related to money laundering, a relevant business shall promptly report the suspicious transaction to the reporting Authority.

Withholding Tax at the rate of 10% of payments is payable on certain remittances abroad. (see Taxation section)

IMPORT/EXPORT REGULATIONS

St. Kitts & Nevis has been a member of GATT since 1995, but it is not a member of the EEC. The country is party to the following regional trade agreements:

Caribbean Single Market & Economy (CSME)
Caribcan (Caribbean-Canada)
Caribbean Basin Initiative (Caribbean-USA)
Economic Partnership Agreement (Caribbean-EU)
CARICOM-Dominican Republic

THE CUSTOMS DEPARTMENT

The St. Kitts & Nevis Customs department's website (www.skncustoms.com) is modern, well-structured, and contains comprehensive up-to-date information about their administration, procedures, tariffs, relevant legislation, exchange rates; and provides various e-documents and forms for viewing or download.

TARIFF & DUTY INFORMATION

The current Customs tariff nomenclature of St. Kitts & Nevis is based on the WCO Harmonized System (HS) Convention. Customs duties and taxes are collected based on the value which is derived from the value stated on the invoice, receipt or other proof of purchase, or such higher value as the Customs Officer assesses as the true value of the goods.

The dollar value must be converted from the foreign currency stated on the proof of purchase document to Eastern Caribbean Dollar XCD. An exchange rate for the conversion of foreign currency to XCD is published by Eastern Caribbean Central Bank. Other foreign currency rates are subject to change and are updated weekly in conjunction with the Central Bank.

Customs Import Duties are applicable according to the rates set out in the Common External Tariff of the Caribbean Common Market. The rates are applied based on the (Cost, Insurance and Freight) -CIF. Rates applicable ranges from 0 to 45% with the majority of commodities attracting a rate of 25%.

MANUFACTURING REQUIREMENTS

There are no manufacturing requirements that stipulate that products must contain locally produced ingredients or components. Therefore, component parts are allowed to be imported.

ENVIRONMENTAL CONSIDERATIONS

There has been increasing attention by the Government in recent years to environmental protection.

Environmental protection is managed under the National Conservation and Environmental Protection Act 1987. This Act established the Department of Environment which is charged with management of conservation areas and of environmental protection in St. Kitts & Nevis.

Conservation and environmental protection are divided into four main categories:

Coast conservation and beach protection
Forestry, soil and water conservation
Protection of wild animals and birds
Protection of antiquities and old buildings Every development proposal which may affect any of the foregoing must include an environment impact assessment.

INTELLECTUAL PROPERTY

Trademarks, copyrights, industrial designs and patents are protected by statute. The relevant statutes are:

The Marks, Collective Marks and Trade Names Act 2000
The Copyright Act 2000
The Patents Act 2000 Protection of trademarks and patents is based on registration; copyright protection is not.

In addition to the foregoing legislative protections, there are common law and equitable rules which protect confidential information even though not falling within any of the categories protected by the above statutes. Such protection could in appropriate circumstances extend to know-how. St. Kitts & Nevis is party to the Paris Convention for the Protection of Industrial Property.

TRADE MARKS

Any mark capable of distinguishing the goods or services of one entity from another is registrable as a trade mark.

Registration is for a period of 10 years and may be renewed for successive periods of 10 years. The owner of the trade mark may license its use but the licence must provide for effective control by the licensor of the quality of goods or services of the licensee in connection with which the mark is to be used.

COPYRIGHTS

Copyright may exist in (a) original literary, dramatic, musical or artistic works, (b) sound recordings, films, broadcasts or cable programs, and (c) typographical arrangements of published editions.

Protection is not based on registration. In general, the author of a protected work is the first owner unless there is an agreement to the contrary.

Copyright protection lasts for 50 years except with regard to typographical arrangements of a published edition for which the period is 25 years.

Copyright may be assigned or licensed.

The Copyright Act authorizes the unaltered simultaneous re-transmission of cable programming in St. Kitts & Nevis without the need to obtain a licence from the copyright owner. However, in such a case, the copyright owner is entitled to equitable remuneration.

PATENTS

Patents may be granted in respect of any invention which is new, involves an inventive step and is capable of industrial application except for (a) scientific theories or mathematical methods, (b) schemes rules or methods for doing business or performing a mental act or playing a game or (c) methods for the treatment of the human or animal body by surgery or therapy as well as diagnostic methods practiced.

A patent lasts for 20 years.

Patents may be assigned or licensed.

At any time after the later of 4 years from the grant of the patent or 3 years from the date of the filing, any interested person may apply to the Court for the grant of a non-voluntary licence under the patent on the ground that the invention is not being exploited or is being insufficiently exploited by working the invention in, or by importation into, St. Kitts-Nevis. If the court grants the non-voluntary licence it must fix the scope and function of the licence, the time limit within which the licensee must begin to exploit the patented invention, and the amount of remuneration to be paid to the patentee.

INVESTMENT INCENTIVES

DESIGNATED DEVELOPMENT AREAS

The Government has designated areas on St. Kitts in which foreign investment in tourism is incentivised. These include the Southeast Peninsula, Frigate Bay and Whitegate Development area. Separate statutory regimes apply to promote investment in these areas.

LAND HOLDING LICENCES

Any non-national individual, and corporate entity formed outside St. Kitts & Nevis, and any corporate entity formed in St. Kitts & Nevis which has any non-national director or of whose shares non-nationals own more than a third, are required to obtain an alien landholding licence to hold title to land except in the Frigate Bay area and on the Southeast Peninsula of St. Kitts, in which latter area up to two acres may be held without such a licence.

An alien landholding licence is required for any such person or entity to hold title to land in Nevis. Any non-national is required to obtain a licence to be a director or shareholder of a Company which carries on business in Nevis, whether the company owns land or not.

INCENTIVES FOR INVESTMENT IN TOURISM

Incentives available to tourism projects (including hotels, condominiums and villa developments) include a tax holiday, waiver of duties on the importation of goods and materials for the construction and operation of the development and waiver of withholding taxes. The period of the tax holiday and waiver is by statute 10 years for developments (other than developments on the Southeast Peninsula) with 30 or more bedrooms and 5 years for developments with 10-29 bedrooms.

INCENTIVES FOR MANUFACTURING

Incentives are available for enterprises engaged in manufacturing and processing which meet criteria based on local value added to the products under manufacture. The legislation allows a tax holiday of up to 10 years and waiver of import duties on components, equipment and other goods used in the manufacturing process and the operation of the business of the manufacturer. Export allowances also apply to manufacturers who qualify for the above incentives.

Goods currently manufactured in St. Kitts & Nevis by manufacturers who benefit from incentives include lighting controls, resolvers, electronics and garments. Data processing services are also incentivized.

Companies may qualify for incentives whether or not they have local investors.

EXPORT INCENTIVES OR GUARANTEES

Government does not provide export guarantees, insurance, subsidies or financing for manufacturers for export. Financing is available from the banking sector.

LEGAL STRUCTURES FOR DOING BUSINESS

A person may carry on business in St. Kitts & Nevis as a sole trader, a partnership, a limited partnership, or a company limited by shares.

SOLE TRADERS

A sole trader is taxed as an individual (see Taxation Section)

LIMITED LIABILITY COMPANIES

(A) LOCAL COMPANIES

Any person or group of persons (under 20 in number) may establish a company to carry on business. Any group of more than 20 persons must incorporate to carry on business.

(B) EXTERNAL COMPANIES

A company which is incorporated in a jurisdiction outside of St. Kitts & Nevis and wishes to carry on business here must register as an external company in the island on which it intends to carry on business. Such registration does not of itself allow the Company to carry on business. Depending on the nature of the business the Company may be required to obtain other licences or permits. There is no legal requirement that a company must have local investment participation in order to register or to be licensed to carry on business in St. Kitts & Nevis.

(C) PUBLIC COMPANIES

A Company which has more than 50 shareholders is deemed to be a public company. A company with fewer shareholders may opt to be registered as or to convert to a public company. The main differences between a private company and a public company are:

1. A public company must have at least 3 directors and at least 2 non-executive directors. A private company may have 1 director.
2. The Secretary of a public company must have certain specified qualifications.
3. A public company must file its audited accounts with the Registrar of Companies
4. A public company must comply with filing and disclosure requirements under the Securities Act.

CORPORATE RECORDS

Every company must maintain a registered office in the island of its incorporation, registers of shareholders, directors and charges and accounting records.

ANNUAL RETURNS

Every registered company (whether private or public, local or external) must file an annual return with the Registrar of Companies.

OFFSHORE COMPANIES

Each island has a separate statutory regime for the incorporation and maintenance of tax-exempt companies. Such companies are exempt from income and withholding taxes provided they do business entirely offshore.

LLC

Nevis also has a regime for the registration of Limited Liability Companies which are exempt from income and withholding taxes provided they do business entirely offshore.

PARTNERSHIPS

A partnership may be established at common law or pursuant to the Partnership Act. No form of registration of partnerships is provided by St. Kitts & Nevis law. Under such partnerships the partners are jointly and severally liable for the debts of the partnership.

LIMITED PARTNERSHIPS

Limited Partnership may be established under the Limited Partnerships Act.

TRUSTS

There is separate legislation in each island for the establishment and registration of trusts.

JOINT VENTURES

There is no business entity known under St. Kitts & Nevis law as a joint venture. Persons wishing to conduct business jointly must use one of the legal entities described above.

BRANCHES

A company registered in a jurisdiction outside of St. Kitts & Nevis may conduct business in St. Kitts & Nevis through a branch office. Such company must register as an external company as indicated in the section on External Companies above. The Company is fully liable for the debts of the branch office. Tax implications are described below.

CAPITALISATION

There is no law applicable generally to the capitalization of companies doing business in St. Kitts & Nevis. There are capitalization requirements for banks and insurance companies under legislation specific to those industries.

REQUIREMENTS FOR THE ESTABLISHMENT OF A BUSINESS

Businesses, other than those providing financial and telecommunications services, are licensed under the Businesses and Occupations Licences Act 1972. Every person, whether a citizen or not, is required to obtain a business licence to carry on any business activity identified in the Act. Generally speaking, aliens will only be granted a business licence where in the judgment of the Government the proposed business activity is not already being undertaken, or adequately undertaken, by citizens.

An application for a business licence is made by submitting the requisite form to the Ministry of Finance and takes between 4 to 8 weeks to process. The successful applicant pays an annual fee to government of between EC$100 to EC$1000 depending on the type of business.

In addition to business licences, every alien must obtain a work permit to work in St. Kitts & Nevis. Application is made by completing and submitting to the Ministry of National Security the requisite form together with (a) passport photograph, (b) notarized copies of applicant's passport and birth certificate; (c) where applicable, notarized copy of marriage certificate and of passports and birth certificates of the applicant's spouse and minor children; (c) police certificate; (d) proof of offer of employment; and (e) in relation to the applicant and his/her spouse and minor children, results of HIV, VDRL and tuberculosis tests and chest x-ray. The application takes 4 – 8 weeks to process.

The work permit expires on December 31 in each year. Application for renewal is made to the Ministry of National Security. There is no need to submit the supporting documentation upon renewal applications. The application to renew must be submitted by January 31. The fee for the work permit is EC$2,500.00 per annum. It is not a legal requirement that businesses carry insurance.

BUSINESS OPERATIONS

Advertising is restricted in certain contexts. Advertising the sale of securities, for example, is regulated by the Securities Act 2000, the Securities (Advertisements) Regulations 2001 and the Securities (Prospectus) Regulations 2001. In the consumer protection context, under the Consumer Affairs Act 2003 suppliers are prohibited from making false representations in connection with the supply of goods and services or in connection with the promotion of the supply of goods or services. A supplier is also prohibited from engaging in bait advertising.

It is not a requirement that an investor have local counsel. However, in almost all instances, an investor will require advice on local law issues. Local counsel can be found by online searches of the following sites:

www.lexmundi.org www.oecsbar.org www.sknvibes.com/legal/lawyers.cfm

The St. Kitts-Nevis Bar Association has promulgated recommended minimum fees in relation to certain specified matters. Most lawyers apply those fees to the specified matters. In relation to matters not specified in the Bar recommendations, fees are negotiated on a case by case basis.

If a local company is formed through which to conduct business, Section 102 of the Companies Act 1996 requires that every company shall keep accounting records which are sufficient to show and explain its transactions and are such as to -(a) disclose with reasonable accuracy, at any time, the financial position of the company at that time; and (b) enable the directors to comply with their statutory duties.

Further, Section 48 of the Income Tax Act 1966 empowers the Comptroller of Inland Revenue, by notice in writing, to require any person or the agent or attorney of any person or the secretary, attorney, manager, agent, or other principal officer of any company to furnish him within the prescribed time with— (a) a return of income; and (b) such accounts (including a balance sheet at the terminal date of such accounts) and particulars as may seem necessary to the Comptroller for the purposes of that Act.

These accounts must be in the English language. Accounts must be prepared in accordance with generally accepted accounting principles.

CONSUMER PROTECTION

As indicated earlier, there is in force in St. Kitts & Nevis the Consumer Affairs Act 2003. The Act established the Bureau of Consumer Affairs which is charged with implementing the Act.

The general thrust of the legislation is to ensure that goods and services supplied to consumers meet certain minimum standards which cannot be excluded by agreement and that suppliers not engage in misleading or unconscionable trade practices.

CONSTRUCTION

The cost of construction depends on numerous factors including whether the building is to be used for residential or commercial purposes, topography and soil type of site, finishing, and construction methodology. Typical costs as of the date of this guide range from US$100 to US$250 per square foot.

No construction can be undertaken until the buildings plans and specification have been approved by the Development Control and Planning Board. Applications are usually dealt with in about 4 – 6 weeks.

CONTRACTS

Subject to the requirement for aliens to obtain a licence to hold any (including security) interests in land in most instances, investors can legally enter into any type of legally enforceable contract.

Contracts entered into here, whether with residents or not, may be stipulated to be governed by the laws of another country so long as that choice is not capricious.

REDUCTIONS OR RETURN ON CAPITAL

Companies formed in St. Kitts & Nevis may only reduce their capital in certain circumscribed cases. In general, they may only do so where the effect will not be to render the company insolvent or unable to meet its obligations as they fall due.

There is no restriction on the repatriation of foreign currency from St. Kitts & Nevis.

TRADE ASSOCIATIONS

The leading business association is the Chamber of Industry & Commerce. Membership is voluntary.

LABOUR LEGISLATION & RELATIONS

The principal legislation governing employer/employee relations is the Protection of Employment Act. However, there are also other laws which impact upon employment relations including the Social Security Act, the Protection of Wages Act, the Labour (Minimum Wage) Act, the Holidays With Pay Act, the Employment of Women, Young Persons & Children Act, and the Labour Act.

Employers must ensure that employees are qualified or trained to perform their duties since employers are vicariously liable for the actions of employees performed in the course of their employment.

Every non-national must obtain a Work Permit or a CARICOM Skilled Nationals Certificate from the Government of St. Kitts & Nevis in order to work in St. Kitts & Nevis.

There are minimum wages stipulated by law in relation to a variety of types of specific employment, eg. hotel workers, casino workers, restaurant workers, security guards and watchmen, domestic helpers, shop employees and manufacturing sector workers. Government has also enacted a national minimum wage of EC$8.00 per hour, which applies to workers other than the aforementioned specific categories.

The minimum wage regulations also provide for overtime to be paid at premium rates after a specified number of hours are exceeded.

The Holidays with Pay Act requires that employees receive a minimum amount of paid vacation annually. This is a minimum of 14 days per year.

A business is not required to employ a minimum number of employees.

Government's policy has always been that non-national employees (who are not owners of the business) would only be granted permits to work in St. Kitts & Nevis where no suitably qualified or capable national can be reasonably employed to perform the particular job.

The common law and the Protection of Employment Act require notice to be given when an employee is being dismissed other than for cause. The required period of notice depends mainly upon the length of service, but the status of the employee and other factors could also be relevant to the determination of what constitutes reasonable notice in any particular case.

In addition to the giving of notice, or payment of salary and benefits in lieu of such notice, employees who are made redundant are also entitled to receive a one-off payment from a

Government-controlled Severance Payments Fund. This Fund is financed by a 1% payroll tax paid monthly by all employers.

Employers will only have continuing obligations to lawfully dismissed employees if the particular employment agreement so provided, e.g. by way of pension rights.

An employee may be dismissed without notice or pay in lieu thereof during the probationary period (which cannot exceed 4 weeks in the case of household employment or 3 months in the case of other employment) or where the employee has engaged in serious misconduct in or in relation to his/her employment.

In addition, notice or payment in lieu of notice is also not required where the employee has received at least two prior written warnings about particular misconduct within the previous 6 months, the latter of which warned of termination in the event of further repetition.

A high degree of freedom of contract is legally available in respect of employment agreements but the Protection of Employment Act makes it unlawful to dismiss an employee on certain specified grounds, including but not limited to: union membership or participation in union activities outside working hours, making a complaint or participating in proceedings against an employer involving an alleged violation of laws or regulations, political opinions or affiliations, race, colour, sex or creed, temporary absence from work due to maternity, illness or injury as certified by a medical practitioner, or absence from work in the performance of jury service.

Where an employer contemplates laying off or terminating more than 9 persons or more than 10% of the employer's workforce (whichever is less), the Protection of Employment Act requires that the Labour Commissioner be notified of this in writing at least 30 days before any such dismissals or lay offs. The Labour Commissioner must be so notified in writing of:

(a)	the reasons for the lay offs or terminations;
(b)	the number and categories of employees affected;
(c)	the period over which the terminations are intended to be carried out; and
(d)	a summary of the results of any consultations with any trade union representing the employees.

The Factories Act imposes certain safety codes in respect of some types of business activities.

Unions are constitutionally and legally recognized as legitimate organizations. Workers cannot be dismissed on account of union activities outside of working hours. The main trade union operating in St. Kitts & Nevis is politically-affiliated to the St. Kitts-Nevis Labour Party, but the two organizations are legally distinct and have their own separate executives.

Legislation provides a mechanism whereby the Labour Commissioner is empowered to conduct polls to determine the percentage of workers in a particular workplace who desire representation by a particular trade union. Employers are not legally obliged to recognize a particular trade union as the bargaining agent for its workers, but the settled industrial relations practice in St. Kitts is for employers to grant such recognition where a majority of employees desire such representation.

Collective agreements are not legally enforceable under St. Kitts & Nevis law unless their terms and conditions are incorporated into the individual contracts of employment.

Traditionally, there are 12 public holidays each year. These include New Year's Day, Carnival Day, Good Friday, Easter Monday, Labour Day, Whit Monday, Emancipation Day, Culturama Day, National Heroes Day, Independence Day, Christmas Day and Boxing Day. In addition, Government sometimes declares additional public holidays to celebrate or mark significant national events.

TAXATION BASICS

The principal forms of taxation currently in effect are corporation tax, payroll taxes, withholding taxes, turnover taxes and transaction taxes. There is no personal income tax on income other than payroll taxes on employees, turnover taxes on unincorporated businesses, and withholding tax on dividends and other specified monies paid to non-residents

TAXATION ON CORPORATIONS

The income tax rate is 35 per cent of taxable profits of all companies which carry on business in St. Kitts & Nevis. Tax is payable by locally incorporated companies on their worldwide income. External companies are liable to tax on taxable profits of their business in St. Kitts & Nevis.

CAPITAL GAINS

Capital gains tax is payable only on profits derived from the sale of a capital item within a year of its acquisition. The rate of tax is 20 per cent of the profit.

TAX REFORM

A review of the system of corporation taxation by the Ministry of Finance is well advanced with a view to a complete overhaul of the system of taxation on companies. It is expected that a new Income Tax Bill will be published within 12 months and the new system will be in place within 24 months.

TRANSACTION TAXES

There is a plethora of transaction taxes to which individuals and companies may be liable.

VAT

From 1st November 2010 most of these taxes are to be replaced by Value Added Tax (VAT). Preparations are underway for the introduction of value added taxes which are expected to replace many of the taxes listed above under the Section "Transaction Taxes". When the legislation is fully enacted we will update this section.

WITHHOLDING TAXES

Withholding tax is payable at the rate of ten per cent of monies paid to non residents on the following: a) Dividend; b) Interest, annuity, premium and discount; c) Rent, lease, contract and royalty payments; d) A natural resource payment; e) Commissions, remuneration, fees and licences f) Charges for the provision of personal services, commercial advice and managerial skills; g) Administration, management and head office expenses; h) Profits; i) Technical, professional, vocational and any other service fees; j) Accounting, actuarial, legal and audit expenses; k) Non-life insurance premiums; l) Any other annual or periodic payment or distribution

PAYROLL TAXES

A Housing and Social Development Levy is payable on all wages as follows:

Housing and Social Development Levy	Employer	Employed Person	Total
Monthly earnings:			
(a) Less than $1083.33 per month	3%	NIL	3% of wages
(b) Between $1083.33 to $6,500	3%	3%	6% of wages
(c) Between $6,500.01 to $8,000	3%	8%	11% of wages
(d) Equal to or greater than $8,000.01	3%	10%	13% of wages

TAX ON INDIVIDUALS

Personal taxation which is commonly applied throughout the world on the income of an individual, however derived, was abolished in 1980. There are however specific taxes payable by individuals. These include payroll and transaction taxes listed above and taxes described in the following sections.

TRADERS TAX

Tax is charged at the rate of 3 per cent on the gross revenue (above EC$8,000) derived by an unincorporated trader from a business carried on by him/her in St. Kitts & Nevis.

CONSUMPTION TAX

Individuals carrying on certain specified professions or trades are liable to this tax at the rate of 4 per cent of gross revenues above EC$8,000 per month.

TAX ON DIRECTORS

A director of a company incorporated in, or a resident director of an external company carrying on business in, St. Kitts is liable to tax at the rate of 8 per cent on directors fees. Directors fees are monies paid to a director for carrying out his corporate responsibility as a director. This tax does not apply to the salary or other remuneration paid to a director for management or other services to the company which are taxable as indicated under section above headed "Payroll Taxes".

CAPITAL GAINS TAX ON INDIVIDUALS

There is no tax on any capital gain made by an individual on the sale of an asset. There are however high rates of stamp duty on the sale of real property. These rates range from 5 per cent of the price or market value on the sale of a condominium to 18.5 per cent on the sale of some real property on the Southeast Peninsula of St. Kitts.

PROPERTY TAX

Property tax is payable by all owners of property with a market value in excess of EC$80,000. The tax is assessed on the market value of the property and payable annually. Rates are 0.3 per cent for commercial property and 0.2 per cent for residential property.

INHERITANCE AND GIFT TAX

There are no death duties or inheritance taxes.

SOCIAL SECURITY SYSTEM

The Social Security system provides pension benefits for eligible contributors as well as sickness and maternity leave benefits and limited funeral expenses.

Rates of contribution are five per cent by the employer and five percent by the employee up to a threshold of EC$6,500 of gross monthly earnings.

Employee contributions on gross earnings are deducted by the employer and paid monthly with employer's contribution and other payroll taxes described above.

Contributions cease to apply when an employee reaches the age of 62.

OTHER PAYROLL TAXES

Employers (only) pay one per cent of their payroll into a Severance Payments Fund from which benefits are paid to employees laid off on the closure of a business or other circumstances stipulated by law (e.g. automation, reorganization, etc.).

An employer (only) pays a tax at the rate of one per cent of his payroll into an Injuries Benefit Fund from which benefits are paid by the Government to employees injured on the job.

There is no compulsory workmens' compensation insurance nor are employers required to pay severance payments to laid off workers provided the employer gives the required notice of the lay off or pay in lieu thereof.

IMMIGRATION AND VISAS

VISAS

Citizens of countries whose nationals do not require visas to enter the Federation of St. Kitts & Nevis must have a valid passport and a return ticket to the country of departure in order to enter the Federation. Permission is granted to remain in the country for 30 days only, however this 30 day period can be extended upon application to the Immigration Department and the payment of a fee which is currently EC$55.

Citizens of countries whose nationals do require a visa to enter the Federation of St. Kitts & Nevis can apply online on the government's official web-site (www.gov.kn), the web-site of the Ministry of Foreign Affairs (www.mofa.gov.kn), or the web-site of Communication's Unit of the office of the Prime Minister (www.cuopm.org).

The following documents are required in support of an application for a visitor's visa:

A valid passport and two passport sized photographs
Return ticket to country of departure
EC$100.00 non-refundable application fee
Bank Statement for past three months

Job letter

All non-English documents must be translated and notarized and all signatures must be notarized

Vaccinations or medical certificates are not required for visitors.

Visitor's Visas are granted for a period of 1-3 months at the discretion of the Minister in charge of Immigration.

IMMIGRATION REQUIREMENTS

As previously stated, foreigners are required to make an application to government for a grant of annual or permanent residence or a work permit in the country.

The following documents or certified photocopies shall be submitted along with any such application –

(a) Birth Certificate
(b) Passport
(c) A Police Certificate or Affidavit (from country where applicant lived for the last six months)
(d) Marriage Certificate (if applicable)
(e) Divorce Decree (if applicable)
(f) Military Record (if applicable)
(g) Affidavit of Support
(h) Evidence of own assets
(i) One (1) Passport size photograph
(j) Birth Certificate of Spouse
(k) Birth Certificate of each unmarried child under 18 years
(l) Evidence of offer of employment (if applicable)
(m) Proof of having passed the H.I.V. Test
(n) VDRL
(o) X-Ray of Chest
(p) Mantoux for Tuberculosis

The processing of residency or work permit applications can take from 6 weeks to 3 months. The government fee for a grant of annual residence is currently EC$1,500.00 and EC$600.00 for temporary residence. An application fee of EC$200.00 is payable upon application for a grant of permanent residence and a further fee of EC$4,800.00 is payable on approval of the application by government. An annual fee of EC$2,500.00 is payable for work permits. These fees are subject to change by government.

A citizen of a Commonwealth country who has ordinarily resided in the country for a period of 14 years immediately preceding the date of his or her application is entitled to apply to be registered as a citizens of St. Kitts & Nevis.

IMMIGRATION CONTROLS

There are no immigration quotas in the country and applications for a grant of annual or permanent residence or for a work permit are dealt with on an individual basis

Each person leaving the country is required to pay departure tax in the sum of EC$50.00 for citizens of the Federation and EC$58.00 for visitors.

CITIZENSHIP BY INVESTMENT

Under the St. Kitts & Nevis Constitution and legislation, persons may qualify to apply for St. Kitts and Nevis citizenship if they make a substantial investment in St. Kitts & Nevis. Cabinet determines what form such qualifying investment must take and the minimum amount of same.

There are presently two main routes to obtain economic citizenship of St. Kitts & Nevis. One route is to purchase a qualifying property (generally US$350,000.00 minimum value) in a development that is specifically approved by Government in relation to the St. Kitts & Nevis economic citizenship programme and ownership of which qualifying property must be retained for a minimum period of at least 5 years. Alternatively, an applicant can make a contribution of at least US$200,000.00 to the Government's Sugar Industry Diversification Foundation, which sum is inclusive of all Government processing fees [ie. disbursements (c) and (d) mentioned two paragraphs below]. The required contributions range from US$200,000.00 (in the case of a single applicant) to US$400,000 (in the case of an applicant with 6 or more dependants).

In relation to the contribution to the Sugar Investment Diversification Fund, the only other disbursement typically incurred in making the application is the cost of the application form (US$250 each), legal fees, courier costs and stamps if a passport is required.

In addition to the purchase price of the property (if the aforementioned real estate route is chosen), there are additional expenses such as: (1) legal fees which are based upon the purchase price of the particular real estate; and (2) Assurance Fund payable to Government of 0.2% of the purchase price of the real estate; and (3) sometimes Purchaser's Stamp Duty, depending upon the location of the property.

In relation to the real estate option, the other outgoings will typically include:

Real Estate Transaction

(a)	the purchase price of the property
(b)	legal fees
(c)	Assurance Fund payable to Government of 0.2% of the purchase price ;
(d)	in some cases (depending on the location of the property), Purchaser's Stamp Duty (6% of the purchase price); and
(e)	survey fees.

Citizenship Application

(a) the costs of obtaining original application forms @ US$250.00 each;
(b) Government's background/due diligence investigation charge of US$3,500.00 in respect of each adult applicant;
(c) Government's registration fees of US$35,000.00 for the main applicant and US$15,000.00 each for spouse and each dependent child, upon approval of the application;
(e) passport stamps costs (unlikely to exceed US$100.00 re each passport); and
(f) courier costs.

MATTERS OF ESPECIAL INTEREST TO EXPATRIATE EMPLOYEES

A temporary St. Kitts & Nevis driver's licence must be obtained before driving in St. Kitts and Nevis but such temporary licences are usually issued in reliance upon a valid foreign driver's licence, without the applicant having to undergo any examination.

A temporary St. Kitts & Nevis driver's licence valid for 3 months costs EC$62.50 (US$23.15).

Educational facilities, both private and public, are available in St. Kitts & Nevis from Pre-School to Tertiary levels. Primary and secondary education is available to citizens of St. Kitts & Nevis free of cost in the public education system. School fees at private educational institutions vary.

St. Kitts & Nevis hosts a University of Veterinary Medicine, a University of Nursing and more than one Medical University. The students at these institutions are predominantly nationals of countries other than St. Kitts & Nevis, including the U.S.A., India and African nations. Except for nursing, the other Universities here require some attendance at Universities in the USA before a degree is issued.

Given the small size of St. Kitts & Nevis, the housing available to investors and visitors is impressive and varied and includes international hotel chains (Marriott and Four Seasons), intimate inns, villas, condominium units and middle-income houses and apartments.

The importation of personal belongings such as motor vehicles and furniture attracts import duties and other similar Governmental charges ranging from 0% to 84%, depending upon the particular items. Personal clothing and other personal effects are not normally charged import duties.

Simple documentation must be submitted to the Customs authorities in order to clear personal effects through Customs. Customs brokers are normally used to process the documentation for the importation of commercial goods.

SELECTED BUSINESS LAWS

IMPORTANT OFFSHORE LAWS AND REGULATIONS

Banking Act 1991
Citizenship Act 1984
Companies Act, 1996 (St Kitts and Nevis)
Confidential Relationships Act of St Christopher & Nevis, 1985
Financial Services (Regulations) Order, 1997 (St Kitts and Nevis)
Fiscal Incentives Act 1974
Foundation Act 2003
Hotel Aids Ordinance
Income Tax Ordinance (St Kitts and Nevis)
Limited Partnerships Act 1996 (St Kitts and Nevis)
Merchant Shipping Act 2002
Nevis Business Corporation Ordinance, 1984
Nevis International Exempt Trust Ordinance, 1994
Nevis International Insurance Ordinance, 2004
Nevis Limited Liability Company Ordinance, 1995
Nevis Multiform Foundations Ordinance, 2004
Nevis Offshore Banking Ordinance, 1996
Trusts Act 1996 (St Kitts and Nevis)

Under the Financial Services Order, 1997, which imposed a licensing and supervisory regime for all offshore financial services businesses, the National Assembly established a Financial Services Department headed by a Director General, whose responsibilities include monitoring the financial sector and examining the affairs or business of any authorized person to make sure of compliance with the law and determining whether the person being investigated is in a sound financial position and carrying on business in a satisfactory manner. In the Department's hierarchy are: (1) the Office of Superintendents, with Superintendents for Deposit-Taking and Investments, Insurance and Assurance, and Trust and Corporate Business; and (2) the Office of Registrars, composed of Registrars for Companies, Limited Partnerships and Trusts.

The law also sets minimum financial resources required by applicants to engage in deposit-taking, insurance and assurance, trust business, investment business, corporate, and holding companies. The minimums do not apply if a lawyer or accountant applies for permission to carry on corporate business.

"Finance business" is defined in the Order as being:

deposit-taking business; (e.g. bankers, financiers, etc.)
investment business; (e.g. stockbrokers, operators of collective investment schemes, etc.)
insurance business; (e.g. insurers)
assurance business; (e.g. insurance agents, insurance brokers, insurance managers, etc.)
trust business; (e.g. professional trustees, protectors, etc.)
corporate business, (e.g. nominee shareholders, professional directors, etc).

Domestic businesses are however specifically excluded from the Order and must be licensed under the Banking Act or the Insurance Act.
The Nevis Mutual Funds Ordinance was enacted on November 16th, 2004.

The Multiform Ordinance allows among other features for the transformation of a trust into a foundation and for consolidation of entities. Two other pieces of legislation, namely the Service Provider, Corporate Management and Trustee (Licensing) Ordinance and the Nevis Segregated Accounts Companies Ordinance, are currently being drafted.

BANKING LAW

Domestic banking is regulated by the Banking Act 1991 and non-domestic banking falls under the Financial Services (Regulations) Order 1997. Nevis has its own Offshore Banking Ordinance 1996.
Two types of banking licenses are granted under the Federation's 1997 Financial Services (Regulations) Order. 'Unrestricted' licenses require minimum financial resources of 1,350,000 East Caribbean dollars ($500,000), while for 'restricted' licenses the level is only 135,000 East Caribbean dollars ($50,000).
A licensee must within 3 months of the end of each of his financial years:

prepare annual accounts in accordance with generally accepted accounting principles, audited by an independent auditor;
deliver to the Director General the annual accounts together with written confirmation from an independent auditor that the annual accounts have been prepared as required under the preceding paragraph and whether or not the auditor's certificate for such accounts is unqualified and if qualified, the nature of the qualification;
deliver to the Director General a certificate of compliance issued by an independent auditor that the information set out in the application for an authorisation, as modified by any subsequent notification of change, remains correct and gives an accurate summary of the business of the authorised person.

Fees for banking licences are as follows:

on filing of first application (not refundable) - for all applications, USD 1,000;
on granting or renewal of authorisation for an unrestricted business, USD 8,000, and for a restricted business, USD 4,000.

The Confidential Relationship Act, 1985 for St. Kitts and Nevis offers complete confidentiality should foreign authorities seek private banking and financial records. Prison terms are mandatory for violation of the statute.
The Nevis Offshore Banking Ordinance 1996 defines offshore banking as follows:

Receiving of foreign funds through the acceptance of foreign money, deposits payable upon receipt demand or after a fixed period or after notice;
The sale or placement of foreign bonds certifcates, notes or other debt obligations or other securities, or
Any other similar activities involving foreign money or foreign securities, and
Either in whole or in part using foreign funds so acquired for loans, advances and investments whether in Nevis or elsewhere.

Licences under the Banking Ordinance are issued to eligible companies or qualified foreign banks. An eligible company must be a wholly owned subsidiary of a local bank regulated by the Eastern Caribbean Central Bank that is licensed under the Banking Act to do business in Nevis. A qualified foreign bank is a foreign bank that is licensed under the Banking Act, or is foreign bank with minimum capitalization and assets, as prescribed by the Minister, that is not licensed under the Banking Act but is licensed to do domestic banking in its jurisdiction of incorporation.

An eligible company must be incorporated under the Companies Act as a company limited by shares, and must have objects or business activity restricted to offshore banking from within Nevis. It must have at least one director who is a citizen of St. Kitts and Nevis with a residence in Nevis. The minimum Authorised Capital must be at least ECD2 Million, of which not less than ECD1 Million has been Subscribed and Paid Up in cash, such cash being deposited in an account maintained by the Permanent Secretary at the Eastern Caribbean Central Bank.
Not later than four months after the close of its financial year, a licensee must forward to the Permanent Secretary copies of its balance sheet and profit and loss account and the full and correct names of the directors of the licensee. The balance sheet and the profit and loss account must bear on its face the certificate of an auditor.

The Minister may by order exempt a licensee in respect of its business from all or so much of any duty payable under the Customs Act in respect of any goods imported by the licensee in respect of its business as the Minister deems expedient, if the licensee in respect of its business satisfies the Minister that the goods concerned are not being made or manufactured in Nevis, are essential as equipment or fixtures for doing business from within Nevis and are not merely goods that will be used up or expended in the ordinary course of business.

Where the Minister is satisfied that a licensee must use the services of specially qualified persons in order to do its business effectively from within Nevis and that (a) it is unable to acquire those services in Nevis, and (b) it is unable to retain or hire those services from outside Nevis without special tax benefits being made available the Minister may authorise an offshore benefit provision for the employment of those specially qualified persons.

An offshore benefit provision is one whereby a prescribed percentage of an employee's or contractor's salary or fees from a licensee (a) is exempt from any duty or tax in Nevis; (b) may be paid in a foreign currency; (c) may be paid in some other prescribed manner in another currency or otherwise; notwithstanding the provision of any other law to the contrary.

INSURANCE LAW

Non-domestic insurance and assurance businesses must be licensed under the Insurance Act. The Federation's 1997 Financial Services (Regulations) Order set the following minimum net assets for applicants wishing to engage in the insurance business: long-term and general insurance business, 810,000 East Caribbean dollars ($300,000), reduced to 540,000 East Caribbean dollars ($20,000) for long-term but not general insurance, and further lowered to 270,000 East Caribbean dollars ($100,000) for general but not long-term insurance.
In July, 2004, the Nevis Ministry of Finance and Development in Nevis announced the passage of the Nevis International Insurance Ordinance. The Ordinance is divided into six sections, and provides for the licensing and regulation of general insurance, captive insurance and reinsurance companies. It is compulsory for insurance companies to have a physical presence in Nevis, whether via a resident manager or a fully trained registered agent, with adequate knowledge and experience of the insurance industry.

TRUST LAW

The St Kitts and Nevis Trusts Act 1996 was a replacement for the 1961 Trustee Ordinance modeled after the 1925 English Trusts Act, and contains modern asset protection provisions. Trusts and their beneficiaries receive the same tax waivers as companies, with the similar proviso that all transactions must be confined to non-residents for the trust to enjoy exempt status. Trusts may have a protector but, with the exception of unit, spendthrift and charitable trusts, the protector needs acceptable professional qualifications. Both the settlor and trustees can be beneficiaries of a trust.

St Kitts and Nevis trusts are exempt from income, withholding, capital gains and stamp taxes as long as all transactions are confined to non-residents, and subject to a statutory declaration of exempt status accompanied by an annual registration fee of US$200.

Section XV of the Act makes it clear that beneficiaries do not lose their exemption if trustees are active in the Federation owning or leasing property for an office or residences for beneficiaries, holding meetings, conducting banking, signing employment contracts, and arranging for goods and services.

Every trust must maintain an office in the Federation for service of papers. At least two trustees must be appointed, unless one trustee is a corporation or only one trustee was originally appointed under previous legislation. One trustee must either be a Federation resident or carry on business from an office within the Federation. Trustees' duties include registering the trust with the Registrar of Trusts (who may also be the Registrar of Companies).

Trusts do not have to be audited, unless trust terms call for this. The annual statement filed by trustees need not include any financial information. Strict confidentiality rules for trustees prevail. In response to a written request, trustees may in a "reasonable time" provide information about the trust's financial situation and management to the Eastern Caribbean Supreme Court, Government inspectors, and, subject to the terms of the trust, the settlor, protector, a beneficiary, and a charitable beneficiary.

Every non-charitable trust is restricted to a 100-year life span. No restriction is imposed on charitable trusts. Trust terms should specify how long the trust might accumulate income.
Asset protection provisions, covered in Part V of the Act dealing with a settlor's rights and responsibilities and applicable to all trust, shield the settlor against forced heirship, compulsory division of matrimonial property, and creditors' suits. A creditor who wants to bring a court action against trust property must first purchase a 25,000 East Caribbean dollars ($9,250) bond from a Federation financial institution and deposit it with the Minister of Finance to cover all costs should the action prove unsuccessful.

The proper law of the trust is the law of the jurisdiction expressed by the trust's terms as the proper law; or, failing that, implied from the trust's terms; or failing either, the jurisdiction with which the trust at the time it was created had the closest connection.
The Federation's 1997 Financial Services (Regulations) Order set the following fees for applicants wishing to engage in the trust business:

on filing of first application (not refundable) - for all applications, USD 200;
on granting or renewal of authorisation for an unrestricted business, USD 2,000;
and for a restricted business, USD 1,000.

Nevis offshore trusts are formed under the Nevis International Exempt Trust Ordinance of 1994, as amended to September 2000. The Trust Ordinance includes special provisions to enhance the use of Nevis as a preferred jurisdiction for the establishment of Asset Protection Trusts.
Highlights of the Trust Ordinance include:

Exemption from all forms of Nevis taxation and exchange controls provided that transactions take place only with non-residents;
The trustee may be either a trust company licensed to do business in Nevis or a company incorporated under the Corporation Ordinance;
The proper law may be the law of Nevis or the law of another jurisdiction;
The rule against perpetuities does not apply;
Forced heirship rules are specifically excluded;
Spendthrift and charitable trusts are permitted;

There is a US$25,000 bond requirement prior to the commencement of an action or proceeding against trust property;
There is no registration requirement other than for the Trust's name, name of Trustee and the registered office address;
Settlor and Beneficiary must be non-residents and may be the same person;
One trustee must be a Nevis offshore company or a trust licensed company;
Protectors are allowed for and may be the same person as the Settlor and Beneficiary of the Trust;
An IET is valid and enforceable notwithstanding that it may be invalid according to the law of the Settlor's domicile or residence or place of current incorporation;
The Trust is not considered fraudulent if settled up to 2 years after the date of the creditor's cause of action;
The creditor must prove the intent of the debtor to defraud with "clear and convincing" evidence;
The Statute of Queen Elizabeth is excluded.

The Nevis registrar maintains a register of international trusts and a register of qualified foreign trusts. Where a trust provides for the law of Nevis to be the governing law of all or any aspects of that trust an application for entry on the register as an international trust shall be made to the registrar within 45 days of the date on which the trust is created, settled or established. Where a trust provides for the law of a jurisdiction other than the Island of Nevis to be the governing law of all aspects of that trust an application for entry on the register as a qualified foreign trust shall be made to the registrar within 45 days of the date on which the trust is created, settled or established.

An application for registration should be accompanied by notice of the name and registered office of the trust, a certificate from a trustee company, a barrister or solicitor certifying that the trust upon registration will be an international trust or a qualified foreign trust, the date on which the trust was created, settled or established, and in the case of a qualified foreign trust, the law under which the trust was settled. Registration has to be renewed annually.

The register is not open for inspection except that a trustee of a trust may in writing authorise a person to inspect the entry of that trust on the register.

A trust registered under the Nevis Ordinance is exempt from all income tax, all estate, inheritance, succession and gift tax payable with respect to the trust property by reason of any death, stamp duty with respect to all instruments relating to the trust property or to transactions carried out by the trustee on behalf of the trust, and all exchange controls.

ANTI-MONEY LAUNDERING LEGISLATION

After St Kitts was listed by the FATF as a tax haven which was unco-operative in fighting money laundering, the government passed the Money Laundering (Prevention) Act 2000, the Financial Services Intelligence Unit Act 2000, the Proceeds of Crime Act 2000 and the Financial Services Commission Act 2000. The latter Act intends to establish the Financial Services Commission as the main regulatory body for the offshore sector. In June 2002, St Kitts and Nevis was removed from the FATF blacklist.

Subsequent legislation has included Anti-Money Laundering Regulations 2002, and the Financial Services (Exchange of Information) Regulations 2002.

COMPANIES LAWS

The Companies (Standard Tables) Order (No. 17 of 1997).
The Companies (Fees) Order (No. 18 of 1997).
The Companies (Application of Share Premium) Order (No. 19 of 1997).
The Companies (Overseas Branch Register) Order (No. 20 of 1997).
The Companies (Purchase of Own Shares) Order, (No. 21 of 1997).
The Companies (Winding Up Provisions) Order, (No. 22 of 1997).
Laws Relevant to Limited Partnerships
The Limited Partnerships Act (No. 24 of 1996).
The Limited Partnerships (Fees) Order (No. 23 of 1997).
Laws Relevant to Trusts
The Trusts Act (No. 23 of 1996).
The Trusts (Fees) Order (No. 24 of 1997).
Laws Relevant to Financial Services
The Financial Services (Regulations) Order (No. 25 of 1997) as amended.
The Financial Services (Fees) Order (No. 26 of 1997).
The Financial Services (Business Names) Order (No. 27 of 1997) as amended.
The Financial Services (Prospectuses) Order (No. 28 of 1997).
The Financial Services (Professional Bodies) Order (No. 29 of 1997).

STATUTORY RULES AND ORDERS

1997, No. 20

The Companies (Overseas Branch Register) Order, 1997.

AN ORDER made by the Minister under sections 49 and 219 of the Companies Act, 1996 - 22.

Citation and commencement

This Order may be cited as the Companies (Overseas Branch Register) Order, 1997.

This Order shall come into force on 3rd of April, 1997.

Application of this Order

This Order applies only to public companies.

Overseas branch register

A company which transacts business in any country, territory or place outside the Federation may cause to be kept in that place a branch register of members resident in that country, territory or place.

A branch register kept pursuant to sub-section (1) shall be known as an "overseas branch register".

An overseas branch register shall be deemed to be part of the company's register of members ("the principal register") and shall be kept in the same manner in which the principal register is by the Act required to be kept.

Notice to be given to the Registrar

A company keeping an overseas branch register shall give to the Registrar notice in such form as he may require of the situation of the office where any overseas branch register is kept and of any change in its situation, and, if it is discontinued, of its discontinuance.

Any such notice shall be given within 14 days of the opening of the office or of the change or discontinuance, as the case may be.

Duplicate of overseas branch register

The company shall -

transmit to its registered office a copy of every entry in its overseas branch register as soon as may be after it is made; and

cause to be kept at the place where the company's principal register is kept a duplicate of its overseas branch register duly entered up from time to time.

Every duplicate of the overseas branch register shall be deemed for all purposes of the Act to be part of the principal register.

Miscellaneous

Subject to the provisions of sub-section 5 with respect to the duplicate register, the shares registered in an overseas branch register shall be distinguished from those registered in the principal register and no transaction with respect to any shares registered in an overseas branch register shall during the continuance of that register be registered in any other register.

A company may discontinue to keep an overseas branch register and thereupon all entries in that register shall be transferred to some other overseas branch register kept in the same country, territory or place, or to the principal register.

Subject to the provisions of this Order, any company may by its articles make such provisions as it thinks fit respecting the keeping of overseas branch registers.

STATUTORY RULES AND ORDERS 1997, No. 21

THE COMPANIES (PURCHASE OF OWN SHARES) ORDER, 1997.

AN ORDER made by the Minister under sections 59 and 219 of the Companies Act, 1996 - 22.

1. Citation and commencement

(1) This Order may be cited as the Companies (Purchase of Own Shares) Order, 1997.

(2) This Order shall come into force on 3rd of April, 1997.

2. Purchase of own shares

For the purposes of sub-paragraph (b) of sub-section (4) of Section 57 of the Act, a resolution authorizing a company to purchase its own shares on a stock exchange may determine either or both the maximum and minimum prices for purchase by -

(a) specifying a particular sum; or

(b) providing a basis or formula for calculating the amount of the price in question without reference to any person's discretion or opinion.

Made by the Minister this 3rd of April, 1997.

Denzil L. Douglas

Minister of Finance

SAINT CHRISTOPHER AND NEVIS

STATUTORY RULES AND ORDERS

1997, No. 22

THE COMPANIES (WINDING UP PROVISIONS) ORDER, 1997.

AN ORDER made by the Minister under sections 188 and 219 of the Companies Act, 1996 - 22.

Citation and commencement

This Order may be cited as the Companies (Winding Up Provisions) Order, 1997.

This Order shall come into force on 3rd of April, 1997.

Qualifications of liquidator

A person is not qualified for appointment as a liquidator of a public company or of a company which is being wound up in accordance with the provisions of Part XXIII of the Act unless he is an accountant.

None of the following persons is so qualified -

a secretary or an officer or servant of the company or a partner or employee of such a person;

a person against whom an order under Section 78 of the Act is in force.

A person is also not so qualified if he is, under sub-section (2), disqualified for appointment as a liquidator of any other body corporate which is that company's subsidiary or holding company or a subsidiary or that company's holding company or would be so disqualified if that body corporate were a company.

Procedure at creditors' meeting

This section applies to creditors' meetings held pursuant to the provisions of Part XXIII of the Act.

Subject to the provisions of this section, every creditor who has been given notice of a creditors' meeting shall be entitled to vote at the meeting or any adjournment of it.

Votes shall be calculated according to the amount of the creditor's debt at the date of the commencement of the winding up.

A creditor shall not vote in respect of a debt for an unliquidated amount, or any debt whose value is not ascertained, except where the chairman of the meeting agrees to put upon the debt an estimated minimum value for the purpose of entitlement to vote.

For any resolution to pass at the creditors' meeting there must be a majority in excess of one-half in value of the creditors present in person or by proxy and voting on the resolution.

A creditors' meeting shall not be competent to act unless there are present in person or by proxy at least three creditors, or all of the creditors if their number does not exceed three, being in either case entitled to vote.

Made by the Minister this 3rd of April, 1997.

Denzil L. Douglas

Minister of Finance

SAINT CHRISTOPHER AND NEVIS

STATUTORY RULES AND ORDERS

1997, No. 27

THE FINANCIAL SERVICES (BUSINESS NAMES) ORDER, 1997.

AN ORDER made by the Minister under sections 13, 219 and 221 of the Companies Act, 1996 - 22; sections 9, 73 and 75 of the Limited Partnerships Act, 1996 - 24; and sections 105 and 107 of the Trusts Act 1996 - 23.

Citation and commencement

This Order may be cited as the Financial Services (Business Names) Order, 1997.

This Order shall come into force on 3rd of April, 1997.

Interpretation

In this Order unless the context otherwise requires -

"the Acts" means the Acts under which this Order is made;

"existing institution" means an institution incorporated or established before the date on which this Order comes into force;

"institution" means any -

company;

partnership; or

trust,

incorporated or established under the law of the Federation or, if incorporated or established under the law of any other country or territory, carrying on business in the Federation or having an address in the Federation which is used regularly for the purpose of its business;

"this Order" means this Order as amended, or as extended or applied, by or under any other Order made under the Acts;

"principal Order" means the Financial Services (Regulations) Order, 1997 - 25, as amended, or as extended or applied, by or under any other Order made under the Acts.

Subject to sub-section (1), any words defined in the Acts and in the principal Order shall, if not inconsistent with the subject or context, bear the same meaning in this Order.

A references in this Order to an enactment is a reference to that enactment as amended, and includes a reference to that enactment as extended or applied by or under any other enactment, including any other provision of that enactment.

Restriction on use of certain words in business names

The words specified in the Schedule hereto or any word, however spelled and whether in the singular or plural form or in the masculine, feminine or neutral gender, or any abbreviation thereof, which may reasonably be understood to convey a similar meaning whether in English or any other language are hereby specified as words for the use of which as, or as part of, an institution's name the permission of the Minister shall be obtained.

Any word in a language other than English ("foreign word") is a word for the use of which as, or as part of, an institution's name the permission of the Minister shall be obtained.

Words in English or in any other language which are used as, or form part of, an institution's name shall be in Roman characters when reproduced in writing or in any substitute for writing.

Restrictions on use of initials in business names

Any initial is an initial for the use of which as, or as part of, an institution's name the permission of the Minister shall be obtained.

Initials which are used as, or form part of, an institution's name shall be in Roman characters or numerals or in Arabic numerals (as may be desired) when reproduced in writing or in any substitute for writing.

References to "initial" in this Order are references to any character or numeral, whether or not preceded or followed by a space or punctuation mark, which can neither by itself nor in combination with any adjacent characters or numerals be reasonably understood to form a word which conveys any meaning in English.

Application for permission

Any institution desirous of obtaining the permission of the Minister under this Order may make application in that behalf by delivering to the Director General a statement signed by or on behalf of a director of the institution setting out -

any name currently used by it;

the name for which the permission of the Minister is being sought together with -

a certified translation of any foreign word; and

a statement explaining the meaning of any initial,

used as, or forming part of, its name;

the intended or, in the case of an existing institution, the current address of its registered office or office for service (as the case may be);

a summary description of the nature of each business intended to be carried out by it or, in the case of an existing institution, currently being carried out by it; and

where a statement is delivered by a person as agent for any director of the institution, the statement shall specify that fact and the person's name and address.

Grant of permission

Subject to section 7, the Minister shall grant permission under this Order and whenever the Minister grants such permission he shall by notice in writing inform the applicant accordingly.

Refusal to grant permission

The Minister may refuse to grant permission under this Order -

if the applicant has not provided information required under section 5;

if it appears to him, as a result of information provided in pursuance of the requirements of section 5 or information otherwise obtained, that the name of the institution for which the application is made would be misleading or otherwise undesirable;

if in connexion with any application made under this Order, the applicant has provided information which is untrue or misleading in any material particular; or

if the name of an institution -

contains one or more initials that have no meaning; or

consists of solely one or more initials. *(paragraph (d) of this sub-section as amended by S.R.O. No. 46 of 1997)*

Whenever the Minister refuses to grant permission under this Order he shall by notice in writing inform the applicant accordingly.

Procedure and rights of appeal

Where the Minister, acting under section 7, refuses to grant permission under this Order to an institution, the applicant may require the Minister to furnish him with a statement in writing of the Minister's reasons for that decision.

Any person aggrieved by such refusal may appeal to the Court, either in term or in vacation, on the ground that the decision of the Minister was unreasonable having regard to all the circumstances of the case.

Punishment of offences

An institution which fails to comply with any provision of this Order which applies to it is guilty of an offence and liable to a fine not exceeding 2,500 dollars and in the case of a continuing offence to a further fine not exceeding 250 dollars for each day on which the offence so continues.

Transitional provision

Any institution in existence prior to the coming into operation of this Order which has a name that does not conform to the provisions of section 3 or 4 of this Order shall change its name or establish that it has obtained the Minister's permission to retain that name under this Order within a period of eighteen months from the day on which this Order comes into operation. *(this section as amended by S.R.O. No. 46 of 1997)*

Made by the Minister this 3rd of April, 1997.

Denzil L. Douglas

Minister of Finance

SCHEDULE

Specification of Restricted Words

A	Agency	D	Deposit		Insurance		Registrar
	Association		Divine		Insurer		Reinsurance
	Assurance		Divinity		Investigation		Reinsurer
	Assurer		Duchess	K	King		Resident
	Authority		Duke		Kittitian (5)		Royal
B	Bank	E	Exchange	L	Licensed		Royale
	Banker	F	Federation		Licensee		Royalty
	Banking		Firm (2) (3)		Licentiate	S	Saint Christopher (5)
	Beneficial		Finance		Limited (1) (2)		Saint Kitts (5)
	Benevolent		Financial	M	Majesty		Security
	Board		Foundation		Municipal		Secured
	Broker		Fund		Mutual		Scheme
	Brokerage	G	Gambling	N	National		School
C	Casino		Gaming		Nevis (5)		Society
	Casualty		Giro		Nevisian (5)		Sovereign
	Chamber		God		Nursing		State
	Charitable		Government	O	Offshore		Stockbroker
	Charity		Governor		Onshore		Subsidiary
	Charter		Group	P	Parliament		Surety
	Chartered		Guarantee		Partnership (2) (3)	T	Trust (4)
	Clinic		Guaranteed		Patent		Trustee
	Club	H	Health		Patentee	U	Underwriter
	Collective		Highness		Police		Union
	College		Holding		Polytechnic		Unit

Commission		Holy		Prince	University
Committee		Holiness		Princess	Unlimited
Company (1) (2) (3)		Hospital		Protection	
Consolidated	I	Imperial	Q	Queen	
Co-operative		Incorporated (1)	R	Reassurance	
Corporate (1)		Indemnity		Reassurer	
Corporation (1)		Institute		Register	
Council		Institution		Registered	

Notes:

Restricted only if the institution (1) is not a company; (2) is not a limited partnership; (3) is not a partnership; (4) is not a trust; or (5) has no majority or principal shareholder controller or no indirect controller who is resident in the Federation.

SAINT CHRISTOPHER AND NEVIS

STATUTORY RULES AND ORDERS 1997, No. 17

THE COMPANIES (STANDARD TABLES) ORDER, 1997.

AN ORDER made by the Minister under sections 7 and 219 of the Companies Act, 1996 - 22.

Citation and commencement

This Order may be cited as the Companies (Standard Tables) Order, 1997.

This Order shall come into force on 3rd of April, 1997.

Standard Tables

The regulations in the Standard Tables in the Schedule to this Order shall be the model articles for the purposes of section 7 of the Companies Act, 1996.

Made by the Minister this 3rd of April, 1997.

Denzil L. Douglas

Minister of Finance

SCHEDULE

Standard Table A

Regulations for the Management of a Company Limited by Shares

Interpretation

In these regulations -

"articles" means the articles of association of the company;

"clear days" in relation to the period of a notice means that period excluding the day when the notice is given or deemed to be given and the day for which it is given or on which it is to take effect;

"executed" includes any mode of execution;

"holder" in relation to shares means the member whose name is entered in the register of members as the holder of the shares;

"office" means the registered office of the company;

"ordinary resolution" means a resolution of the company in general meeting adopted by a simple majority of the votes cast at that meeting;

"seal" means the common seal of the company;

"secretary" means the secretary of the company or any other person appointed to perform the duties of the secretary of the company, including a joint, assistant or deputy secretary;

"the Act" means the Companies Act 1996 including any statutory modification or re-enactment thereof for the time being in force.

Unless the context otherwise requires, words or expressions contained in these regulations bear the same meaning as in the Act but excluding any statutory modification thereof not in force when these regulations become binding on the company.

SHARE CAPITAL

Subject to the provisions of the Act -

without prejudice to any rights attached to any issued shares, any share may be issued with such rights or restrictions as the company may by special resolution determine;

the company may -

issue, or

convert any existing non-redeemable shares, whether issued or not, into, shares which are to be redeemed, or are liable to be redeemed at the option of the company or the shareholder, on such terms and in such manner as may be determined by special resolution;

unissued shares shall be at the disposal of the directors who may allot, grant options over or otherwise dispose of them to such persons and on such terms as the directors think fit.

The company may exercise the powers of paying commissioners conferred by the Act. Subject to the provisions of the Act, any such commission may be satisfied by the payment of cash or by the allotment of fully or partly paid shares or partly in one way and partly in the other.

Except as required by law, no person shall be recognised by the company as holding any share upon any trust and (except as otherwise provided by the articles or by law) the company shall not be bound by or recognise any interest in any share except an absolute right to the entirety thereof in the holder.

SHARE CERTIFICATES

Every member, upon becoming the holder of any shares, shall be entitled without payment to one certificate for all the shares of each class held by him (and, upon transferring a part of his holding of shares of any class, to a certificate for the balance of such holding) or several certificates each for one or more of his shares upon payment for every certificate after the first of such reasonable sum as the directors may determine. Every certificate shall be sealed with the seal and shall specify the number, class and distinguishing numbers (if any) of the shares to which it relates. The company shall not be bound to issue more than one certificate for shares held jointly by several persons and delivery of a certificate to one joint holder shall be a sufficient delivery to all of them.

If a share certificate is defaced, worn out, lost or destroyed, it may be renewed on such terms (if any) as to evidence and indemnity and payment of the expenses reasonably incurred by the company in investigating evidence as the directors may determine but otherwise free of charge, and (in the case of defacement or wearing out) on delivery up of the old certificate.

Where the company is authorised under the Act to issues bearer certificates such certificates may be issued by the company upon such terms and subject to such conditions as shall be determined by the directors. The provisions of the articles with respect to transfer and transmission of shares shall not apply in respect of the shares to which a bearer certificate relates.

Lien

The company shall have a first and paramount lien on every share (not being a fully paid share) for all moneys (whether presently payable or not) payable at a fixed time or called in respect of that share. The directors may at any time declare any share to be wholly or in part exempt from the provisions of this regulation. The company's lien on a share shall extend to any amount payable in respect of it.

The company may sell in such manner as the directors determine any shares on which the company has a lien if a sum in respect of which the lien exists is presently payable and is not paid within 14 clear days after notice has been given to the holder of the share or to the person entitled to it in consequence of the death or bankruptcy of the holder, demanding payment and stating that if the notice is not complied with the shares may be sold.

To give effect to a sale the directors may authorise some person to execute an instrument of transfer of the shares sold to, or in accordance with the directions of, the purchaser. The title of the transferee to the shares shall not be affected by an irregularity in or invalidity of the proceedings in reference to the sale.

The net proceeds of the sale, after payment of the costs, shall be applied in payment of so much of the sum for which the lien exists as is presently payable, and any residue shall (upon surrender to the company for cancellation of the certificate for the shares sold and subject to a like lien for any moneys not presently payable as existed upon the shares before the sale) be paid to the person entitled to the shares at the date of the sale.

CALLS ON SHARES AND FORFEITURE

Subject to the terms of allotment, the directors may make calls upon the members in respect of any moneys unpaid on their shares (whether in respect of stated value or premium) and each member shall (subject to receiving at least 14 clear days' notice specifying when and where payment is to be made) pay to the company as required by the notice the amount called on his shares. A call may be required to be paid by instalments. A call may, before receipt by the company of any sum due thereunder, be revoked in whole or part and payment of a call may be postponed in whole or part. A person upon whom a call is made shall remain liable for calls made upon him notwithstanding the subsequent transfer of the shares in respect whereof the call was made.

A call shall be deemed to have been made at the time when the resolution of the directors authorising the call was passed.

The joint holders of a share shall be jointly and severally liable to pay all calls in respect thereof.

If a call remains unpaid after it has become due and payable the person from whom it is due and payable shall pay interest on the amount unpaid from the day it became due and payable until it is paid at the rate fixed by the terms of allotment of the share or in the notice of the call or at such rate not exceeding ten per cent per annum as the directors may determine but the directors may waive payment of the interest wholly or in part.

An amount payable in respect of a share on allotment or at any fixed date, whether in respect of stated value or premium or as an instalment of a call, shall be deemed to be a call and if it is not paid the provisions of the articles shall apply as if that amount had become due and payable by virtue of a call. The company may accept from a member the whole or a part of the amount remaining unpaid on shares held by him, although no part of that amount has been called up.

Subject to the terms of allotment, the directors may make arrangements on the issue of shares for a difference between the holders in the amounts and times of payment of calls on their shares.

If a call remains unpaid after it has become due and payable the directors may give to the person from whom it is due not less than 14 clear days' notice requiring payment of the amount unpaid together with any interest which may have accrued. The notice shall name the place where payment is to be made and shall state that if the notice is not complied with the shares in respect of which the call was made will be liable to be forfeited.

If the notice is not complied with any share in respect of which it was given may, before the payment required by the notice has been made, be forfeited by a resolution of the directors and the forfeiture shall include all dividends or other moneys payable in respect of the forfeited shares and not paid before the forfeiture.

Subject to the provisions of the Act, a forfeited share may be sold, re-allotted or otherwise disposed of on such terms and in such manner as the directors determine either to the person who was before the forfeiture the holder or to any other person and at any time before sale, re-allotment or other disposition, the forfeiture may be cancelled on such terms as the directors think fit. Where for the purposes of its disposal a forfeited share is to be transferred to any person the directors may authorise some person to execute an instrument of transfer of the share to that person.

A person any of whose shares have been forfeited shall cease to be a member in respect of them and shall surrender to the company for cancellation the certificate for the shares forfeited but shall remain liable to the company for all moneys which at the date of forfeiture were presently payable by him to the company in respect of those shares with interest at the rate at which interest was payable on those moneys before the forfeiture, or at such rate not exceeding ten per cent per annum as the directors may determine, from the date of forfeiture until payment, but the directors may waive payment wholly or in part or enforce payment without any allowance for the value of the shares at the time of forfeiture or for any consideration received on their disposal.

A declaration under oath by a director or the secretary that a share has been forfeited on a specified date shall be conclusive evidence of the facts state in it as against all persons claiming to be entitled to the share and the declaration shall (subject to the execution of an instrument of transfer if necessary) constitute a good title to the share and the person to whom the share is disposed of shall not be bound to see to the application of the consideration, if any, nor shall his title to the share be affected by any irregularity in or invalidity of the proceedings in reference to the forfeiture or disposal of the share.

Transfer of shares

The instrument of transfer of a share may be in any usual form or in any other form which the directors may approve and shall be executed by or on behalf of the transferor and, unless the shares are fully paid, by or on behalf of the transferee.

The directors may refuse to register the transfer of a share which is not fully paid to a person of whom they do not approve and they may refuse to register the transfer of a share on which the company has a lien. They may also refuse to register a transfer unless the instrument of transfer -

is lodged at the office or at such other place as the directors may appoint and is accompanied by the certificate for the shares to which it relates and such other evidence as the directors may reasonably require to show the right of the transferor to make the transfer;

is in respect of only one class of shares; and

is in favour of not more than four transferees.

If the directors refuse to register a transfer of a share, they shall within 2 months after the date on which the instrument of transfer was lodged with the company send to the transferor and the transferee notice of the refusal.

The registration of transfers of shares or of transfers of any class of shares may be suspended at such times and for such periods (not exceeding 30 days in any year) as the directors may determine.

No fee shall be charged for the registration of any instrument of transfer or other document relating to or affecting the title to any share.

The company shall be entitled to retain any instrument of transfer which is registered, but any instrument of transfer which the directors refuse to register shall be returned to the person lodging it when notice of the refusal is given.

Transmission of shares

If a member dies, the survivor or survivors where he was a joint holder, and his personal representatives where he was a sole holder or the only survivor of joint holders, shall be the only persons recognised by the company as having any title to his interest; but nothing herein contained shall release the estate of a deceased member from any liability in respect of any share which had been jointly held by him.

A person becoming entitled to a share in consequence of the death or bankruptcy of a member may, upon such evidence being produced as the directors may properly require, elect either to become the holder of the share or to have some person nominated by him registered as the transferee. If he elects to become the holder he shall give notice to the company to that effect. If he elects to have another person registered he shall execute an instrument of transfer of the share to that person. All the articles relating to the transfer of shares shall apply to the notice or instrument of transfer as if it were an instrument of transfer executed by the member and the death or bankruptcy of the member had not occurred.

A person becoming entitled to a share in consequence of the death or bankruptcy of a member shall have the rights to which he would be entitled if he were the holder of the share, except that he shall not, before being registered as the holder of the share, be entitled in respect of it to attend or vote at any meeting of the company or at any separate meeting of the holders of any class of shares in the company.

Consolidation of shares

Whenever as a result of a consolidation of shares any members would become entitled to fractions of a share, the directors may, on behalf of those members, sell the shares representing the fractions for the best price reasonably obtainable to any person (including, subject to the provisions of the Act, the company) and distribute the net proceeds of sale in due proportion among those members, and the directors may authorise some person to execute an instrument of transfer of the shares to, or in accordance with the directions of, the purchaser. The transferee shall not be bound to see to the application of the purchase money nor shall his title to the shares be affected by any irregularity in or invalidity of the proceedings in reference to the sale.

General meetings

All general meetings other than annual general meetings shall be called extraordinary general meetings.

The directors may call general meetings and, on the requisition of members pursuant to the provisions of the Act, shall forthwith proceed to call a general meeting for a date not later than 2 months after the receipt of the requisition. If there are not sufficient directors to call a general meeting, any director or any member of the company may call such a meeting.

Notice of general meetings

An annual general meeting or a general meeting called for the passing of a special resolution or a resolution appointing a person as a director shall be called by at least 21 clear days' notice. All other meetings shall be called by at least 14 clear days' notice but a general meeting may be called by shorter notice if it is so agreed-

in the case of an annual general meeting, by all the members entitled to attend and vote thereat; and

in the case of any other meeting by a majority in number of the members having a right to attend and vote at the meeting being a majority together holding not less than 95 per cent in stated value of the shares giving that right.

The notice shall specify the day, time and place of the meeting and the general nature of the business to be transacted and, in the case of an annual general meeting, shall specify the meeting as such.

Subject to the provisions of the articles and to any restrictions imposed on any shares, the notice shall be given to all the members, to all persons entitled to a share in consequence of the death or bankruptcy of a member and to the directors and auditors, if any.

The accidental omission to give notice of a meeting to, or the non-receipt of notice of a meeting by, any person entitled to receive notice shall not invalidate the proceedings at the meeting.

Proceedings at General Meetings

In the case where a company has only one member, or where all the issued shares of any class of shares in any company are held by only one member, that member present in person or by proxy shall be deemed to constitute a meeting. In any other case, no business shall be transacted at any meeting unless a quorum is present and, subject as hereinafter otherwise provided, two persons entitled to vote upon the business to be transacted, each being a member or a proxy for a member or a duly authorised representative of a body corporate, shall be a quorum.

If a quorum is not present within half an hour from the time appointed for the meeting, or if during a meeting such quorum ceases to be present, the meeting shall stand adjourned to the same day in the next week at the same time and place or such day, time and place as the directors may determine. If at such adjourned meeting, a quorum is not present within half an hour from the time appointed for the meeting, or if during such adjourned meeting a quorum ceases to be present, then any member present in person or by proxy shall be a quorum.

The chairman, if any, of the board of directors or in his absence some other director nominated by the directors shall preside as chairman of the meeting, but if neither the chairman nor such other director (if any) is present within 15 minutes after the time appointed for holding the meeting and willing to act, the directors present shall elect one of their number to be chairman and, if there is only one director present and willing to act, he shall be chairman.

If no director is willing to act as chairman, or if no director is present within 15 minutes after the time appointed for holding the meeting, those present and entitled to be counted in a quorum shall choose one of their number to be chairman.

A director shall, notwithstanding that he is not a member, be entitled to attend and speak at any general meeting and at any separate meeting of the holders of any class of shares in the company.

The chairman may, with the consent of a meeting at which a quorum is present (and shall if so directed by the meeting), adjourn the meeting from time to time and from place to place, but no business shall be transacted at an adjourned meeting other than business which might properly have been transacted at the meeting had the adjournment not taken place. When a meeting is adjourned for 14 days or more, at least 7 clear days' notice shall be given specifying the day, time and place of the adjourned meeting and the general nature of the business to be transacted. Otherwise it shall not be necessary to give any such notice.

A resolution put to the vote of a meeting shall be decided on a show of hands unless before, or on the declaration of the result of, the show of hands a poll is duly demanded. Subject to the provisions of the Act, a poll may be demanded -

by the chairman; or

by at least two members having the right to vote on the resolution; or

by a member or members representing not less than one-tenth of the total voting rights of all the members having the right to vote on the resolution; or

by a member or members holding shares conferring a right to vote on the resolution being shares on which an aggregate sum has been paid up equal to not less than one-tenth of the total sum paid up on all the shares conferring that right,

and a demand by a person as proxy for a member shall be the same as a demand by the member.

Unless a poll is duly demanded a declaration by the chairman that a resolution has been carried or carried unanimously, or by a particular majority, or lost, or not carried by a particular majority and an entry to that effect in the minutes of the meeting shall be conclusive evidence of the fact without proof of the number or proportion of the votes recorded in favour of or against the resolution.

The demand for a poll may, before the poll is taken, be withdrawn but only with the consent of the chairman and a demand so withdrawn shall not be taken to have invalidated the result of a show of hands declared before the demand was made.

A poll shall be taken as the chairman directs and he may appoint scrutineers (who need not be members) and fix a day, time and place for declaring the result of the poll. The result of the poll shall be deemed to be the resolution of the meeting at which the poll was demanded.

In the case of an equality of votes, whether on a show of hands or on a poll, the chairman shall be entitled to a casting vote in addition to any other vote he may have.

A poll demanded on the election of a chairman or on a question of adjournment shall be taken forthwith. A poll demanded on any other question shall be taken either forthwith or at such day, time and place as the chairman directs not being more than 30 days after the poll is demanded. The demand for a poll shall not prevent the continuance of a meeting for the transaction of any business other than the question on which the poll was demanded. If a poll is demanded before the declaration of the result of a show of hands and the demand is duly withdrawn, the meeting shall continue as if the demand had not been made.

No notice need be given of a poll not taken forthwith if the day, time and place at which it is to be taken are announced at the meeting at which it is demanded. In any other case, at least 7 clear days' notice shall be given specifying the day, time and place at which the poll is to be taken.

Votes of members

Subject to any rights or restrictions attached to any shares, on a show of hands every member who (being an individual) is present in person or (being a body corporate) is present by a duly authorised representative, not being himself a member entitled to vote, shall have one vote and on a poll every member shall have one vote for every share of which he is the holder.

In the case of joint holders the vote of the senior who tenders a vote, whether in person or by proxy, shall be accepted to the exclusion of the votes of the other joint holders; and seniority shall be determined by the order in which the names of the holders stand in the register of members.

A member in respect of whom an order has been made by any court having jurisdiction (whether in the Federation or elsewhere) in matters concerning mental disorder may vote, whether on a show of hands or on a poll, by his curator or other person authorised in that behalf appointed by that court, and any such curator or other person may, on a poll, vote by proxy. Evidence to the satisfaction of the directors of the authority of the person claiming to exercise the right to vote shall be deposited at the office, or at such other place within the Federation as is specified in accordance with the articles for the deposit of instruments of proxy not less than 48 hours before the time appointed for holding the meeting or adjourned meeting at which the right to vote is to be exercised and in default the right to vote shall not be exercisable.

No member shall vote at any general meeting or at any separate meeting of the holders of any class of shares in the company, either in person or by proxy, in respect of any share held by him unless all moneys presently payable by him in respect of that share have been paid.

No objection shall be raised to the qualification of any voter except at the meeting or adjourned meeting at which the vote objected to is tendered, and every vote not disallowed at the meeting shall be valid. Any objection made in due time shall be referred to the chairman whose decision shall be final and conclusive.

On a poll votes may be given either personally or by proxy. A member may appoint more than one proxy to attend on the same occasion.

An instrument appointing a proxy shall be in writing in the usual form, or as approved by the directors, and shall be executed by or on behalf of the appointor.

The instrument appointing a proxy and any authority under which it is executed or a copy of such authority certified notarially or in some other way approved by the directors may -

be deposited at the office or at such other place within the Federation as is specified in the notice convening the meeting or in any instrument of proxy sent out by the company in relation to the meeting not less than 48 hours before the time for holding the meeting or adjourned meeting at which the person named in the instrument proposes to vote; or

in the case of a poll taken more than 48 hours after it is demanded, be deposited as aforesaid after the poll has been demanded and not less than 24 hours before the time appointed for the taking of the poll; or

where the poll is not taken forthwith but is taken not more than 48 hours after it was demanded, be delivered at the meeting at which the poll was demanded to the chairman or to the secretary or to any director,

and an instrument of proxy which is not deposited or delivered in a manner so permitted shall be invalid.

A vote given or poll demanded by proxy or by the duly authorised representative of a body corporate shall be valid notwithstanding the previous determination of the authority of the person voting or demanding a poll unless notice of the determination was received by the company at the office or at such other place at which the instrument of proxy was duly deposited before the commencement of the meeting or adjourned meeting at which the vote is given or the poll demanded or (in the case of a poll taken otherwise than on the same day as the meeting or adjourned meeting) the time appointed for taking the poll.

Number of directors

Unless otherwise determined by special resolution, the number of directors (other than alternate directors) shall not be subject to any maximum number but shall not be less than the minimum number specified in the Act.

Alternate directors

Any director (other than an alternate director) may appoint any other director, or any other person approved by resolution of the directors and willing to act, to be an alternate director and may remove from office an alternate director so appointed by him.

An alternate director shall be entitled to receive the same notice of meetings of directors and of all meetings of committees of directors of which his appointor is a member as his appointor is entitled to receive, to attend and vote at any such meeting at which the director appointing him is not personally present, and generally to perform all the functions of his appointor as a director in his absence, but shall not be entitled to receive any remuneration from the company for his services as an alternate director.

An alternate director shall cease to be an alternate director if his appointor ceases to be a director, but, if a director is reappointed, any appointment of an alternate director made by him which is in force immediately prior to his reappointment shall continue after his reappointment.

Any appointment or removal of an alternate director shall be by notice to the company signed by the director making or revoking the appointment or in any other manner approved by the directors.

Save as otherwise provided in the articles, an alternate director shall be deemed for all purposes to be a director and shall alone be responsible for his own acts and defaults and he shall not be deemed to be the agent of the director appointing him.

Powers of directors

Subject to the provisions of the Act, the memorandum and the articles and to any directions given by special resolution, the business of the company shall be managed by the directors who may exercise all the powers of the company. No alteration of the memorandum or articles and no such direction shall invalidate any prior act of the directors which would have been valid if that alteration had not been made or that direction had not been given. The powers given by this regulation shall not be limited by any special power given to the directors by the articles and a meeting of directors at which a quorum is present may exercise all powers exercisable by the directors.

The directors may, by power of attorney or otherwise, appoint any person to be the agent of the company for such purposes and on such conditions as they determine, including authority for the agent to delegate all or any of his powers.

Delegation of directors' powers

The directors may delegate any of their powers to any committee consisting of one or more directors and (if thought fit) one or more other persons, but a majority of the members of the committee shall be directors. No resolution of the committee shall be effective unless a majority of those present when it is passed are directors. They may also delegate to any managing director or any director holding any other executive office such of their powers as they consider desirable to be exercised by him. Any such delegation may be made subject to any conditions the directors may impose, and either collaterally with or to the exclusion of their own powers and may be revoked or altered. Subject to any such conditions, the proceedings of a committee with two or more members shall be governed by the articles regulating the proceedings of directors so far as they are capable of applying.

Appointment of directors

The first directors of the company shall be appointed in writing by the subscribers of the memorandum or a majority of them.

No person shall be appointed a director at any general meeting unless -

he is recommended by the directors; or

not less than 14 nor more than 35 clear days before the date appointed for the meeting, notice executed by a member qualified to vote at the meeting has been given to the company of the intention to propose that person for appointment stating the particulars which would, if he were so appointed, be required to be included in the company's register of directors together with notice executed by that person of his willingness to be appointed.

Not less than 7 nor more than 28 clear days before the date appointed for holding a general meeting notice shall be given to all who are entitled to receive notice of the meeting of any person who is recommended by the directors for appointment or reappointment as a director at the meeting or in respect of whom notice has been duly given to the company of the intention to propose him at the meeting for appointment as a director. The notice shall give the particulars of that person which would, if he were so appointed, be required to be included in the company's register of directors.

Subject as aforesaid, the company may by ordinary resolution appoint a person who is willing to act to be a director either to fill a vacancy or as an additional director.

The directors may appoint a person who is willing to act as a director, either to fill a vacancy or as an additional director, provided that the appointment does not cause the number of directors to exceed any number fixed by or in accordance with the articles as the maximum number of directors. A director so appointed shall hold office only until the next following annual general meeting but shall be eligible for reappointment. If not reappointed at such annual general meeting, he shall vacate office at the conclusion thereof.

Disqualification and removal of directors

The office of a director shall be vacated if -

he ceases to be a director by virtue of any provision of the Act or he becomes prohibited by law from or disqualified for being a director; or

he becomes bankrupt or makes any arrangement or composition with his creditors generally; or he resigns his office by notice to the company; or

he shall for more than six consecutive months have been absent without permission of the directors from meetings of directors held during that period and the directors resolve that his office be vacated; or

the company so resolves by ordinary resolution.

Remuneration of directors

The directors shall be entitled to such remuneration as the company may by ordinary resolution determine and, unless the resolution provides otherwise, the remuneration shall be deemed to accrue from day to day.

Directors' expenses

The directors may be paid all travelling, hotel, and other expenses properly incurred by them in connexion with their attendance at meetings of directors or committees of directors or general meetings or separate meetings of the holders of any class of shares or of debentures of the company or otherwise in connexion with the discharge of their duties.

Directors' appointments and interests

Subject to the provisions of the Act, the directors may appoint one or more of their number to the office of managing director or to any other executive office under the company and may enter into an agreement or arrangement with any director for his employment by the company or for the provision by him of any services outside the scope of the ordinary duties of a director. Any such appointment, agreement or arrangement may be made upon such terms as the directors determine and they may remunerate any such director for his services as they think fit. Any appointment of a director to an executive office shall terminate if he ceases to be a director but without prejudice to any claim to damages for breach of the contract of service between the director and the company.

Subject to the provisions of the Act, and provided that he has disclosed to the directors the nature and extent of any material interests of his, a director notwithstanding his office -

may be a party to, or otherwise interested in, any transaction or arrangement with the company or in which the company is otherwise interested;

may be a director or other officer of, or employed by, or a party to any transaction or arrangement with, or otherwise interested in, any body corporate promoted by the company or in which the company is otherwise interested; and

shall not, by reason of his office, be accountable to the company for any benefit which he derives from any such office or employment or from any such transaction or arrangement or from any interest in any such body corporate and no such transaction or arrangement shall be liable to be avoided on the ground of any such interest or benefit.

For the purposes of regulation 0 -

a general notice given to the directors that a director is to be regarded as having an interest of the nature and extent specified in the notice in any transaction or arrangement in which a specified person or class of persons is interested shall be deemed to be a disclosure that the director has an interest in any such transaction of the nature and extent so specified; and

an interest of which a director has no knowledge and of which it is unreasonable to expect him to have knowledge shall not be treated as an interest of his.

Directors' gratuities and pensions

The directors may provide benefits, whether by the payment of gratuities or pensions or by insurance or otherwise, for any person who has held but no longer holds any executive office or employment with the company or with any body corporate which is or has been a subsidiary of the company or a predecessor in business of the company or of any such subsidiary, and for any member of his family (including a spouse and a former spouse) or any person who is or who was dependent on him, and may (as well before as after he ceases to hold such office or employment) contribute to any fund and pay premiums for the purchase or provision of any such benefit and may include rights in respect of any such benefit in the terms of engagement of any such person notwithstanding that he may be or may have been a director of the company.

Proceedings of directors

Subject to the provisions of the articles, the directors may regulate their proceedings as they think fit. A director may, and the secretary at the request of a director shall, call a meeting of the directors. Questions arising at a meeting shall be decided by a majority of votes. In the case of an equality of votes, the chairman shall have a second or casting vote. A director who is also an alternate director shall be entitled in the absence of his appointor to a separate vote on behalf of his appointor in addition to his own vote.

Subject to the Act, where the subscribers to the memorandum or a majority of them have appointed only one director or where the company has by special resolution determined that the maximum number of directors shall be one, that director present in person shall constitute a meeting. In any other case, the quorum for the transaction of the business of the directors shall be two or such higher number as may be fixed by the directors. A person who holds office only as an alternate director shall, if his appointor is not present, be counted in the quorum.

The continuing directors or a sole continuing director may act notwithstanding any vacancies in their number, but, if the number of directors is less than the number fixed as the quorum, the continuing directors or director may act only for the purpose of filling vacancies or of calling a general meeting.

The directors may appoint one of their number to be the chairman of the board of directors and may at any time remove him from that office. Unless he is unwilling to do so, the director so appointed shall preside at every meeting of directors at which he is present. If there is no director holding that office, or if the director holding it is unwilling to preside or is not present within five minutes after the time appointed for the meeting, the directors present shall appoint one of their number to be chairman of the meeting.

All acts done by a meeting of directors, or of a committee of directors, or by a person acting as a director shall, notwithstanding that it be afterwards discovered that there was a defect in the appointment of any director or that any of them were disqualified for holding office, or had vacated office, or were not entitled to vote, be as valid as if every such person had been duly appointed and was qualified and had continued to be a director and had been entitled to vote.

A resolution in writing signed by all the directors entitled to receive notice of a meeting of directors or of a committee of directors shall be valid and effectual as if it had been passed at a meeting of directors or (as the case may be) a committee of directors duly convened and held and may consist of several documents in the like form each signed by one or more directors; but a resolution signed by an alternate director need not also be signed by his appointor and, if it is signed by a director who has appointed an alternate director, it need not be signed by the alternate director in that capacity.

Save as otherwise provided by the articles, a director shall not vote at a meeting of directors or of a committee of directors on any resolution concerning a matter in which he has, directly or indirectly, an interest or duty which is material and which conflicts or may conflict with the interests of the company unless his interest or duty arises only because the case falls within one or more of the following paragraphs -

the resolution relates to the giving to him of a guarantee, security, or indemnity in respect of money lent to, or an obligation incurred by him for the benefit of, the company or any of its subsidiaries;

the resolution relates to the giving to a third part of a guarantee, security or indemnity, in respect of an obligation of the company or any of its subsidiaries for which the director has assumed responsibility in whole or part and whether alone or jointly with others under a guarantee or indemnity or by the giving of security;

his interest arises by virtue of his subscribing or agreeing to subscribe for any shares, debentures or other securities of the company or any of its subsidiaries, or by virtue of his being, or intending to become, a participant in the underwriting or sub-underwriting of an offer of any such shares, debentures, or other securities by the company or any of its subsidiaries for subscription, purchase or exchange;

the resolution relates in any way to a retirement benefits scheme which has been approved, or is conditional upon approval, by the Comptroller of Income Tax for taxation purposes;

the resolution relates to an agreement for the benefit of employees of the company or any of its subsidiaries which does not accord to him any privilege or advantage not generally accorded to the employees to whom the arrangement relates.

A director shall not be counted in the quorum present at a meeting in relation to a resolution on which he is not entitled to vote.

The company may by ordinary resolution suspend or relax to any extent, either generally or in respect of any particular matter, any provisions of the articles prohibiting a director from voting at a meeting of directors or of a committee of directors.

Where proposals are under consideration concerning the appointment of two or more directors to offices or employments with the company or any body corporate in which the company is interested the proposals may be divided and considered in relation to each director separately and (provided he is not for another reason precluded from voting) each of the directors concerned shall be entitled to vote and be counted in the quorum in respect of each resolution except that concerning his own appointment.

If a question arises at a meeting of directors or of a committee of directors as to the right of a director to vote, the question may, before the conclusion of the meeting, be referred to the chairman of the meeting and his ruling in relation to any director other than himself shall be final and conclusive.

Secretary

Subject to the provisions of the Act, the secretary shall be appointed by the directors for such term, at such remuneration and upon such conditions as they may think fit; and any secretary so appointed may be removed by them.

Minutes

The directors shall cause minutes to be made in books kept for the purpose in accordance with the Act.

The seal

The seal shall only be used by the authority of the directors or of a committee of directors authorised by the directors. The directors may determine who shall sign any instrument to which the seal is affixed and unless otherwise so determined it shall be signed by two directors or by a director and the secretary.

Dividends

Subject to the provisions of the Act, the company may by ordinary resolution declare dividends in accordance with the respective rights of the members, but no dividend shall exceed the amount recommended by the directors.

Subject to the provisions of the Act, the directors may pay interim dividends if it appears to them that they are justified by the profits of the company available for distribution. If the share capital is divided into different classes, the directors may pay interim dividends on shares which confer deferred or non-preferred rights with regard to dividend as well as on shares which confer preferential rights with regard to dividend, but no interim dividend shall be paid on shares carrying deferred or non-preferred rights if, at the time of payment, any preferential dividend is in arrear. The directors may also pay at intervals settled by them any dividend payable at a fixed rate if it appears to them that the profits available for distribution justify the payment. Provided the directors act in good faith, they shall not incur any liability to the holders of shares conferring preferred rights for any loss they may suffer by the lawful payment of an interim dividend on any shares having deferred or non-preferred rights.

Except as otherwise provided by the rights attached to shares, all dividends shall be declared and paid according to the amounts paid up on shares on which the dividend is paid. All dividends shall be apportioned and paid proportionately to the amounts paid up on the shares during any portion or portions of the period in respect of which the dividend is paid, but, if any share is issued on terms providing that it shall rank for dividend as from a particular date, that share shall rank for dividend accordingly.

A general meeting declaring a dividend may, upon the recommendation of the directors, direct that it shall be satisfied wholly or partly by the distribution of assets and, where any difficulty arises in regard to the distribution, the directors may settle the same and in particular may issue fractional certificates and fix the value for distribution of any assets and may determine that cash shall be paid to any member upon the footing of the value so fixed in order to adjust the rights of members and may vest any assets in trustees.

Any dividend or other moneys payable in respect of a share may be paid by cheque or by warrant sent by post to the registered address of the person entitled or, if two or more persons are the holders of the share or are jointly entitled to it by reason of the death or bankruptcy of the holder, to the registered address of one of those persons who is first named in the register of members or to such person and to such address as the person or persons entitled may in writing direct. Every cheque or warrant shall be made payable to the order of the person or persons entitled or to such other person as the person or persons entitled may in writing direct and payment of the cheque or warrant shall be a good discharge to the company. Any joint holder or other person jointly entitled to a share as aforesaid may give receipts for any dividend or other moneys payable in respect of the share.

No dividend or other moneys payable in respect of a share shall bear interest against the company unless otherwise provided by the rights attached to the share.

Any dividend which has remained unclaimed for 10 years from the date when it became due for payment shall, if the directors so resolve, be forfeited and cease to remain owing by the company.

No member shall (as such) have any right of inspecting any accounting records or other book or document of the company except as conferred by law or authorised by the directors or by ordinary resolution of the company.

The company shall appoint auditors to examine the accounts and report thereon in accordance with the Act.

Capitalisation of profits

The directors may with the authority of an ordinary resolution of the company -

subject as hereinafter provided, resolve to capitalise any undivided profits of the company not required for paying any preferential dividend (whether or not they are available for distribution) or any sum standing to the credit of the company's share premium account or capital redemption reserve;

appropriate the sum resolved to be capitalised to the members in proportion to the stated amounts of the shares (whether or not fully paid) held by them respectively which would entitle them to participate in a distribution of that sum if the shares were fully paid and the sum were distributable and were distributed by way of dividend and apply such sum on their behalf either in or towards paying up the amounts, if any, for the time being unpaid on any shares held by them respectively, or in paying up in full unissued shares of the company of a stated amount or debentures of the company of a stated amount equal to that sum, and allot the shares or debentures credited as fully paid to those members, or as they may direct, in those proportions, or partly in one way and partly in the other; but the share premium account, the capital redemption reserve, and any profits which are not available for distribution may, for the purposes of this regulation, only be applied in paying up unissued shares to be allotted to members credited as fully paid up;

make such provision by the issue of fractional certificates or by payment in cash or otherwise as they determine in the case of shares or debentures becoming distributable under this regulation in fractions; and

authorise any person to enter on behalf of all the members concerned into an agreement with the company providing for the allotment to them respectively, credited as fully paid, of any shares or debentures to which they are entitled upon such capitalisation, any agreement made under such authority being binding on all such members.

Notices

Any notice to be given to or by any person pursuant to the articles shall be in writing except that a notice calling a meeting of the directors need not be in writing.

A member shall be entitled to receive any notice to be given to him pursuant to the articles notwithstanding that his registered address is not within the Federation. The company may give notice to a member either personally or by sending it by post in a prepaid envelope addressed to the member at his registered address or by leaving it at that address. In the case of joint holders of a share, all notices shall be given to the joint holder whose name stands first in the register of members in respect of the joint holding and notice so given shall be sufficient notice to all the joint holders.

Proof that an envelope containing a notice was properly addressed, prepaid and posted shall be conclusive evidence that the notice was given. A notice shall be deemed to be given at the expiration of 48 hours after the envelope containing it was posted.

Where the company has issued any bearer certificate, the directors shall arrange for any notice to be given by the company pursuant to the articles to be published in one or more newspapers circulated in the Federation (but the directors may also arrange for such notice to be published in one or more newspapers circulated elsewhere than in the Federation) and such notice shall be deemed to be duly given to all holders of bearer certificates issued by the company on the day on which it appears in any such newspaper.

A member present, either in person or by proxy, at any meeting of the company or of the holders of any class of shares in the company shall be deemed to have received notice of the meeting and, where requisite, of the purposes for which it was called.

Every person who becomes entitled to a share shall be bound by any notice in respect of that share which, before his name is entered in the register of members, has been duly given to a person from which he derives his title.

A notice may be given by the company to the persons entitled to a share in consequence of the death or bankruptcy of a member by sending or delivering it, in any manner authorised by the articles for the giving of notice to a member, addressed to them by name, or by the title of representatives of the deceased, or trustee of the bankrupt or by any like description at the address supplied for that purpose by the persons claiming to be so entitled. Until such an address has been supplied, a notice may be given in any manner in which it might have been given if the death or bankruptcy had not occurred.

Winding up

If the company is wound up, the company may, with the sanction of a special resolution and any other sanction required by the Act, divide the whole or any part of the assets of the company among the members *in specie* and the liquidator or, where there is no liquidator, the directors may, for that purpose, value any assets and determine how the division shall be carried out as between the members or different classes of members, and with the like sanction, vest the whole or any part of the assets in trustees upon such trusts for the benefit of the members as he with the like sanction determines, but no member shall be compelled to accept any assets upon which there is a liability.

Indemnity

In so far as the Act allows, every present or former officer of the company shall be indemnified out of the assets of the company against any loss or liability incurred by him by reason of being or having been such an officer.

Standard Table B

Regulations for the Management of
a Company Limited by Guarantee

Interpretation

In these regulations -

"articles" means the articles of association of the company;

"clear days" in relation to the period of a notice means that period excluding the day when the notice is given or deemed to be given and the day for which it is given or on which it is to take effect;

"executed" includes any mode of execution;

"office" means the registered office of the company;

"ordinary resolution" means a resolution of the company in general meeting adopted by a simple majority of the votes cast at that meeting;

"seal" means the common seal of the company;

"secretary" means the secretary of the company or any other person appointed to perform the duties of the secretary of the company, including a joint, assistant or deputy secretary;

"the Act" means the Companies Act 1996 including any statutory modification or re-enactment thereof for the time being in force.

Unless the context otherwise requires, words or expressions contained in these regulations bear the same meaning as in the Act but excluding any statutory modification thereof not in force when these regulations become binding on the company.

Members

The subscribers to the memorandum of association and such other persons as the directors shall admit to membership shall be members of the company.

General meetings

All general meetings other than annual general meetings shall be called extraordinary general meetings.

The directors may call general meetings and, on the requisition of members pursuant to the provisions of the Act, shall forthwith proceed to call a general meeting for a date not later than 2 months after the receipt of the requisition. If there are not sufficient directors to call a general meeting, any director or any member of the company may call such a meeting.

Notice of general meetings

An annual general meeting or a general meeting called for the passing of a special resolution or a resolution appointing a person as a director shall be called by at least 21 clear days' notice. All other meetings shall be called by at least 14 clear days' notice but a general meeting may be called by shorter notice if it is so agreed-

in the case of an annual general meeting, by all the members entitled to attend and vote thereat; and

in the case of any other meeting by a majority in number of the members having a right to attend and vote at the meeting being a majority together representing not less than 95 per cent of the total voting rights at that meeting of all the members.

The notice shall specify the day, time and place of the meeting and the general nature of the business to be transacted and, in the case of an annual general meeting, shall specify the meeting as such.

Subject to the provisions of the articles, the notice shall be given to all the members, to all persons entitled to receive the notice in consequence of the death or bankruptcy of a member and to the directors and auditors, if any.

The accidental omission to give notice of a meeting to, or the non-receipt of notice of a meeting by, any person entitled to receive notice shall not invalidate the proceedings at the meeting.

Proceedings at General Meetings

In the case where a company has only one member, or where there is only one member of any class of members of the company, that member present in person or by proxy shall be deemed to constitute a meeting. In any other case, no business shall be transacted at any meeting unless a quorum is present and, subject as hereinafter otherwise provided, two persons entitled to vote upon the business to be transacted, each being a member or a proxy for a member or a duly authorised representative of a body corporate, shall be a quorum.

If a quorum is not present within half an hour from the time appointed for the meeting, or if during a meeting such quorum ceases to be present, the meeting shall stand adjourned to the same day in the next week at the same time and place or such day, time and place as the directors may determine. If at such adjourned meeting, a quorum is not present within half an hour from the time appointed for the meeting, or if during such adjourned meeting a quorum ceases to be present, then any member present in person or by proxy shall be a quorum.

The chairman, if any, of the board of directors or in his absence some other director nominated by the directors shall preside as chairman of the meeting, but if neither the chairman nor such other director (if any) is present within 15 minutes after the time appointed for holding the meeting and willing to act, the directors present shall elect one of their number to be chairman and, if there is only one director present and willing to act, he shall be chairman.

If no director is willing to act as chairman, or if no director is present within 15 minutes after the time appointed for holding the meeting, those present and entitled to be counted in a quorum shall choose one of their number to be chairman.

A director shall, notwithstanding that he is not a member, be entitled to attend and speak at any general meeting and at any separate meeting of any class of members of the company.

The chairman may, with the consent of a meeting at which a quorum is present (and shall if so directed by the meeting), adjourn the meeting from time to time and from place to place, but no business shall be transacted at an adjourned meeting other than business which might properly have been transacted at the meeting had the adjournment not taken place. When a meeting is adjourned for 14 days or more, at least 7 clear days' notice shall be given specifying the day, time and place of the adjourned meeting and the general nature of the business to be transacted. Otherwise it shall not be necessary to give any such notice.

A resolution put to the vote of a meeting shall be decided on a show of hands unless before, or on the declaration of the result of, the show of hands a poll is duly demanded. Subject to the provisions of the Act, a poll may be demanded -

by the chairman; or

by at least two members having the right to vote on the resolution; or

by a member or members representing not less than one-tenth of the total voting rights of all the members having the right to vote on the resolution,

and a demand by a person as proxy for a member shall be the same as a demand by the member.

Unless a poll is duly demanded a declaration by the chairman that a resolution has been carried or carried unanimously, or by a particular majority, or lost, or not carried by a particular majority and an entry to that effect in the minutes of the meeting shall be conclusive evidence of the fact without proof of the number or proportion of the votes recorded in favour of or against the resolution.

The demand for a poll may, before the poll is taken, be withdrawn but only with the consent of the chairman and a demand so withdrawn shall not be taken to have invalidated the result of a show of hands declared before the demand was made.

A poll shall be taken as the chairman directs and he may appoint scrutineers (who need not be members) and fix a day, time and place for declaring the result of the poll. The result of the poll shall be deemed to be the resolution of the meeting at which the poll was demanded.

In the case of an equality of votes, whether on a show of hands or on a poll, the chairman shall be entitled to a casting vote in addition to any other vote he may have.

A poll demanded on the election of a chairman or on a question of adjournment shall be taken forthwith. A poll demanded on any other question shall be taken either forthwith or at such day, time and place as the chairman directs not being more than 30 days after the poll is demanded. The demand for a poll shall not prevent the continuance of a meeting for the transaction of any business other than the question on which the poll was demanded. If a poll is demanded before the declaration of the result of a show of hands and the demand is duly withdrawn, the meeting shall continue as if the demand had not been made.

No notice need be given of a poll not taken forthwith if the day, time and place at which it is to be taken are announced at the meeting at which it is demanded. In any other case, at least 7 clear days' notice shall be given specifying the day, time and place at which the poll is to be taken.

Votes of members

On a show of hands or on a poll every member who (being an individual) is present in person or (being a body corporate) is present by a duly authorised representative, not being himself a member entitled to vote, shall have one vote.

A member in respect of whom an order has been made by any court having jurisdiction (whether in the Federation or elsewhere) in matters concerning mental disorder may vote, whether on a show of hands or on a poll, by his curator or other person authorised in that behalf appointed by that court, and any such curator or other person may, on a poll, vote by proxy. Evidence to the satisfaction of the directors of the authority of the person claiming to exercise the right to vote shall be deposited at the office, or at such other place within the Federation as is specified in accordance with the articles for the deposit of instruments of proxy not less than 48 hours before the time appointed for holding the meeting or adjourned meeting at which the right to vote is to be exercised and in default the right to vote shall not be exercisable.

No member shall vote at any general meeting or at any separate meeting of any class of members in the company, either in person or by proxy, unless all moneys presently payable by him to the company have been paid.

No objection shall be raised to the qualification of any voter except at the meeting or adjourned meeting at which the vote objected to is tendered, and every vote not disallowed at the meeting shall be valid. Any objection made in due time shall be referred to the chairman whose decision shall be final and conclusive.

On a poll votes may be given either personally or by proxy. A member may appoint more than one proxy to attend on the same occasion.

An instrument appointing a proxy shall be in writing in the usual form, or as approved by the directors, and shall be executed by or on behalf of the appointor.

The instrument appointing a proxy and any authority under which it is executed or a copy of such authority certified notarially or in some other way approved by the directors may -

be deposited at the office or at such other place within the Federation as is specified in the notice convening the meeting or in any instrument of proxy sent out by the company in relation to the meeting not less than 48 hours before the time for holding the meeting or adjourned meeting at which the person named in the instrument proposes to vote; or

in the case of a poll taken more than 48 hours after it is demanded, be deposited as aforesaid after the poll has been demanded and not less than 24 hours before the time appointed for the taking of the poll; or

where the poll is not taken forthwith but is taken not more than 48 hours after it was demanded, be delivered at the meeting at which the poll was demanded to the chairman or to the secretary or to any director,

and an instrument of proxy which is not deposited or delivered in a manner so permitted shall be invalid.

A vote given or poll demanded by proxy or by the duly authorised representative of a body corporate shall be valid notwithstanding the previous determination of the authority of the person voting or demanding a poll unless notice of the determination was received by the company at the office or at such other place at which the instrument of proxy was duly deposited before the commencement of the meeting or adjourned meeting at which the vote is given or the poll demanded or (in the case of a poll taken otherwise than on the same day as the meeting or adjourned meeting) the time appointed for taking the poll.

Number of directors

Unless otherwise determined by special resolution, the number of directors (other than alternate directors) shall not be subject to any maximum number but shall not be less than the minimum number specified in the Act.

Alternate directors

Any director (other than an alternate director) may appoint any other director, or any other person approved by resolution of the directors and willing to act, to be an alternate director and may remove from office an alternate director so appointed by him.

An alternate director shall be entitled to receive the same notice of meetings of directors and of all meetings of committees of directors of which his appointor is a member as his appointor is entitled to receive, to attend and vote at any such meeting at which the director appointing him is not personally present, and generally to perform all the functions of his appointor as a director in his absence, but shall not be entitled to receive any remuneration from the company for his services as an alternate director.

An alternate director shall cease to be an alternate director if his appointor ceases to be a director, but, if a director is reappointed, any appointment of an alternate director made by him which is in force immediately prior to his reappointment shall continue after his reappointment.

Any appointment or removal of an alternate director shall be by notice to the company signed by the director making or revoking the appointment or in any other manner approved by the directors.

Save as otherwise provided in the articles, an alternate director shall be deemed for all purposes to be a director and shall alone be responsible for his own acts and defaults and he shall not be deemed to be the agent of the director appointing him.

Powers of directors

Subject to the provisions of the Act, the memorandum and the articles and to any directions given by special resolution, the business of the company shall be managed by the directors who may exercise all the powers of the company. No alteration of the memorandum or articles and no such direction shall invalidate any prior act of the directors which would have been valid if that alteration had not been made or that direction had not been given. The powers given by this regulation shall not be limited by any special power given to the directors by the articles and a meeting of directors at which a quorum is present may exercise all powers exercisable by the directors.

The directors may, by power of attorney or otherwise, appoint any person to be the agent of the company for such purposes and on such conditions as they determine, including authority for the agent to delegate all or any of his powers.

Delegation of directors' powers

The directors may delegate any of their powers to any committee consisting of one or more directors and (if thought fit) one or more other persons, but a majority of the members of the committee shall be directors. No resolution of the committee shall be effective unless a majority of those present when it is passed are directors. They may also delegate to any managing director or any director holding any other executive office such of their powers as they consider desirable to be exercised by him. Any such delegation may be made subject to any conditions the directors may impose, and either collaterally with or to the exclusion of their own powers and may be revoked or altered. Subject to any such conditions, the proceedings of a committee with two or more members shall be governed by the articles regulating the proceedings of directors so far as they are capable of applying.

Appointment of directors

The first directors of the company shall be appointed in writing by the subscribers of the memorandum or a majority of them.

No person shall be appointed a director at any general meeting unless -

he is recommended by the directors; or

not less than 14 nor more than 35 clear days before the date appointed for the meeting, notice executed by a member qualified to vote at the meeting has been given to the company of the intention to propose that person for appointment stating the particulars which would, if he were so appointed, be required to be included in the company's register of directors together with notice executed by that person of his willingness to be appointed.

Not less than 7 nor more than 28 clear days before the date appointed for holding a general meeting notice shall be given to all who are entitled to receive notice of the meeting of any person who is recommended by the directors for appointment or reappointment as a director at the meeting or in respect of whom notice has been duly given to the company of the intention to propose him at the meeting for appointment as a director. The notice shall give the particulars of that person which would, if he were so appointed, be required to be included in the company's register of directors.

Subject as aforesaid, the company may by ordinary resolution appoint a person who is willing to act to be a director either to fill a vacancy or as an additional director.

The directors may appoint a person who is willing to act as a director, either to fill a vacancy or as an additional director, provided that the appointment does not cause the number of directors to exceed any number fixed by or in accordance with the articles as the maximum number of directors. A director so appointed shall hold office only until the next following annual general meeting but shall be eligible for reappointment. If not reappointed at such annual general meeting, he shall vacate office at the conclusion thereof.

Disqualification and removal of directors

The office of a director shall be vacated if -

he ceases to be a director by virtue of any provision of the Act or he becomes prohibited by law from or disqualified for being a director; or

he becomes bankrupt or makes any arrangement or composition with his creditors generally; or

he resigns his office by notice to the company; or

he shall for more than six consecutive months have been absent without permission of the directors from meetings of directors held during that period and the directors resolve that his office be vacated; or

the company so resolves by ordinary resolution.

Remuneration of directors

The directors shall be entitled to such remuneration as the company may by ordinary resolution determine and, unless the resolution provides otherwise, the remuneration shall be deemed to accrue from day to day.

Directors' expenses

The directors may be paid all travelling, hotel, and other expenses properly incurred by them in connexion with their attendance at meetings of directors or committees of directors or general meetings or separate meetings of the holders of any class of shares or of debentures of the company or otherwise in connection with the discharge of their duties.

Directors' appointments and interests

Subject to the provisions of the Act, the directors may appoint one or more of their number to the office of managing director or to any other executive office under the company and may enter into an agreement or arrangement with any director for his employment by the company or for the provision by him of any services outside the scope of the ordinary duties of a director. Any such appointment, agreement or arrangement may be made upon such terms as the directors determine and they may remunerate any such director for his services as they think fit. Any appointment of a director to an executive office shall terminate if he ceases to be a director but without prejudice to any claim to damages for breach of the contract of service between the director and the company.

Subject to the provisions of the Act, and provided that he has disclosed to the directors the nature and extent of any material interests of his, a director notwithstanding his office -

may be a party to, or otherwise interested in, any transaction or arrangement with the company or in which the company is otherwise interested;

may be a director or other officer of, or employed by, or a party to any transaction or arrangement with, or otherwise interested in, any body corporate promoted by the company or in which the company is otherwise interested; and

shall not, by reason of his office, be accountable to the company for any benefit which he derives from any such office or employment or from any such transaction or arrangement or from any interest in any such body corporate and no such transaction or arrangement shall be liable to be avoided on the ground of any such interest or benefit.

For the purposes of regulation 0 -

a general notice given to the directors that a director is to be regarded as having an interest of the nature and extent specified in the notice in any transaction or arrangement in which a specified person or class of persons is interested shall be deemed to be a disclosure that the director has an interest in any such transaction of the nature and extent so specified; and

an interest of which a director has no knowledge and of which it is unreasonable to expect him to have knowledge shall not be treated as an interest of his.

Directors' gratuities and pensions

The directors may provide benefits, whether by the payment of gratuities or pensions or by insurance or otherwise, for any person who has held but no longer holds any executive office or employment with the company or with any body corporate which is or has been a subsidiary of the company or a predecessor in business of the company or of any such subsidiary, and for any member of his family (including a spouse and a former spouse) or any person who is or who was dependent on him, and may (as well before as after he ceases to hold such office or employment) contribute to any fund and pay premiums for the purchase or provision of any such benefit and may include rights in respect of any such benefit in the terms of engagement of any such person notwithstanding that he may be or may have been a director of the company.

Proceedings of directors

Subject to the provisions of the articles, the directors may regulate their proceedings as they think fit. A director may, and the secretary at the request of a director shall, call a meeting of the directors. Questions arising at a meeting shall be decided by a majority of votes. In the case of an equality of votes, the chairman shall have a second or casting vote. A director who is also an alternate director shall be entitled in the absence of his appointor to a separate vote on behalf of his appointor in addition to his own vote.

Subject to the Act, where the subscribers to the memorandum or a majority of them have appointed only one director or where the company has by special resolution determined that the maximum number of directors shall be one, that director present in person shall constitute a meeting. In any other case, the quorum for the transaction of the business of the directors shall be two or such higher number as may be fixed by the directors. A person who holds office only as an alternate director shall, if his appointor is not present, be counted in the quorum.

The continuing directors or a sole continuing director may act notwithstanding any vacancies in their number, but, if the number of directors is less than the number fixed as the quorum, the continuing directors or director may act only for the purpose of filling vacancies or of calling a general meeting.

The directors may appoint one of their number to be the chairman of the board of directors and may at any time remove him from that office. Unless he is unwilling to do so, the director so appointed shall preside at every meeting of directors at which he is present. If there is no director holding that office, or if the director holding it is unwilling to preside or is not present within five minutes after the time appointed for the meeting, the directors present shall appoint one of their number to be chairman of the meeting.

All acts done by a meeting of directors, or of a committee of directors, or by a person acting as a director shall, notwithstanding that it be afterwards discovered that there was a defect in the appointment of any director or that any of them were disqualified for holding office, or had vacated office, or were not entitled to vote, be as valid as if every such person had been duly appointed and was qualified and had continued to be a director and had been entitled to vote.

A resolution in writing signed by all the directors entitled to receive notice of a meeting of directors or of a committee of directors shall be valid and effectual as if it had been passed at a meeting of directors or (as the case may be) a committee of directors duly convened and held and may consist of several documents in the like form each signed by one or more directors; but a resolution signed by an alternate director need not also be signed by his appointor and, if it is signed by a director who has appointed an alternate director, it need not be signed by the alternate director in that capacity.

Save as otherwise provided by the articles, a director shall not vote at a meeting of directors or of a committee of directors on any resolution concerning a matter in which he has, directly or indirectly, an interest or duty which is material and which conflicts or may conflict with the interests of the company unless his interest or duty arises only because the case falls within one or more of the following paragraphs -

the resolution relates to the giving to him of a guarantee, security, or indemnity in respect of money lent to, or an obligation incurred by him for the benefit of, the company or any of its subsidiaries;

the resolution relates to the giving to a third part of a guarantee, security or indemnity, in respect of an obligation of the company or any of its subsidiaries for which the director has assumed responsibility in whole or part and whether alone or jointly with others under a guarantee or indemnity or by the giving of security;

his interest arises by virtue of his subscribing or agreeing to subscribe for any shares, debentures or other securities of the company or any of its subsidiaries, or by virtue of his being, or intending to become, a participant in the underwriting or sub-underwriting of an offer of any such shares, debentures, or other securities by the company or any of its subsidiaries for subscription, purchase or exchange;

the resolution relates in any way to a retirement benefits scheme which has been approved, or is conditional upon approval, by the Comptroller of Income Tax for taxation purposes;

the resolution relates to an agreement for the benefit of employees of the company or any of its subsidiaries which does not accord to him any privilege or advantage not generally accorded to the employees to whom the arrangement relates.

A director shall not be counted in the quorum present at a meeting in relation to a resolution on which he is not entitled to vote.

The company may by ordinary resolution suspend or relax to any extent, either generally or in respect of any particular matter, any provisions of the articles prohibiting a director from voting at a meeting of directors or of a committee of directors.

Where proposals are under consideration concerning the appointment of two or more directors to offices or employments with the company or any body corporate in which the company is interested the proposals may be divided and considered in relation to each director separately and (provided he is not for another reason precluded from voting) each of the directors concerned shall be entitled to vote and be counted in the quorum in respect of each resolution except that concerning his own appointment.

If a question arises at a meeting of directors or of a committee of directors as to the right of a director to vote, the question may, before the conclusion of the meeting, be referred to the chairman of the meeting and his ruling in relation to any director other than himself shall be final and conclusive.

Secretary

Subject to the provisions of the Act, the secretary shall be appointed by the directors for such term, at such remuneration and upon such conditions as they may think fit; and any secretary so appointed may be removed by them.

Minutes

The directors shall cause minutes to be made in books kept for the purpose in accordance with the Act.

The seal

The seal shall only be used by the authority of the directors or of a committee of directors authorised by the directors. The directors may determine who shall sign any instrument to which the seal is affixed and unless otherwise so determined it shall be signed by two directors or by a director and the secretary.

Accounts and audit

The company shall appoint auditors to examine the accounts and report thereon in accordance with the Act.

Notices

Any notice to be given to or by any person pursuant to the articles shall be in writing except that a notice calling a meeting of the directors need not be in writing.

A member shall be entitled to receive any notice to be given to him pursuant to the articles notwithstanding that his registered address is not within the Federation. The company may give notice to a member either personally or by sending it by post in a prepaid envelope addressed to the member at his registered address or by leaving it at that address.

Proof that an envelope containing a notice was properly addressed, prepaid and posted shall be conclusive evidence that the notice was given. A notice shall be deemed to be given at the expiration of 48 hours after the envelope containing it was posted.

A member present, either in person or by proxy, at any meeting of the company or at any separate meeting of any class of members of the company shall be deemed to have received notice of the meeting and, where requisite, of the purposes for which it was called.

A notice may be given by the company to the persons entitled to receive the notice in consequence of the death or bankruptcy of a member by sending or delivering it, in any manner authorised by the articles for the giving of notice to a member, addressed to them by name, or by the title of representatives of the deceased, or trustee of the bankrupt or by any like description at the address supplied for that purpose by the persons claiming to be so entitled. Until such an address has been supplied, a notice may be given in any manner in which it might have been given if the death or bankruptcy had not occurred.

Winding up

If the company is wound up, the company may, with the sanction of a special resolution and any other sanction required by the Act, divide the whole or any part of the asses of the company among the members *in specie* and the liquidator or, where there is no liquidator, the directors may, for that purpose, value any assets and determine how the division shall be carried out as between the members or different classes of members, and with the like sanction, vest the whole or any part of the assets in trustees upon such trusts for the benefit of the members as he with the like sanction determines, but no member shall be compelled to accept any assets upon which there is a liability.

Indemnity

In so far as the Act allows, every present or former officer of the company shall be indemnified out of the assets of the company against any loss or liability incurred by him by reason of being or having been such an officer.

FINANCIAL SERVICES ACT

SAINT CHRISTOPHER AND NEVIS No. 26 OF 2008

AN ACT to require the licensing and regulation of money services businesses and to make provision for related matters.

[*Published 21st August 2008, Extra-Ordinary Gazette No. 40 of 2008.*]

BE IT ENACTED by the Queen's Most Excellent Majesty by and with the advice and consent of the National Assemblyof Saint Christopher and Nevis, and by the authority of the same as follows:

PART I PRELIMINARY

1. This Act may be cited as the Money Services Business Short title and commencement.

Act, 2008, and shall come into operation on such date as the Minister may, by Order, appoint.

2. In this Act Interpretation.

"affiliate" in relation to a licensee ("L") means

(a) a company which is or has at any relevant time been (i.) a holding company or subsidiary of L; (ii.) a subsidiary of a holding company of L; or (iii.) a holding company of a holding company or a

subsidiary of a subsidiary of L; or

(b) any company or firm over which L has control;

(c) any company or firm over which L and any person associated with L has control;

(d) any company or firm which has common ownership with L;

(e) any company or firm which has the same beneficial owner and shares common management and interlinked businesses with L.

"applicant" means a person applying for a license under section 6;

"Authority" means Financial Services Commission created pursuant to the Financial Services Commission Act, 2000;

"Central Bank" means the Eastern Caribbean Central Bank established under Article 3 of the Eastern Caribbean Central Bank Agreement 1983;

"Court" means the High Court of Justice established by the Supreme Court Order 1967;

"designated licensee" means a licensee who has been designated as a funds transfer system under the Payment System Act, 2008;

"financial year" means, in relation to a licensee, a period of not more than twelve (12) months for which the audited financial statements of a licensee is prepared in accordance with this Act;

"licence" means a Money Services Business Licence granted under section 6 (4)(a)(i);

"licensee" means a person holding a licence under this Act;

"Minister" means the Minister responsible for Finance;

"money services business" means

(a) the business of providing (as a primary business) any one or more of the following:

(i) transmission of money or monetary value in any form;

(ii) cheque cashing;

(iii) currency exchange;

(iv) the issuance, sale or redemption of money orders or traveller's cheques;

(v) pay day advances;

(vi) any other services or businesses that the Minister may specify by Order published in the ***Gazette***; or

(b) the business of operating as an agent or franchise holder of any of the businesses mentioned in paragraph (a);

"net worth" means excess assets over liabilities as presented under international accounting standards subject to adjustment for non-admitted assets as determined by the Authority;

"pay day advances" means any advances made prior to the payment of a person's salary, where the salary to be paid is used as collateral for the advance;

"significant shareholder" means a person who either alone or with an affiliate or related or connected person, is entitled to exercise or control ten percent or more of the voting power at any general meeting of the licensee or another company of which the licensee is a subsidiary.

3. (1) This Act does not apply to:

(a) a person licensed under the Banking Act, 2004 and any exempt company or entity incorporated under the CompaniesAct, 1996, the NevisOffshore Banking Ordinance, 1996 or the Nevis Business Corporation Ordinance, 1984 unless such person, exempt company or entity is operating as agent or franchise holder of a money services business;

(b) the Central Bank;

(c) an organisation licensed as a clearing agency under the Securities Act, 2001;

(d) an operator of a clearing house or funds transfer system.

(2) A money services business which is licensed under this Act is not required to be licensed under the Licenses on Businesses and Occupations Act, 1972.

(3) This Act does not apply to or affect the validity of any money services business transaction in existence at the date of commencement of this Act.

PART II LICENCES

4. (1) Subject to subsections (2) and (5) a person shall not carry on money services business in Saint Christopher and Nevis unless that person holds a licence in accordance with this Act.

(2) A person who immediately before the date of commencement of this Act was carrying on money services business, shall upon that date be deemed to be duly licensed under this Act for a period of four months, or such other period as the Authority approves and shall require a licence in order to carry on money services business after the expiry of that period.

(3) A person holding funds which that person has obtained by conducting money services business without being in possession of

Application of the Act.

Requirement for licence.

Classes of licences.

a licence granted under this Act shall settle his obligations in accordance with Regulations issued by the Minister.

(4) A person who contravenes subsection (1) commits an offence and is liable on summary conviction to a fine of fifty thousand dollars or to imprisonment for a term of two years or to both such fine and imprisonment.

(5) The Minister may by Order exempt any person from the licence requirement contained in subsection (1) if.

(**a**) that person is a local government body or agency;

(b) it is considered that the exemption would be beneficial to the economic needs of Saint Christopher and Nevis.

5. (1) There shall be several classes of licences as specified in Schedule 1, which may be applied for and granted subject to the provisions of this Act.

(2) The several classes of licences issued under this Act shall authorise the holders, for the period specified in the licence, to carry on money services business as specified under this section and not otherwise –

(a) a “Class A” licence permits the holder to carry on any or all of the following businesses –

(i) transmission of money or monetary value in any form;

(ii) the issuance, sale or redemption of money orders ortraveller’s cheques;

(iii) cheque cashing; (iv) currency exchange;

(b) a “Class B” licence permits the holder to carry on any or all of the following businesses:

(i) the issuance, sale or redemption of money orders or traveller’s cheques;

(ii) cheque cashing;

(iii) currency exchange;

(c) a “Class C” licence permits the holder to carry on the business of cheque cashing;

(d) a “Class D” licence permits the holder to carry on the business of currency exchange;

(e) a “Class E” licence permits the holder to carry on the business of pay day advances.

(3) The Minister may by Order published in the ***Gazette*** amend Schedule 1 to add to, vary or remove the classes of licences.

6. (1) In order to obtain a licence as a money services business, a person shall apply in writing to the Authority and submit the documents and other information as specified in Schedule 2 and pay the application fee prescribed in Schedule 4.

(2) In considering an application for a licence, the Authority shall conduct such investigation as it may deem necessary at the expense of the applicant, to ascertain:

(a) the validity of the documents submitted in accordance with Schedule 2,

(b) the financial condition and history of the applicant,

(c) the nature of the business of the applicant,

(d) the experience of the persons who are to constitute its management,

(e) the source of initial capital, and

(f) the convenience and needs of the community to be served by the granting of the licence,

(3) In considering an application for a Class A or Class B licence, the Authority shall, in addition to the matters specified in subsection (2), take into consideration

(a) the adequacy of capital structure, and

(b) the earning prospects of the applicant.

(4) Within a reasonable time of its receipt of the application for a licence the Authority shall:

(a) if it is satisfied that an application under subsection (1) is in order and that the applicant is a fit and proper person to be licensed to conduct money services business and that it can fulfill the obligations of a licensee under this Act:

(i) approve the application and issue a licence to the applicant in the form set out in Schedule 3, subject to the applicant paying the prescribed licence fee set out in Schedule 4 and making the prescribed statutory deposit in accordance with section 8, and subject to such other terms, conditions and restrictions it considers necessary;

Application for licence, formalities and consideration.

(ii) on issuing the licence to the applicant submit a copy of the licence to the Central Bank and recommend to the Central Bank that the licensee be designated in accordance with section 11 of the Payment Systems Act, 2008; or,

(b) if it is of the opinion that it would be undesirable in the public interest to grant the licence or that the applicant is not a fit and proper person to be licensed to conduct money services business, it may refuse to grant the same and shall inform the applicant that it has refused to grant the licence.

(5) In considering whether an applicant is a fit and proper person to be licensed, the Authority:

(a) shall have regard to, in respect of each of its significant shareholders, directors, executive management, agents and officers:

(i) his financial status;

(ii) his educational or other qualifications or experience having regard to the nature of his application;

(iii) his ability to perform his proposed function efficiently, honestly and fairly; and (iv) his reputation, character, financial integrity and reliability; and

(b) may take into account any matter relating to:

(i) any person who is or is to be employed by, or associated with, the applicant for the purposes of the business to which the application relates;

(ii) any person who will be acting as a principal or representative in relation to such business; and

(iii) any significant shareholder, director or officer of the applicant, any other company or firm in the same group of companies or to any director or officer of any such company or firm.

(6) For the purposes of this section, the Authority may have regard to any information in its possession whether furnished by the applicant or not.

(7) A licence to carry on money services business under this Act is not transferable.

(8) The Authority may at any time vary or repeal the conditions or restrictions it imposed pursuant to subsection (4).

(9) The Minister may amend or replace Schedules 2 and 4 by Order and the amendment or replacement shall be published in the ***Gazette***.

7. An applicant shall forthwith give written notice to the Authority of:

(a) any proposed alteration to, or

(b) the occurrence of any event which it knows affects or may affect in a material respect, information supplied to the Authority in relation to the application, being a proposal or event made or occurring while the application is pending a decision by the Authority.

8. (1) A licensee shall maintain adequate capital in such form and based on such formula as the Minister may by Order prescribe.

(2) A licensee shall make a statutory deposit of a portion of the prescribed capital referred to in subsection (1) with the Authority to be held in trust in an interest bearing account with a bank or other financial institution approved by the Authority for the benefit of holders of outstanding payment instruments, in the event that the licensee becomes bankrupt or for any other reason is unable to meet its contractual obligations to its customers.

(3) A trust referred to in subsection (2) shall be created by trust deed.

(4) The Authority shall retain the deposit for a period of at least six months after the licensee ceases money services business in Saint Christopher and Nevis subject to any court order made in respect of the said deposit.

(5) Where there is a deficiency in the prescribed capital, the Authority shall require the licensee to present a plan that is satisfactory to the Authority to reconstitute its capital within thirty days or such longer period as may be determined by the Authority.

(6) Where the licensee:

(a) fails to present a satisfactory plan pursuant to subsection (5); or

(b) fails to implement a plan presented pursuant to subsection (5) the Authority shall take such remedial action as it deems necessary in accordance with section 38.

Alteration of facts disclosed in application.

Adequacy of capital.

Period of licence and licence fee.

Authorisation of location and approval of new business premises.

Display of licence certificate.

(7) The requirements of this section shall not apply to the holder of a Class C, Class D or Class F licence.

(8) The Minister may by Order exempt any other licensee from the requirements of this section.

9. (1) Every licensee shall pay the prescribed annual licence fee according to the classification of the licence as set out in Schedule 4.

(2) A licence to carry on money services business is valid from the date of first issue to the 31st December of that year and is renewable each year on payment of the prescribed annual fee on or before the 15th day of January.

(3) All licence fees paid under this Act shall be payable to the Accountant General and form part of the Consolidated Fund, except that where the money services business concerned is to be conducted on the Island of Nevis, the licence fees and any other fees to be collected shall be paid by the licensee to the Nevis Island Administration and shall form part of the Consolidated Fund of the Island of Nevis.

10. (1) A licence granted under this Act authorises the licensee to carry on money services business in Saint Christopher and Nevis at the place of business designated in the licence.

(2) Where different places of business are kept in the name of the same person, a separate licence shall be taken out for each such place of business.

(3) No licensee shall open a new place of business or change the location of an existing place of business in Saint Christopher and Nevis without the prior approval of the Authority and no licensee shall close an existing place of business in Saint Christopher and Nevis without having given thirty days prior written notification to the Authority.

(4) A licensee which is formed under the laws of Saint Christopher and Nevis shall not open a place of business elsewhere than in Saint Christopher and Nevis without the prior written approval of the Authority.

(5) A licensee which is formed under the laws of Saint Christopher and Nevis shall not close a place of business outside of Saint Christopher and Nevis without having given twenty-one days prior written notification to the Authority.

11. A licensee shall display or cause to be displayed and shall keep displayed a copy of the certificate of its licence granted under this Act in a conspicuous place in the public part of any place of business of the licensee.

12. (1) No licensee shall be granted or continue to hold a licence under a name which:

(a) is identical to that of any company, firm or business house, whether within Saint Christopher and Nevis or not, or that so nearly resembles that name as to be misleading;

(b) falsely suggests, the patronage of or connection with some person or Minister, whether within Saint Christopher and Nevis or not;

(c) falsely suggests, that the money services business has a special status in relation to or derived from the Government, has the official backing of or acts on behalf of the Government or any department, branch, agency or organ of Government, or of any officer of Government or is recognised in Saint Christopher and Nevis as a national or central money services business.

(2) The Authority may refuse to grant a licence to or revoke the licence of a person who contravenes subsection (1).

(3) A person who contravenes subsection (1) commits an offence and is liable on summary conviction to a fine of fifty thousand dollars or to imprisonment for a term of two years or to both such fine and imprisonment.

13. (1) No person, other than a licensee or any entity to which this Act does not apply pursuant to section 3, shall

(a) use any English or foreign words in the description or title under which the person carries on business within Saint Christopher and Nevis, representing that that person is carrying on money services business;

(b) make any representation in any billhead, letter, letterhead, circular, paper, notice or advertisement or in any other manner that that person is carrying on money services business within Saint Christopher and Nevis; or

(c) in any manner solicit or receive money from any person for the purpose of carrying on money services business within Saint Christopher and Nevis.

(2) A person who contravenes subsection (1) commits an offence and is liable on summary conviction to a fine of fifty thousand dollars or to imprisonment for a term of two years or both such fine and imprisonment.

Restrictions of names likely to mislead.

Advertisement.

Actions of fundamental change requiring approval.

Change in directorship.

14. Unless the approval of the Authority is first obtained no licensee shall:

(a) change its name;

(b) change its principal office;

(c) transfer the whole or any substantial part of its assets or liabilities in Saint Christopher and Nevis other than in the ordinary course of its business; or

(d) enter into a merger or consolidation within Saint Christopher and Nevis.

15. (1) A licensee must, no less than thirty days prior to the proposed date of appointment of a director or other senior officer:

(a) submit to the Authority a completed Form B in Schedule 2 and the prescribed application form in respect of each proposed appointee; and

(b) obtain approval of the Authority for appointment of the proposed appointee as director or other senior officer.

(2) Upon receipt of the completed Form B in Schedule 2 and the prescribed application form the Authority shall conduct an investigation at the expense of the applicant to determine whether the proposed appointee satisfies the fit and proper criteria established in section 6 (5).

(3) Within six weeks of the receipt of the completed Form B in Schedule 2 and the prescribed application form the Authority shall:

(a) approve the appointment of the proposed appointee to the proposed post and notify the licensee; or

(b) inform the licensee that the proposed appointee does not satisfy the fit and proper criteria and refuse approval for appointment of the proposed appointee as director or other senior officer.

(4) Notwithstanding subsection (1), where prior notification of the appointment of a proposed appointee as director or other senior officer of a licensee is not possible, the licensee:

(a) may appoint the proposed appointee as director or other senior officer as the case may be, conditional on the approval of the Authority in accordance with subsection (3); and

(b) shall within five days of such appointment submit to the Authority the forms prescribed under subsection (1) and a letter specifying the reasons for the appointment of the proposed appointee without prior approval.

PART III AUDIT,INFORMATIONANDEXAMINATION

16. (1) A licensee shall appoint annually an auditor who must be a chartered accountant, a certified public accountant, a member of the Institute of Chartered Accountants of the Eastern Caribbean (ICAEC) or some other professionally qualified accountant, satisfactory to the Authority whose duties shall:

(**a**) be to examine the books and records and to make a report on the annual financial statements and financial position; and

(b) include all or any of the following duties as may from time to time be imposed on the auditor by the licensee at the request of the Authority:

(i) to submit such additional information in relation to the audit of the licensee as the Authority considers necessary;

(ii) to carry out any other examination or establish any procedure in any particular case;

(iii) to submit a report on any of the matters referred to in sub-paragraphs (i) and (ii);

(iv) to submit a report on the financial and accounting systems and risk management controls of the licensee;

(v) to provide an opinion on whether suitable measures to counter money laundering and to combat the financing of terrorism have been adopted by the licensee and are being implemented in accordance with the applicable laws.

(2) A licensee shall within three months of the end of the financial year, forward the audited financial statements referred to in subsection (1) to the Authority unless prior written approval for an extension has been granted by the Authority.

(3) The audited financial statements referred to in subsection (1) shall cover a period of not more than eighteen months beginning on the date the licensee was incorporated, or if the licensee has previously prepared audited financial statements, beginning at the end of the period covered by the most recent audited financial statements.

Annual audit, report and publication of financial statements and results.

(4) A designated licensee shall submit audited financial statements annually to the Central Bank in accordance with the provisions of the Payment SystemsAct, 2008 and shall submit a copy of such audited financial statements to the Authority.

(5) A licensee shall remunerate the auditor in respect of the discharge by the auditor of all or any of the duties set out in subsection (1).

(6) If in the course of the performance of an auditor's duties an auditor is satisfied that:

(a) there has been a serious breach of or non-compliance with the provisions of this Act or any regulations, notice, order, guidelines or directions issued under this Act;

(b) there is evidence:

(i) that a criminal offence involving fraud or other dishonesty may have been committed; or

(ii) of any suspicious transaction as defined in the Anti-Money Laundering Regulations 2001, issued pursuant to the Proceeds of Crime Act, 2000, the auditor shall immediately report the matter to the licensee and the Authority.

(7) The Authority may request copies of reports submitted to the licensee by both its internal and external auditors.

(8) An auditor shall report to the Authority any matter it is required to report on any licensee to any investigative, regulatory or other institution, simultaneously with its report to that institution.

(9) A licensee who fails to secure compliance with a request under subsection (1) (b) commits an offence and is liable on summary conviction to a fine not exceeding fifty thousand dollars for each such failure.

(10) If a licensee fails to appoint an auditor satisfactory to the Authority, the Authority may appoint an auditor for such licensee. The remuneration of the auditor so appointed shall be determined by the

Authority and paid by the licensee.

(11) The Authority may appoint an auditor to conduct an independent audit of a licensee, in accordance with the instructions of the Authority, and to report the findings or results to the Authority.

(12) No auditor shall be liable for breach of any duty solely by reason of compliance with the provisions of subsections (1), (6) or (8), of this section or any other request for information by the Authority.

(13) (a) No person having an interest in any licensee otherwise than as a depositor and no director, manager, secretary, employee or agent of a licensee shall be eligible for appointment as auditor for such licensee; and

(b) any person appointed as auditor who shall, after an appointment, acquire any interest in a licensee, or become a director, manager, secretary, employee or agent of such licensee shall immediately cease to be such auditor.

(14) The Minister may by Order:

(a) exempt any licensee or any class of licensee from the audit requirement contained in subsection (1) of this section;

(b) waive the audit requirement contained in subsection (1) of this section in respect of any licensee or any class of licensee;

(c) require that the Authority conduct an ad hoc audit of any licensee or any class of licensee in respect of which the audit requirement is waived or lifted under paragraphs (a) and (b) of this subsection.

(15) The Authority may assess a licensee for the reasonable expenses of conducting any ad hoc audit ordered by the Minister under paragraph (c) of subsection (14).

A licensee must notify the Authority in writing of its intention to terminate the appointment of its auditor, or not to reappoint its auditor for a new term, and state the reasons for its decision in the notification.

(1) A licensee must in accordance with this section, in respect of its money services business:

keep accounting records; and

establish and maintain systems

of internal control and record keeping, and

for inspection and report.

(2) The systems of control, inspection and report shall ensure that the money services business is so conducted and its records so kept that:

Notice of termination of auditor's appointment.

Accounting records and systems of business control.

Returns.

Extension of time for providing information.

Retention of records.

(a) the information necessary to enable the directors and the business to discharge their duties and functions is sufficiently accurate, and is available with sufficient regularity or as needed and with sufficient promptness, for those purposes; and

(b) the information obtained by or furnished to the Authority under or for the purposes of this Act is sufficiently accurate for the purpose for which it is obtained or furnished.

(3) A licensee shall institute procedures to ensure that its accounting records and systems of business control comply with the requirements of the Anti-Money Laundering Regulations 2001, issued pursuant to the Proceeds of Crime Act, 2000.

19. (1) The holder of a Class A or Class B licence, must, in the format provided by the Authority, file quarterly returns with the Authority within fifteen days of the end of a quarter, along with a written declaration that the information set out in the application for the licence remains correct and gives a full and fair picture of its money services business.

(2) The holder of a Class C, Class D or Class E licence must, within fifteen days of the end of the financial year, file an annual return with the Authority along with a written declaration that the information set out in the application for the licence remains correct and gives a full and fair picture of its money services business.

(3) A designated licensee must submit a copy of its returns to the Central Bank within the stipulated time.

(4) A licensee who fails to file the returns within the time stipulated in subsections (1) or (2) commits an offence and is liable on summary conviction to a fine of fifty thousand dollars or to imprisonment for a term of two years or to both such fine and imprisonment.

At the request of a licensee, the Authority may extend, from time to time, any period within which such licensee is, in accordance with the provisionsof thisAct, obliged to furnishanydocument or information

(1) A licensee shall retain for a period of at least five years from the date of creation of each particular record, all records created and obtained by them, in particular records of each

transaction executed by them, records of each outstanding transaction, bank reconciliation records and bank statements received during the course of operation and administration of its money services business.

(2) The retention of records under subsection (1) may be effected by electronic means.

22. (1) The Authority, shall examine or cause an examination to be made of each licensee from time to time or whenever in its judgment such examination is necessary or expedient in order to determine that such licensee is in a sound financial condition and that the requirements of this Act have been complied with in the conduct of its business.

(2) For the purpose of determining the condition of a licensee and its compliance with this Act, the Authority may at any time examine or cause an examination to be made of any affiliate of the licensee in Saint Christopher and Nevis to the same extent that an examination may be made of the licensee.

(3) The Authority may assess a licensee for the reasonable expenses of conducting an examination under subsections (1) and (2).

(4) The Authority shall forward copies of balance sheets, statements and reports on the results of any examination to the licensee.

(5) A licensee refusing to make available for examination any books, accounts and records having been requested to do so by the Authority commits an offence and is liable on summary conviction to a fine not exceeding fifty thousand dollars or imprisonment for a term not exceeding two years or to both such fine and imprisonment.

23. No person who has acquired knowledge in his capacity as director, manager, secretary, officer, employee or agent of any licensee or as its auditor or receiver or official liquidator or as director, officer, employee or agent of the Authority, shall disclose to any person or governmental authority the identity, assets, liabilities, transactions or other information in respect of a customer of the licensee except:

(a) with the written authorisation of the customer or of his heirs or legal personal representatives; or

(b) for the purpose of the performance of his duties within the scope of his employment in conformity with the provisions of this Act; or

(c) when lawfully required to make disclosure by any court of competent jurisdiction within Saint Christopher and Nevis; or

(d) under the provisions of any law of Saint Christopher and Nevis.

24. Notwithstanding section 23, the Authority may:

(a) share any information received or any report prepared by it in the performance of its duties under this Act, with the Central Bank or any foreign authority responsible for the supervision or regulation of

Examination by Authority.

Confidential information.

Exchange of information.

affiliates of a licensee, or for maintaining the integrity

Segregated accounts.

Bankruptcy or insolvency of licensee.

Utilisation of deposits, etc.

of the financial system; or

(b) provide access, to any officer of the Central Bank or a foreign authority responsible for the supervision or regulation of affiliates of a licensee in order to assess the safety and soundness of an affiliate;

on a reciprocal basis and subject to

(i) an agreement of confidentiality and a Memorandum of Understanding between the Authority and the Central Bank or such authorities; and

(ii) any law on the protection of confidential information.

PART IV SEGREGATEDACCOUNTS, BANKRUPTCYORINSOLVENCYOFLICENSEE

25. (1) A licensee on receipt of funds from a customer shall immediately and irrevocably segregate the amount intended for transmission or delivery to the payee customer exclusively for the purpose of the proper payment of the funds in due course to the payee customer.

(2) Any funds which are not delivered or transmitted to the payee customer by or on behalf of the licensee shall be a first charge on the assets of a bankrupt or otherwise insolvent licensee and shall be:

(**a**) re-paid to the payor customer; or

(b) paid to the payee customer;

by the licensee, receiver, liquidator or administrator out of the segregated account to which it was placed or was deemed to have been placed.

26. (1) Alicensee must notifythe Authorityas soon as practicable after bankruptcy or insolvency proceedings are instituted.

(2) A person does not contravene subsection (1) if he took reasonable steps to comply with that subsection.

(3)

A person who contravenes subsection (1) commits an offence and is liable on summary conviction to a fine not exceeding fifty thousand dollars.

27. (1) Notwithstanding anything to the contrary in the Bankruptcy Act, Chapter 9, the Companies Act, 1996, or the Companies Ordinance No. 4 of 1999, any funds delivered to a licensee by or on behalf of a customer, prior to the issue of any bankruptcy, winding-up or receivership order against that licensee shall be utilised by the licensee, receiver or liquidator solely to discharge the licensee's contractual obligations to the customer.

(2) Notwithstanding anything to the contrary in the Bankruptcy Act, Chapter 9, the Companies Act, 1996, or the Companies Ordinance No. 4 of 1999, if a licensee goes into bankruptcy, receivership or is wound up any provision contained in a written agreement between that licensee and a customer is binding upon the liquidator, receiver or administrator in respect of any payment or settlement obligation.

(3) A person who contravenes the provisions of this subsection (1) commits an offence and is liable on summary conviction to a fine not exceeding fifty thousand dollars.

PART V ABANDONEDPROPERTY

28. (1) Subject to subsection (2) the following items which are held or owing by a licensee shall be presumed to be abandoned:

(**a**) any funds paid in Saint Christopher and Nevis toward the purchase of shares or other interests in a licensee, together with any interest or dividend, but excluding any lawful charges;

(b) any sum payable on written instruments issued in Saint Christopher and Nevis on which a licensee is directly liable or;

(c) any sum delivered to the licensee for transmittal to a person in Saint Christopher and Nevis or in another jurisdiction for and on behalf of a payee.

(2) The items enumerated in subsection (1) shall not be presumed to be abandoned if the owner has

(a) corresponded in writing with the licensee concerning the items; or

(b) otherwise indicated an interest in the items as evidenced by a memorandum concerning them written by a licensee within two years of the date of deposit, payment of funds or issuance of instruments, as the case may be.

29. (1) A licensee who holds any of the items enumerated in section 28 shall within ninety days after the end of its financial year report such holdings to the Authority, and subsequently pay or deliver to the Authority all property presumed to be abandoned listed in the report in accordance with Regulations issued by the Minister under this Act.

Abandoned property.

Report, publication and disposal of abandoned property.

Sale and handling of proceeds of sale of abandoned property.

Claims on abandoned property.

Penalties for failure to file abandoned property report.

(2) Upon paying or delivering such property identified in subsection (1) into the custody of the Authority a licensee is relieved of all liability to the extent of the value of the property for any claim in that respect.

(3) Within thirty days after the end of its financial year but before the filing of the report to the Authority required by subsection (1), a licensee shall publish in the ***Gazette*** and a newspaper circulating in Saint Christopher and Nevis the name of the owner and particulars concerning the property and shall mail a notice to the owner at his last known address containing particulars concerning the property.

30. (1) A licensee may sell at public sale all property other than money presumed to be abandoned after the expiration of sixty days from the later date of publication or mailing required by section 29(3) following such advertisement of the sale as the Minister may prescribe.

(2) A purchaser shall receive title to the property free from all claims of the owner or prior holder and from all persons claiming through or under him.

(3) A licensee shall deposit with the Authority the proceeds of the sale of property in accordance with subsection (1) less all reasonable costs incurred by it in connection with the sale, mailing of notices, and service as it may deem appropriate to assure the prompt payment of claims which may subsequently be made and approved by the Minister.

(4) Any property remaining unsold shall be delivered to the Authority and shall be disposed of by the Authority in such manner as the Minister may direct.

31. (1) Any person claiming an interest in any property which has been paid to, or delivered into the custody of the Authority or in the proceeds from the sale may file a claim, with the Authority and, after an appropriate hearing the decision of which shall be communicated to the claimant and made a public record, the Authority may deliver up the property or make payment.

(2) Any person aggrieved by a decision of the Authority may commence an action in the High Court to establish his claim within thirty days following the decision of the Authority.

32. (1) A licensee shall not willfully fail to file the report or to pay or deliver property presumed to be abandoned into the custody of the Authority in accordance with section 29 (1) or 30 (4).

(2) A licensee who contravenes subsection (1) commits an offence, and it and each of its directors shall be liable on summary conviction to a fine not exceeding one thousand dollars or to imprisonment for a term not exceeding three months or to both such fine and imprisonment.

PART VI ENFORCEMENT

33. (1) The Authority may revoke any licence to carry on money services business in Saint Christopher and Nevis if the licensee:

(**a**) fails to commence operations within a period of three (3) months following the granting of the licence;

(b) fails to comply with the conditions or restrictions of its licence;

(c) is in breach of any of the provisions of this Act;

(d) ceases to carry on money services business in Saint Christopher and Nevis for a period in excess of ten months;

(e) is conducting its affairs in a manner detrimental to the public interest or to the interest of its customers;

(f) goes into liquidation or is wound up or otherwise dissolved; or

(g) by reason of any other circumstance, is no longer a fit and proper person to hold a licence.

(2) The Authority shall terminate a licence at the request of the licensee.

(3) Before revoking a licence under subsection (1), the Authority shall give the licensee concerned notice in writing of its intention to do so, specifying therein the grounds upon which it proposes to make the revocation and shall require the licensee to submit to it within a specified period being not less than thirty days, a statement of objections to the making of the revocation and thereafter, the Authority shall advise the licensee of its decision.

(4) Notice under subsection (3) shall be served at the licensee's last known address and shall be published in the ***Gazette*** or in any local newspaper.

(5) If any licensee is aggrieved by any decision made under subsection (1), that licensee may appeal to the High Court within fourteen days of such decision, setting out the grounds of such appeal, and the High Court may revoke or confirm the said decision.

(6) Where a licence to carry on money services business in Saint Christopher and Nevis has been revoked, the Authority shall, as soon as possible thereafter cause a notice of the revocation to be Revocation and termination of licence.

Suspension of licence.

Persons carrying on money services business without a licence.

published in the ***Gazette*** and a newspaper circulating in Saint Christopher and Nevis and cause such other steps to be taken as are deemed to be necessary to inform the public of such revocation.

04. (1) The Authority may, if it thinks it necessary.

(a) as a matter of urgency for the protection of the public, or

(b) as a result of any investigation under this Act or Regulations made under this Act;

suspend a licence granted under this Act for such period, or until the happening of an event, as the Authority considers appropriate.

(2) A person whose licence is suspended under this Act shall be notified accordingly by the Authority and shall, for the purpose of this Act, be deemed not to be licensed from the date of notification of suspension.

(3) Notice under subsection (2) shall be served at the licensee's last known address and shall be published in the ***Gazette*** or in any newspaper circulating in Saint Christopher and Nevis

(4) If any licensee is aggrieved by any decision made under subsection (1), that licensee may appeal to the High Court within fourteen days of such decision, setting out the grounds of such appeal, and the High Court may revoke or confirm the said decision.

35. (1) If the Authority has reasonable cause to suspect that

(a) any person is carrying on money services business without a licence granted under this Act; and

(b) evidence of contravention of section 4(1) is to be found on any premises in Saint Christopher and Nevis,

the Authority may lay information on oath before a Magistrate as regards its suspicions.

(2) Upon filing of the information in subsection (1), the Magistrate may, by warrant, authorise an officer of the Authority named in such warrant to enter and search such premises with the assistance of the police and seize any books, accounts, records, vouchers and other documents, cheques, securities and any cash as may be found on the premises relating to the conduct of money services business, to ascertain whether the person is carrying on money services business without a licence.

(3) Any such warrant may authorise:

(a) the Authority to detain the books, accounts, records, vouchers and other documents, cheques, securities and any cash for a period not exceeding thirty days;

(b) the officer to make copies of the books, accounts, records, vouchers and other documents, cheques, securities and any cash; and

(c) the Authority to retain copies of the books, accounts, records, vouchers and other documents, cheques, securities and any cash.

(4) The person authorised by a warrant to search any premises may:

(a) seize any books, accounts, records, vouchers and other documents, cheques, securities and any cash found:

(i) in the premises; or

(ii) in the possession of any person described in paragraph (b) of this sub-section;

if he has reasonable grounds for believing that any of those books, accounts, records, vouchers and other documents, cheques, securities and any cash relate to the conduct of money services business on those premises.

(b) search every person who:

(i) is found in those premises; or

(ii) has recently left or is about to enter those premises;

whom he has reasonable grounds to believe is in possession of any books, accounts, records, vouchers and other documents, cheques, securities and any cash in respect of the conduct of money services business on those premises.

(5) In pursuance of any warrant issued under this section, no person shall be searched by an officer of the opposite sex.

(6) Where under this section a person has the power to enter any premises, he may if necessaryuse reasonable force to enter the premises.

(7) A person who obstructs the Authority or any other person in the exercise of any powers conferred under this section commits an offence and is liable on summary conviction to a fine of five thousand dollars or to imprisonment for a term of six months or both such fine and imprisonment.

36. (1) Without prejudice to section 4(1), where a person is found under section 35 (1) to be conducting money services business without a licence, the Authority mayapply to the court for appointment of a receiver to liquidate the business.

Appointment of receiver.

Authority may apply to court to preserve customers' interests.

Powers of the Authority in respect of licensees.

(2) Before applying for the appointment of a receiver under subsection (1), the Authority shall give the person concerned notice in writing of its intention to do so and shall require the person to comply with the requirements of this Act within a specified period being not less than thirty days and thereafter the Authority shall advise the person of its decision.

37.(1) The Authority may, in a case where a licensee, or a person who has at any time been a licensee, is being wound up voluntarily, apply to the Court if the Authority considers that the winding up is not being conducted in the best interests of the licensee's customers or creditors, and the Court shall make any order it considers appropriate.

(2) If it appears to the Authority that there is reasonable ground for suspecting that an offence against this Act has been or is being committed by any person, the Authority may, with the approval of the court, take any action it considers necessary, in the interest of the person's customers or creditors, to preserve any assets held by that person.

38. (1) Whenever the Authority is of the opinion that:

(a) a licensee is or appears likely to become unable to meet its obligations as they fall due;

(b)

a licensee is carrying on business in a manner detrimental to the public interest or the interest of its customers or creditors;

(c) a licensee has contravened this Act;

(d) a licensee has failed to comply with a condition of its licence;

(e) there has been or is, on the part of a licensee or its directors, a failure to satisfy any one or more of the criteria of prudent management set out in section 41;

(f) a licensee, director, manager, secretary or other officer concerned in the management of a licensee refuses to cooperate with the Authority in the performance of its functions under section 40;

(g) a licensee is carrying on business in an unlawful manner;

(h) a licensee has failed to maintain the prescribed capital; or

(i) is violating any law, regulation or guideline to which the licensee or person is subject;

the Authority may take one or more of the measures set out in subsection (2).

(2) Without prejudice to sections 33 and 34, the measures that the Authority may take in pursuance of subsection (1) are as follows:

(a) impose conditions, or further conditions, as the case may be, upon the licence and may amend or revoke any of the conditions;

(b) require the suspension or removal of a director or officer of the licensee;

(c) at the expense of the licensee, appoint a person to advise the licensee on the proper conduct of its affairs and to report to the Authority within three months of the date of his appointment, or any extension of appointment and at such intervals as the Authority may require;

(d) at the expense of the licensee, appoint a person to assume control of the licensee's affairs who shall, have all the powers of a person appointed as a receiver or manager under the Bankruptcy Act, Chapter 9, who shall report to the Authority within three months of the date of his appointment, or any extension of appointment and at such intervals as the Authority may require;

(e) require a licensee, to take, refrain from, or discontinue any action as the Authority considers necessary;

(f) revoke the licence.

(3) The Authority may, on receipt of a report under subsection (2):

(a) revoke the appointment of the person appointed under subsection (2)(c) or (d);

(b) extend the period of appointment of a person appointed under subsection 2 (c) or (d);

(c) subject to any conditions that the Authority may impose, allow the licensee to reorganise its affairs in a manner approved by the Authority; or,

(d) revoke the licence.

(4) The Authority must comply with the procedures established in subsections (3), (4), (5) and (6) of section 33 if it decides to revoke a licence pursuant to subsections 2(f) and 3(d).

(5) If any licensee is aggrieved by any decision made under subsection (2), that licensee may appeal to the High Court within fourteen days of such decision, setting out the grounds of such appeal, and the High Court may revoke or confirm the decision.

Transactions effected prior to suspension or revocation of licence.

Powers and duties of the Authority.

The suspension or revocation of a license under this Act does not void or affect any agreement, transaction or arrangement relating to a provision of money services business entered into by the licensee before the suspension or revocation of the licence and does not affect any right, obligation, or liability arising under any such agreement, transaction or arrangement.

(1) The Authority shall ensure the proper administration of this Act and without limiting the generality of the foregoing, shall:

maintain a general review of money services business practice in Saint Christopher and Nevis;

whenever it thinks fit, examine the affairs or business of any licensee carrying on business within Saint Christopher and Nevis for the purpose of satisfying itself that this Act has been or is being complied with and that the licensee is in a sound financial position and is managing its business in a prudent manner;

assist in the investigation of any offence against the laws of Saint Christopher and Nevis which it has reasonable grounds to believe has or may have been committed by a licensee or by any of its directors or officers in their capacity as directors or officers;

examine

returns furnished to it under section 19, and

audited financial statements forwarded to it under section 16, and report on them to the Minister whenever it thinks fit;

require or perform consolidated supervision of affiliates whenever it thinks fit; and

cooperate with and facilitate the Central Bank in consolidated supervision of designated licensees.

(2) In the performance of its functions under this Act the Authority is entitled at all reasonable times:

(a) to have access to the premises, books, records, vouchers, documents, cash and securities of any licensee;

(b) to remove and make copies of any books, records, vouchers and documents found on the premises of a licensee;

(c) to request the information, matter or thing from any person who it has reasonable grounds to believe is carrying on money services business in contravention of section 4(1); and

(d) to call upon the manager of the licensee or any similar person, or an officer designated by either of them, for any information or explanation, the Authority may require for the purpose of enabling it to perform its functions under this Act; and information requested under this subsection shall be provided in such form as the Authority may require.

(3) A person who fails to comply with a requirement under subsection (2) by the Authority commits an offence and is liable on summary conviction to a fine of fifty thousand dollars or to imprisonment for a term of two years or both such fine and imprisonment.

41. For the purpose of section 40(1)(b), the criteria of prudent management are as follows:

(a) maintenance of

(i) adequate reserves and other capital resources in amounts which may be prescribed by the Minister;

(ii) adequate assets in liquid form in amounts which may be prescribed by the Minister;

(iii) a system for managing and containing risks to the net worth of the licensee's business and risks to its net income, whether arising from fluctuations in interest or exchange rates or from other factors;

(iv) the requisite accounting records;

(v) systems of internal control and record keeping; and

(vi) systems for inspection and report;

(b) management conducted with prudence and integrity by a sufficient number of persons, having regard to the range and scale of the business, who are fit and proper to be directors or, as the case may be, officers of the licensee in accordance with the criteria established under section 6(5); and

(c) conduct of the licensee's business with adequate professional skills.

Criteria of prudent management.

Management's duty of compliance with the requirements of the law.

False or misleading information.

Removal and disqualification of officers.

A director, manager, secretary or other officer concerned in the management of a licensee who fails to take all reasonable steps to secure compliance by the licensee with the requirements of this Act commits an offence and is liable on summary conviction to a fine not exceeding fifty thousand dollars or to imprisonment for a term not exceeding two years or to both such fine and imprisonment.

A licensee, director or an officer of a licensee who knowingly or willfully supplies false or misleading information to the Authority commits an offence and is liable on summary conviction to a fine of fifty thousand dollars or to imprisonment for a term of two years or both such fine and imprisonment.

(1) Any person who is a director, manager or other officer concerned with the management of a licensee shall cease to hold office upon:

notification by its management team of a finding by two-thirds of its members of his permanent incapacity or serious neglect of, or misconduct in, office; or

his being declared bankrupt or compounding with, or suspending payment to, his creditors; or

his conviction in a court of law of any offence involving fraud or dishonesty; or

his being sentenced for an offence involving a term of imprisonment of at least six months or the payment of a fine in default of such a term of imprisonment,; or

his being deemed not to be a fit and proper person in accordance with the criteria established under section 6(5).

(2) No person who has been a director of, or directly or indirectly concerned, in, the management of a licensee, the licence of which has been revoked shall, without the approval of the Authority, act or continue to act as a director, or be directly or indirectly concerned in the management of any licensee.

(3) A person who contravenes subsection (1) or (2) commits an offence and is liable on summary conviction to a fine not exceeding fifty thousand dollars or to imprisonment for a term not exceeding two years or to both such fine and imprisonment.

45. (1) Where an offence under this Act has been committed by a body of persons which is:

(a) a body corporate, society or other body of persons, every person who at the time of the commission of the offence was a director, manager, secretary or other officer of the body corporate, society or other body of persons as well as that body corporate, society or other body of persons commits the offence;

(b) a partnership or firm, every partner of the partnership or firm as well as that partnership or firm commits the offence, and is liable to be proceeded against and punished accordingly.

(2) No person referred to in subsection (1) shall be convicted of an offence under that subsection where he proves, that:

(a) the act constituting the offence took place without his knowledge or consent, or

(b) he exercised all due diligence to prevent the commission of the offence.

46. A person who contravenes any provision or requirement of this Act for which no offence is specifically created or penalty provided commits an offence and is liable on summary conviction to a fine not exceeding fifty thousand dollars or to imprisonment for a term of two years or both such fine and imprisonment.

PART VII IMMUNITIES,REGULATIONSANDGUIDELINES

Neither the Authority nor an employee of the Authority shall be liable for anything done or omitted in the discharge or purported discharge of its functions under this Act unless it is shown that the act or omission was in bad faith.

The Authority in administering the provisions of this Act may issue prudential guidelines and related orders and without limiting the generality of the foregoing may issue prudential guidelines and related orders respecting:

policies, practices and procedures for evaluating the quality of assets;

policies, procedures and systems for identifying, monitoring and controlling transfer risk, market risk, operational risk; and such other risks as the Authority shall specify;

corporate governance;

auditors;

procedures to be adopted by licensees and the Authority; and

Offences by officers of corporate bodies.

General penalty.

Immunity.

Prudential guidelines.

(f) anti-money laundering and combating the financing of

terrorism matters.

49. The Minister may make Regulations for giving effect to the provisions of this Act, and without limiting the generality of the foregoing, may make Regulations respecting:

Regulations.

(**a**) the form of advertising by licensees;

(b) registers and records to be kept under this Act;

(c) forms to be used by licensees;

(d) fees payable under this Act; and

(e) any other matter required to be prescribed under this Act.

SCHEDULE 1 [SECTION 5]

Classes of Licences

Class of Licence Description of Licence Class A Money Transmission Class B Issuance, Sale and Redemption of Payment Instruments Class C Cheque Cashing Class D Currency Exchange Class E Pay day advances

SCHEDULE 2 FORM A [SECTION 6]

INFORMATION TO BE CONTAINED INAND TO ACCOMPANY AN APPLICATIONFOR THE GRANT OFALICENCE

The name and address of the money services business in respect of which the licence is sought.

The name and address of the applicant.

The type of money services business the applicant proposes to conduct.

The source and quantum of funds for initial capital or acquisition of the money services business.

The address of the principal office of the applicant and of its registered office if different.

If the applicant is a corporation, limited liability company, partnership or other entity the applicant must provide –

the date and place of incorporation or formation and a copy of the memorandum andarticlesof association,Act, charter, partnershipagreement or other instrument constituting and defining the constitution of the applicant verified by a declaration made by one of its directors or partners or its secretary; and

a brief description of the structure or organisation of the applicant including any parent or subsidiary of the applicant.

The name and address of each person who –

owns or controls the money services business;

is a director or officer of the money services business;

is an agent of the applicant;

otherwise participates in the conduct of the affairs of the money services business.

The following information is also required from the named persons in Item 7 and each significant shareholder –

legal name and any alias and residential address;

occupation (over the previous five years) and business address;

date of birth;

citizenship;

[social security] [NIS] number;

passport number;

two (2) character references, a police or other certificate satisfactory to the Authority that the person has not been convicted of a serious crime or any offence involving dishonesty.

The name and address of any depository institution at which a transaction account is maintained for the purposes of the money services business.

Where appropriate a statement in writing in a form acceptable to the Authority from the body responsible for the administration of the laws relating to money services businesses and the supervision of the businesses in the country in which the applicant or its parent company is incorporated that the body has no objection to the application being made.

11. If the applicant is a company the following information is required (where applicable) –

(a) the annual accounts for the two year period immediately preceding the date of the application, of each significant shareholder which is a body corporate, together with similar accounts for the parent body, if any, of each of the bodies corporate or the annual accounts for the current year, in the case of a body corporate which is in existence for less than two years,

(b) two or more references verifying the good financial standing of each significant shareholder who is a natural person;

(c) the name and address of its proposed auditor;

(d) a statement giving the date for the drawing up of the annual accounts of the applicant;

(e) confirmation in writing under the hand of the presiding officer of the applicant and the presiding officer of its parent body, if any, that they concur in the making of the application;

(f) three business references of which at least one shall be from a bank;

(g) a detailed business plan, containing details of the current money services business activities, if any, of the applicant and its proposed activities if the licence applied for is granted, including;

(i) the reasons for applying for the licence;

(ii) the business aims of the applicant in respect of the money services business and its potential client base;

(iii) a detailed statement setting out its proposed initial assets and its proposed assets and expected liabilities at the end of each of the two years next succeeding the date of such grant together with an estimate of expected income;

(iv) particulars of its management structure and personnel;

(v) the names and addresses of the registered offices of all subsidiary companies of the applicant together with a statement as to how much of the capital of each company constitutes an asset of the applicant;

(vi) a chart showing the relationship to its subsidiaries and affiliates and any holding company; and

(vii) a brief description of each of its subsidiaries and affiliates; (viii) details of the identified economic needs that the applicant intends to meet, growth prospects in that service area over the next five years, the exact nature and source of capital financing to be made available to the company for start-up and ongoing operations;

(h) details of the applicant's proposals for establishing and maintaining, in respect of the money services business, systems of control, inspection and report, if the licence applied for is granted;

(i) in the case of a company incorporated outside the State, the name and address of the supervisory or regulatory authority responsible for the supervision of each of the applicant's agents operating outside the State.

If the applicant is a franchise holder the contract and any other documents relating to the operation of the franchise.

General requirements –

the applicant must submit a description of any money services business, other than that which is the subject of the application, previously or currently engaged in by the applicant;

the applicant must submit completed copies of a Personal Questionnaire for each executive officer, director and significant shareholder;

the applicant must submit copies of the applicant's audited financial statements.

Any other information requested by the Authority.

FORM B

PERSONALQUESTIONNAIRE [Fit and Proper Test] PARTA

NAME:

PREVIOUS NAMES(IFANY):

ALIASES: ______________________DATE OF BIRTH: ________________

CITIZENSHIP:

PLACE OF BIRTH

[SOCIALSECURITY][NIS] NUMBER:

PASSPORT NUMBER: ADDRESS (Home & Business):

OCCUPATION:

Have you at any time been charged or convicted of any offence by a civil, criminal or military court? (excluding minor Road Traffic offences). If so, please give details of charge, and if convicted, the date of conviction and full particulars of the offence and the penalty imposed.

Have you ever been the subject of investigation/disciplinary procedures, censured, disciplined by any professional body to which you belong or have belonged? If so, give particulars.

Have you ever been refused entry to any profession or vocation? If so, give particulars.

Have you ever been dismissed or requested to resign from any office or employment? If so, give particulars.

Have you ever been censured, disciplined by, or made the subject of a court order at the instigation of

any regulatory authority?

any officially appointed enquiry?

(c) any other established body concerned with the regulation of a relevant activity (as described in the glossary at the end of this form) ? If so, give particulars.

In connection with the formation or management of any corporation, have you been adjudged by a court civilly or criminally liable for any fraud, misfeasance or other misconduct towards that corporation or any member of the corporation? If so, give particulars.

In connection with the formation or management of any corporation have you been disqualified by a court from being a director or from acting in the management or conduct of the affairs of any corporation? If so, give particulars.

Have you ever –

been adjudged bankrupt by a court in any jurisdiction?

had a receiving order made against you?

had your estate sequestrated?

entered into a deed of arrangement, or other composition or arrangement with your creditors?

Has a bankruptcy petition ever been served on you? If pending, give details of the circumstances and if not pending, how was the matter resolved?

If so, give particulars.

Have you, your company or your employer, previously dealt on a regular basis with any person carrying on a relevant activity (as described in the glossary at the end of this form) who has, to your knowledge at any time, indicated that he is unwilling to effect further transactions with you, your company or your employer, by reason of any act or omission by you? If so, give particulars.

Will you be actively engaged in the business or the entity to which this application relates and devote the major portion of your time to it?

PART B RELATEDOROTHERINTEREST

1. Are you a director of any company, partnership, corporate body or any other business organisation engaged in money services business? If so, state –

(a) name of company/corporation/etc;

(b) nature of business;

(c) date of commencement of directorship;

(d) whether or not employed on service contract (e.g. managing directorship)i n any case.

2. Have you been a director of a deposit taking institution, credit extending institution, other financial service provider, any other limited company or corporation other than those stated in the previous questions? If so, state –

(a) name of company/corporation;

(b) nature of business;

(c) date of commencement of directorship;

(d) date of cessation of directorship.

3. Are you or have you been engaged –

(a) in partnership?; or

(b) in business as a principal on your own account? If so, give particulars.

Are you a beneficial owner of any controlling interest in any unlisted private or public company? If so, give particulars.

Have you ever been a director of, or directly concerned with the management of a bank or other financial institution –

that has been wound up by a court?

the licence of which has been revoked?

which has been placed in receivership?

which has entered into a composition with its creditors?

whose business had been adjudged to have been conducted imprudently or fraudulently?

which has failed to meet the solvency requirements prescribed by law?

If so, give particulars.

6. Have you ever been a director, or been directly concerned with the management or conduct of affairs of any company which has gone into liquidation, whilst you were, or within one year of your being a director, or so concerned? If so, give details of the circumstances including the following –

(a) name of company;

(b) name of liquidator;

(c) address of liquidator.

7. Have you ever been concerned with the management or conduct of affairs of any corporation which, by reason of any matter relating to a time when you were so concerned, has been censured or disciplined by –

(a) any regulatory authority?

(b) any official appointed enquiry?

(c) any other body concerned with regulation of a relevant activity? If so, give particulars.

8. Do you (in your personal capacity or through any entity controlled by you) have outstanding debt of any amount sixty or more days in arrears? If so, state the following –

(a) form

(b) amount

(c) source

(d) maturity date

Has any person, firm or company guaranteed the indebtedness? If so, give particulars (see previous question).

Are you at present guaranteeing the debts and obligations of any third parties? If so, give particulars.

I,... certify that all the statements contained in this questionnaire are true, accurate and fair to the best of my knowledge and belief.

....

Signature

***AUDITEDFINANCIALSTATEMENTS**

If the applicant is a business that was in existence and operating prior to the date of application, copies of audited financial statements (balance sheet, profit and loss, auditor's report and notes to accounts) for the five consecutive years immediately preceding its application, except however that where such applicant has been functioning for less than five years, a copy of its audited financial statements for each year it has been in operation shall be sufficient.

Where item 1 is not applicable the opening balance sheet, (audited).

Operating projections for the proposed licensee's first five years of business. This should include balance sheet, income statement and cash flow projections prepared in an acceptable accounting format. Details of any financial or economic assumptions on which these projections are based should be clearly indicated.

Where applicant is a subsidiary or affiliate of another company, submit in addition to item 1 or 2, audited financial statements of the parent company and all other "connected" companies.

***GLOSSARY**

"connected" in relation to a company means two or more companies or groups of companies with interests which are so interrelated that they should be considered as a single unit;

"corporation" means a body corporate, incorporated in Saint Christopher and Nevis or elsewhere;

"relevant activity" means:

(a) banking, finance, insurance, money-lending, money management, debt financing, hire purchase financing, leasing or other financial activities;

(b) dealing in securities;

(c) providing investment or financial advice and management.

SCHEDULE 3 [Section 6] FORMOFLICENCE SAINT CHRISTOPHER AND NEVIS MONEY SERVICES BUSINESSACT, 2008

LICENCE No.

....is licensed under the Money Services Business Act, 2008 to carry on the business of ***[money transmission/issuance, sale and redemption of payment instruments/cheque cashing/currency exchange]**** within the State subject to the following conditions/restrictions:

....

The licensee shall forthwith notify the Authority of any change in the information supplied in the application for this licence.

....

Granted this day of , at [address].

Authority

**** Delete as necessary***

SCHEDULE4 [Sections 6 and 9] FEES

Class of Licence	Description of Licence	Fees	
		Application Fee	Annual Licence Fee
Class A	Transmission of money or monetary value in any form, the issuance, sale or redemption of money orders or traveller's cheques, cheque cashing, currency exchange	$1000,00	$5000,00
Class B	Issuance, sale or redemption of money orders or traveller's cheques, cheque cashing, currency exchange	$1000,00	$5000,00
Class C	Cheque Cashing	$1000,00	$5000,00
Class D	Currency Exchange	$1000,00	$5000,00
Class E	Pay day advances	$1000,00	$5000,00

ANTI-MONEY LAUNDERING REGULATIONS, 2001 NO. OF 2001 ARRANGEMENT OF REGULATIONS

The Minister, with the concurrence of the Premier of Nevis, hereby makes these Regulations in exercise of the powers conferred on him by section 67 of the Proceeds of Crime Act, No. 16 of 2000.

CITATION. These Regulations may be cited as the Anti-money Laundering Regulations 2001.

INTERPRETATION. (1) In these Regulations, unless the context otherwise requires,

No. 16 of 2000. "Act" means the Proceeds of Crime Act, 2000;

"applicant for business" means a person seeking to form a business relationship or carry out a one-off transaction with a relevant person who is carrying on relevant business in or from the Federation;

"business relationship" means arrangement between two or more persons where

(a) at least one of those persons is acting in the course of a business;

(b) the purpose of the arrangement is to facilitate the carrying out of transactions between the persons concerned on a frequent, habitual or regular basis; and

(c) the total amount of any payment or payments to be made by any person to any other in the course of that

arrangement is not known or capable of being ascertained at the time the arrangement is made;

"CFATF" means the Caribbean Financial Action Task Force on money laundering;

"Commission" means the Financial Services Commission established by section 3 of Financial Services Commission Act, 2000;

"Compliance Officer" also known as "Reporting Officer" means a senior office of a relevant person appointed under paragraph 12;

"FATF" means the Financial Action Task Force on money laundering;

"Guidance Notes" means the Guidance Notes on the Prevention of Money;

"one–off transaction" means a transaction other than a transaction carried out in the course of an established business relationship formed by a relevant person;

"regulated person" means any person carrying on a regulated business activity as defined under the No.16 of 2000. Proceeds of Crime Act.

"relevant business" means engaging by way of business in one or more of the businesses or transactions referred to in relation to a regulated person;

"relevant person" means a person carrying on relevant business;

"Reporting Authority" means the Financial Intelligence Unit established by section 3 of the Financial No. 15 of 2000. Intelligence Unit Act, 2000.

(2) For the purposes of these Regulations,

(a) a business relationship formed by any relevant person is an established business relationship where that person has obtained, under procedures maintained in accordance with these Regulations, satisfactory evidence of the identity of the person who, in relation to the formation of that business relationship, was the applicant for business;

(b) the question as to what constitutes satisfactory evidence of identity may be determined in accordance with the Guidance Notes; and

(c) key staff is a member of staff, who at any time in the course of his duties, has or may have, access to any information which may be relevant in determining whether any person is engaged in money laundering.

3. GENERAL REQUIREMENTS. (1) In conducting relevant business, a relevant person shall not form a business relationship or carry out a one-off transaction with or for another person unless the relevant person

(a) maintains

(i) identification procedures in accordance with regulations 4 to 6;

(ii) record keeping procedures in accordance with regulations 7 to 11;

(iii) internal reporting procedures in accordance with regulation 14; and

(iv) internal controls and communication procedures which are appropriate for the purposes of forestalling and preventing money laundering;

(b) takes appropriate measures from time to time for the purpose of making employees aware of

(i) the procedures maintained under sub-regulation (a); and

(ii) the provisions of the Act, any regulations made thereunder and any directives issued under these Regulations; and

(c) provides training for employees to assist them

(i) in the recognition and handling of transactions carried out by, on or behalf of, any person who is, or appears to be, engaged in money laundering;

(ii) in dealing with customers where such transactions have been reported to the Reporting Authority in accordance with the provisions of the Act.

(2) For the avoidance of doubt, it is declared that the requirements of sub-regulation (1) (a) shall apply in relation to a person with whom, prior to the coming into force of these Regulations, a business relationship or one-off transaction was formed or carried out and such relationship or transaction is subsisting or continues upon the coming into force of these Regulations and in such a case the reference in regulation 4, 5 and 6 as to the period when contact is first made shall be construed as if contact was made upon the coming into force of these Regulations.

(3) A relevant person shall submit for the approval of the Reporting Authority the identification procedures, record keeping procedures, internal reporting procedures and internal controls and communication procedures required to be maintained under sub-regulation (1)(a) and the Reporting Authority may keep, for its own use, copies of such documents.

4. IDENTIFICATION PROCEDURES IN RELATION TO NEW AND CONTINUING RELATIONSHIPS (1) A relevant person shall establish and maintain identification procedures which, as soon as is reasonably practicable after contact is first made between that person and business particular business relationship, require: an applicant for business concerning any

(a) the production by the applicant for business of a satisfactory evidence of his identity; or

(b) the taking of such measures as are specified in these Regulations as will produce satisfactory evidence of his identity

(2) Sub-regulation (1) shall not apply if there are reasonable grounds for believing that the applicant for business is

(a) a regulated person; or

(b) an authorized financial institution in a country or territory which is a member of the FATF or CFATF has anti-money laundering laws and procedures that are at least equivalent to those of the Federation.

(3) Sub-regulation (1) shall not apply if there are reasonable grounds for believing that the applicant for business

(a) acts in the course of a business in relation to which a regulatory authority outside the Federation exercises regulatory functions; and

(b) is based or incorporated in or formed under the law of a country or territory outside the Federation (which is a member of the FATF or CFATF) in which there are in force anti-money laundering laws and procedures that are at least equivalent to those of the Federation.

(4) For the purposes of sub-regulations (2) (b) and (3) (b), a country or territory outside the Federation shall be deemed to have in force anti-money laundering laws and procedures that are at least equivalent to those of the Federation if it is recognized by the Commission as specified in the Guidance Notes.

(5)A relevant person shall establish and maintain procedures which, in respect of transactions undertaken after a business relationship has been established in compliance with sub-regulation (1), require

(a) the satisfactory verification of evidence of identity produced under sub-regulation (1) (a) or

(b) the taking of such measures as are specified in the procedures as will produce satisfactory verification of evidence or identity produced under sub-regulation (1) (b), as soon as reasonably practicable after transactions are undertaken which are significantly different from the normal pattern of previous business.

(6) Procedures comply with this regulation if they require that when satisfactory evidence of identity or satisfactory verification of evidence of identity is not obtained or produced, the business relationship and transactions shall not proceed any further.

(7) A regulated person shall not, in the course of a business relationship, operate or keep open or keep anonymous account or accounts which are in fictitious names.

5. IDENTIFICATION PROCEDURES IN RELATION TO ONE-OFF TRANSACTIONS.

(1) A relevant person shall establish and maintain identification procedures which, as soon as reasonably practicable after contact is first made between that person and an applicant for business concerning any one-off transaction, require

(a) the production by the applicant of satisfactory evidence of his identity; or

(b) the taking of such measures as are specified in the procedures as will produce satisfactory evidence of his identity.

(2) Sub-regulation (1) shall not apply if there are reasonable grounds for believing that the applicant for business is a person specified in regulation 4 (2) or (3), and regulation 4 (4) shall apply accordingly.

(3) Procedures comply with this regulation if they require that when satisfactory evidence of identity is not obtained or produced, the business relationship and transaction shall not proceed any further.

6. IDENTIFICATION PROCEDURES IN RELATION TO INTRODUCED PERSONS.

(1) Where an applicant for business is introduced to a relevant person by a third party (in this regulation referred to as " the introducer") the relevant person shall establish and maintain identification procedures which, as soon as reasonably practicable after contact is first made between the relevant person and the introducer, require

(a) the production by the introducer of satisfactory evidence of the identity of the applicant; or

(b) the taking of such measures as are specified in these regulations as will produce satisfactory evidence of the identity of the applicant.

(2) Sub-regulation (1) shall not apply if there are reasonable grounds for believing that

(a) the introducer is a person specified in regulation 4 (2);or

(b) the relevant person and the applicant for business are bodies corporate in the same group.

(3) In sub-regulation (2) (b) the term "group", in relation to a body corporate, means that body corporate, any other body corporate which is its holding company or subsidiary and any other body corporate which is a subsidiary of that holding company, and "subsidiary" and "holding company" shall be

No. 22 of 1996. construed in accordance with the Companies Act.

(4) Sub-regulation (1) shall not apply it there are reasonable grounds for believing that

(a) the introducer acts in the course of a business in relation to which regulatory authority outside the Federation exercises regulatory functions; and

(b) the introducer is based or incorporated in or formed under the law of a country or territory outside the Federation which is a member of the FATF or CFATF and in which there are in force anti-money laundering laws and procedures that are at least equivalent to those of the Federation; and

(c) the introducer will comply with terms of business made in accordance with sub-regulation (6).

(5) Regulation 4 (4) applies to sub-regulation (4)(b) as if the reference to sub-regulation (2) (b) and (3) (b) in regulation 4 (4) were a reference to sub-regulation (4)(b).

(6) Written terms of business between the relevant person and the introducer shall, notwithstanding sub-regulation (2), in all cases require the introducer

(a) to verify the identity of all applicants for business introduced to the relevant person sufficiently to comply with the requirements of the Act, and Regulations made thereunder.

(b) to maintain a record of the evidence of verification of identity and records of all transactions for at least five years calculated in accordance with regulation 9 (1);

(c) to supply to the relevant person forthwith upon request evidence of the verification of identity in any particular case; and

(d) to inform the relevant person specifically of each case where the introducer is not required or has been unable to verify the identity of the applicant.

(7) Procedures comply with this regulation if they require that when satisfactory evidence of identity is not obtained or produced, the business relationship and transactions shall not proceed any further.

7. MAINTAINING A RECORD OF VERIFICATION OF IDENTITY.

Where a relevant person is required under these Regulations to verify the identity of a person, the relevant person

. shall establish and maintain a record in the Federation which

(a) indicates the nature of the evidence obtained; and

(b) comprises a copy of the evidence or, where this is not reasonably practicable, contains such information as would enable a copy of the evidence to be obtained.

8. MAINTAINING A RECORD OF TRANSACTIONS. Where a relevant person is required under these Regulations to verify the identity of a person, the relevant person shall maintain a record of all transactions carried out by or on behalf of that person (such as records sufficient to identify the source and recipient of payments from which investigating authorities will be able to compile an audit trail for suspected money laundering).

9. LIMITATION PERIOD FOR RETENTION OF RECORDS.

(1) A relevant person shall maintain the records required by regulations 6, 7 and 8 for at least five years from the date

(a) when all activities relating to one-off transaction or a series of linked transactions were completed;

(b) when the business relationship was formally ended; or

(c) where the business relationship was not formally ended, when the last transaction was carried out.

(2) Where a report has been made to the Reporting Authority in pursuance of regulation 14 (1) (f), or the relevant person knows or believes that a matter is under investigation, that person shall without prejudice to sub-regulation (1), retain all relevant records for as long as may be required by the Reporting Authority.

(3) For the purposes of this regulation, the question as to what records may be relevant in the investigation process may be determined in accordance with the Guidance Notes.

10. FORMAT AND RETRIEVAL OF RECORDS.

(1) A relevant person shall ensure that any records required to be maintained under these Regulations are capable of retrieval in legible form without undue delay.

(2) A relevant person may rely on the records of a third party in respect of the details of payments and transactions by customers, provided that it is satisfied that the third party is willing and able to retain and, if asked, to produce in legible form, copies of the records required.

11. MAINTAINING A REGISTER OF MONEY LAUNDERING ENQUIRIES. (1) A relevant person shall maintain a register of all enquiries made of it by the Commission and other law enforcement authorities acting under powers provided by the Act or any other Acts and any regulations made thereunder.

(2) The register maintained under sub-regulation (1) shall be kept separate from other records and shall contain as a minimum the date and nature of the enquiry, the name and agency of the inquiring officer, the powers being exercised, and details of the accounts or transactions involved.

12. DUTY TO APPOINT COMPLIANCE OFFICER.

(1) A relevant person shall appoint or designate one of his staff, as may be approved by the Commission as a Compliance Officer for the purposes of these Regulations.

(2) A Compliance Officer shall

(a) be a senior officer with relevant qualifications and experience to enable him to respond sufficiently well to enquiries relating to the relevant person and the conduct of its business;

(b) be responsible for establishing and maintaining such manual of compliance procedures in relation to the business of the relevant person as the Regulator may require;

(c) be responsible for ensuring compliance by staff of the relevant person with

(i) the provisions of these Regulations and any other law relating to money laundering;

(ii) the provisions of any manual of compliance procedures established under sub-regulation (b); and

(iii) the internal reporting procedures established under regulation 14;

(d) act as the liaison between the relevant person and the Regulator in matters relating to compliance with the provisions of these Regulations and any other law or directive with respect to money laundering; and

(e) prepare and submit to the Regulator written reports on the relevant person's compliance with the provisions of these Regulations and any other law or directive relating to money laundering, and the reports shall be prepared in such form and submitted at such time as the Regulator may determine.

(3) For the purposes of sub-regulation (2)(a), the question as to whether a senior officer of a relevant person has relevant qualifications and experience shall be determined in accordance with such guidelines as the Commission may determine.

DUE DILI\GENCE AUDIT. Without prejudice to regulation 12 or any enactment relating to the conduct of inspections to verify compliance, the Regulator may conduct an inspection of any relevant person to determine compliance by that person with the requirements of these Regulations and any other law or directive relating to money laundering.

ESTABLISHMENT OF PROCEDURES FOR RECOGNISINGAND REPORTING SUSPICIOUS TRANSACTIONS.

(1) A relevant person shall establish written internal reporting procedures which, in relation to its relevant business, will

enable all its directors or, as the case may be, partners, all other persons involved in its management, and all key staff to know to whom they should report any knowledge or suspicion of money laundering activity;

ensure that there is a clear reporting chain under which suspicions of money laundering activity will be passed to the Compliance Officer.

identify a Compliance Officer to whom a report is to be made of any information or

other matter which comes to the attention of the person handling that business and which in that person's opinion give rise to knowledge or suspicion that another person is engaged in money laundering;

require the Compliance Officer to consider any report in the light of all other relevant information available to him for the purpose of determining whether or not it gives rise to a knowledge or suspicion of money laundering;

ensure that the Compliance Officer has reasonable access to any other information which may be of assistance to him and which is available to the relevant person; and

require that the information or other matter contained in a report is disclosed promptly to the Reporting Authority where the Compliance Officer knows or suspects that another person is engaged in money laundering.

(2) A relevant person shall maintain a register of all reports made to the Compliance Officer in pursuance of sub-regulation (1)(f).

(3) The register maintained under sub- Regulation (2) shall contain details of the date on which the report is made, the person who makes the report and information sufficient to identify the relevant documents.

15. REPORTING OF SUSPICIOUS BUSINESS TRANSACTIONS BY RELEVANT PERSON.

(1) A regulated person shall pay special attention to all complex, unusual or large business transactions, whether completed or not, and to all unusual patterns of transactions and to insignificant but periodic transactions, which have no apparent economic or lawful purpose.

(2) Upon reasonable suspicion that the transaction described in sub-regulation (1) could constitute or be related to money laundering, a relevant business shall promptly report the suspicious transaction to the Reporting Authority.

(3) When the report referred to in sub-regulation

(2)is made in good faith, a relevant person and its employees, staff, directors, owners or other representatives as authorized by law shall be exempted from criminal, civil or administrative liability, as the case may be, for complying with these regulations or for breach of any restriction on disclosure of information imposed by contract or by any legislative, regulatory of administrative provision, regardless of the result of the communication.

(5) A criminal offence is committed by a relevant person or its employees, staff, directors, owners or other authorized representatives who, acting as such, willfully fail to comply with the obligations in this regulation, or who willfully make a false or falsified report referred to above.

16. STAFF TRAINING. (1) A relevant person shall provide education and training for all directors or, as the case may be, partners, all other persons involved in its management, and all key staff to ensure that they are aware of

(a) the provisions of the Act and regulations made thereunder;

(b) their personal obligations under those enactments;

(c) the manual of compliance procedures established under regulation 12(2)(b) and the internal reporting procedures established under regulation 14;

(d) the procedures maintained by the relevant person in compliance with the duties imposed under these Regulations, and

(e) their personal liability for failure to report information or suspicions in accordance with internal procedures.

(2) A relevant person shall, in addition, provide training in accordance with the requirements of this regulation to all new key staff as soon as practicable after their appointment.

17. TRAINING FOR SENIOR AND SPECIALIST STAFF. A relevant person shall also provide education and training appropriate to particular categories of staff in:

(a) its policies and procedures to prevent money laundering;

(b) its customer identification, record keeping and other procedures; and

(c) the recognition and handling of suspicious transactions.

REQUIREMENT FOR REFRESHER TRAINING. A relevant person shall, at least once in every year, make arrangements for refresher training to remind key staff of their responsibilities and to make them aware of any changes in the laws relating to money laundering and the internal procedures of the relevant person.

OFFENCES AND PENALTIES. (1) A person who fails to comply with the requirements of these Regulations or any directive issued under regulation 20 commits an offence and is liable on summary conviction to a fine not exceeding fifty thousand dollars, and, if in the case of a continuing offence, the contravention continues after such conviction, he commits a further offence and is liable to an additional fine of five thousand dollars for each day on which the contravention continues.

(2) In determining whether a person has complied with the requirements of these Regulations or any directive issued under regulation 20, a court may take account

(a) of any provision in the Guidance Notes which may apply to that person;

(b) in a case where sub-regulation (a) does not apply, of any other relevant guidance issued by a body that regulates, or is representative of, any trade, business, profession or employment carried on by that person.

(3) In proceedings against a person for an offence under these Regulations, it shall be a defence for the person to prove that he took all reasonable steps and exercised due diligence to comply with the requirements of these Regulations or any directive issued under regulation 20 in respect of which he is charged.

(4) Where an offence under these Regulations has been committed by a body corporate the directors as well as the corporate body shall be guilty of that offence and liable to be proceeded against and punished accordingly.

(5) Where the affairs of a body corporate are managed by its members, sub-regulation (4) applies in relation to the acts and defaults of a member in connection with his functions of management as if he were a director of the body corporate.

(6) Where an offence under these Regulations committed by a partnership, or by an unincorporated association other than a partnership, is proved to have been committed with the consent or connivance of, or is attributable to the failure to exercise due diligence by, a partner in the partnership or, as the case may be, a person concerned in the management or control of the association, he, as well as the partnership or association, shall be guilty of that offence and liable to be proceeded against and punished accordingly.

DIRECTIVES. The Commission may, for the purposes of these Regulations, issue such directives as it considers necessary and such directives, when issued, shall be published in the *Gazette* and at least one locally circulated newspaper.

USE OF GUIDANCE NOTES. In the preparation of procedures required to be maintained in accordance with the provisions of these Regulations, a relevant person may adopt or have regard to the provisions of the Guidance Notes.

NEGATIVE RESOLUTION. These Regulations shall be subject to negative resolution of the National Assembly of Saint Christopher and Nevis.

COMMENCEMENT. These Regulations shall come into operation on the day of , 2001.

TRAVEL TO THE COUNTRY

TOURIST INFORMATION

TOTAL NUMBER OF VISITORS
214.415 (Including 123,148 cruise ship passengers).

TOTAL TOURIST EXPENDITURES
US$67.7 million

AVERAGE TOURIST DOLLAR SPENT
US$397

PRIMARY COUNTRIES OF ORIGIN
United States, Other Caribbean, Canada, United Kingdom

TOTAL NUMBER OF HOTEL ROOMS
1,593

VISA/ ENTRY REQUIREMENTS

Passports are not required by citizens of Canada and the United States, subject to proof of identity. Maximum length of stay is 6 months and assured onward passage. Visas are not required by citizens of the United Kingdom, Commonwealth countries, the United States, Canada, Western Europe and certain other countries.

IN SAINT KITTS AND NEVIS

Saint Kitts-Nevis Chamber of Industry & Commerce;
P.O Box 332,
Basseterre,
Telephone; (869) 465-4490
Fax; (869) 465-7746

Saint Kitts-Nevis Hotel Association;
P.O Box 392,
Basseterre,
Telephone; (869) 465-5304
Fax; (869) 465-7746

Saint Kitts-Nevis Manufacturers Association;
P.O Box 392,
Basseterre,
Telephone; (869) 465-6626

Nevis Industrial Development Unit;
Treasury Building,

Main Street,
Charlestown,
Nevis,
Telephone; (869) 469-5485

IN THE UNITED KINGDOM

OECS High Commission;
10 Kensington Court,
London,
W85 DL,
United Kingdom,
Telephone; (44) 71-937-5514

IN THE UNITED STATES

Eastern Caribbean Investment Promotion Service (ECIPS);
3216 New Mexico Avenue,
N.W,
Washington D.C 20016
Telephone; (202) 363-0229
Fax; (202) 363-4328

Consulate of Saint Kitts and Nevis;
Economic Affairs Division,
414 East 75th Street,
New York,
NY 10021
Telephone; (212) 535-1234
Fax; (212) 535-6854

Embassy of Saint Kitts and Nevis;
OECS Building,
3216 New Mexico Avenue,
N.W,
Washington D.C 20016
Telephone; (202) 686-2636
Fax; (202) 686- 5740

U.S Department of Commerce;
Andean/ Caribbean Division,
Room 3035,
Washington D.C 20230
Telephone; (202) 482-1658
Fax; (202) 482-0464

US STATE DEPARTMENT SUGGESTIONS

COUNTRY DESCRIPTION: St. Kitts and Nevis is a developing Caribbean island nation. Tourist facilities are widely available.

ENTRY/EXIT REQUIREMENTS: A valid U.S. passport or certified U.S. birth certificate and a picture identification that contains both name and date of birth are required of U.S. citizens entering St. Kitts and Nevis. Visitors should also have a valid return ticket. St. Kitts and Nevis immigration recommends that visitors put their full home address in the U.S. on their arrival cards in order to facilitate the entry process. Stays of up to one month are granted at immigration. Anyone requiring an extension must apply to the Ministry of National Security. There is an airport departure tax. For further information, travelers can contact the Embassy of St. Kitts and Nevis, 3216 New Mexico Avenue, N.W., OECS Building, Washington, D.C. 20016, telephone (202) 686-2636, the Permanent Mission to the UN in New York at (212) 535-1934, or the Internet at http://www.stkittsnevis.org

SAFETY/SECURITY: There may be demonstrations by small but vociferous groups during election periods. While there is no evidence that these demonstrations are anti-American, it is a good security practice to avoid all demonstrations. Contact the Consular Section for additional information.

CRIME INFORMATION: U.S. citizens have occasionally been victims of armed robbery, assault, burglary, and other petty street crime. Valuables left unattended on beaches are subject to theft.

The loss or theft of a U.S. passport overseas should be reported to the local police and the nearest U.S. Embassy or consulate. A lost or stolen U.S. birth certificate and/or driver's license generally cannot be replaced outside the U.S. U.S. citizens may refer to the Department of State's pamphlets, *A Safe Trip Abroad*, and *Tips for Travelers to the Caribbean* for ways to promote a more trouble-free journey. The pamphlet is available by mail from the Superintendent of Documents, U.S. Government Printing Office, Washington, D.C. 20402, via the Internet at http://www.access.gpo.gov/su_docs, or via the Bureau of Consular Affairs home page at http://travel.state.gov.

MEDICAL FACILITIES: Medical care is limited. Serious medical problems requiring hospitalization and/or medical evacuation to the U.S. can cost thousands of dollars or more. Doctors and hospitals often expect immediate cash payment for health services.

MEDICAL INSURANCE: U.S. medical insurance is not always valid outside the U.S. U.S. Medicare and Medicaid programs do not provide payment for medical services outside the U.S. Uninsured travelers who require medical care overseas may face extreme difficulties. Please check with your own insurance company to confirm whether your policy applies. Please ascertain whether payment will be made to the overseas hospital or doctor, or whether you will be reimbursed later for expenses that you incur. Some insurance policies also include coverage for psychiatric treatment and for disposition of remains in the event of death. Useful information on medical emergencies abroad, including overseas insurance programs, is provided in the Department of State's Bureau of Consular Affairs brochure, *Medical Information for Americans Traveling Abroad*, available via the Bureau of Consular Affairs home page or autofax: (202) 647-3000.

OTHER HEALTH INFORMATION: Information on vaccinations and other health precautions may be obtained from the Centers for Disease Control and Prevention's hotline for international travelers at 1-877-FYI-TRIP (1-877-394-8747); fax 1-888-CDC-FAXX (1-888-232-3299), or via CDC's Internet site at http://www.cdc.gov.

TRAFFIC SAFETY/ROAD CONDITIONS: While in a foreign country, U.S. citizens may encounter road conditions that differ significantly from those in the U.S. The information below concerning

St. Kitts and Nevis is provided for general reference only, and may not be totally accurate in a particular location or circumstance.

Safety of Public Transportation: Good
Urban Road Conditions/Maintenance: Good
Rural Road Conditions/Maintenance: Poor
Availability of Roadside Assistance: Poor

Traffic in St. Kitts and Nevis moves on the left-hand side of the road. Main roads and most secondary roads are in reasonably good condition. More detailed information on roads and traffic safety can be obtained from the Ministry of Tourism, Culture and the Environment, Bay Road, Pelican Mall, P.O. Box 132, Basse Terre, St. Kitts, telephone 1-869-647-8970.

For specific information concerning St. Kitts and Nevis driver's permits, vehicle inspection, road tax and mandatory insurance in St. Kitts and Nevis, contact the St. Kitts and Nevis National Tourist Organization offices in New York via the Internet.

AVIATION OVERSIGHT: The U.S. Federal Aviation Administration (FAA) has assessed the government of St. Kitts and Nevis' civil aviation authority as Category 2 -- not in compliance with international aviation safety standards for oversight of St. Kitts and Nevis' air carrier operations. While consultations to correct the deficiencies are ongoing, St. Kitts and Nevis' air carriers are permitted to conduct limited operations to the U.S. subject to heightened FAA surveillance.

For further information, travelers may contact the Department of Transportation within the U.S. at 1-800-322-7873, or visit the FAA's Internet website at http://www.faa.gov/avr/iasa/. The U.S. Department of Defense (DOD) does not permit its personnel to use air carriers from Category 2 countries for official business except for flights originating from or terminating in the U.S. For information regarding the DOD policy on specific carriers, travelers may contact DOD at (618) 229-4801.

CUSTOMS REGULATIONS: St. Kitts and Nevis customs authorities may enforce strict regulations concerning temporary import or export of various items. It is advisable to contact the Embassy of St. Kitts and Nevis in Washington, D.C. or the Permanent Mission in New York for specific information on customs requirements.

CRIMINAL PENALTIES: While in a foreign country, a U.S. citizen is subject to that country's laws and regulations, which sometimes differ significantly from those in the U.S. and may not afford the protections available to the individual under U.S. law. Penalties for breaking the law can be more severe than in the U.S. for similar offenses. Persons violating St. Kitts and Nevis laws, even unknowingly, may be expelled, arrested or imprisoned. Penalties for possession, use, or trafficking in illegal drugs in St. Kitts and Nevis are strict and convicted offenders can expect jail sentences and heavy fines.

CONSULAR ACCESS: There is no U.S. Embassy or Consulate in St. Kitts and Nevis. The U.S. Embassy in Bridgetown, Barbados is responsible for these islands. U.S. citizens are encouraged to carry their U.S. citizenship evidence with them at all times, so if questioned by local officials, proof of identity and U.S. citizenship are readily available.

DISASTER PREPAREDNESS: St. Kitts and Nevis is a hurricane-prone country. General information about natural disaster preparedness is available via the Internet from the U.S. Federal Emergency Management Agency (FEMA) at http://www.fema.gov.

CHILDREN'S ISSUES: For information on international adoption of children and international parental child abduction, please refer to our Internet site at http://travel.state.gov/children's_issues.html or telephone (202) 736-7000.

REGISTRATION/EMBASSY AND CONSULATE LOCATIONS: U.S. citizens living in or visiting St. Kitts and Nevis are encouraged to register at the Consular Section of the U.S. Embassy in Bridgetown, Barbados and obtain updated information on travel and security within St. Kitts and Nevis. Consular Section hours are 9:00 am-12 noon and 2:00 pm-4:00 pm, Monday-Friday except local and U.S. holidays. The U.S. Embassy is located in the American Life Insurance (ALICO) building, Cheapside, Bridgetown, Barbados, telephone 1-246-431-0225, fax 1-246-431-0179, e-mail address: ConsularBridge@state.gov or Internet home page: http://usembassy.state.gov/posts/bb1/wwwhcons.html.

There is also a U.S. Consular Agent for the area in English Harbor, Antigua, tel. 1-268-463-6521, fax 1-268-460-1569, e-mail address: ryderj@candw.ag. Office hours are 9:00 am-4:00 pm, Monday-Friday except local and U.S. holidays.

IMPORTANT INFORMATION FOR TRAVELERS

Tipping/Gratuities: Same as in the US--10% to 15%, depending on the service. Some restaurants and hotels will automatically add a 10% gratuity. If you are in doubt, do not feel uncomfortable asking. Usually, porters and bellhops receive 50 cents per bag, taxi drivers 10-15% of the fare.

Telephones: Calling the U.S. is easy from St. Kitts & Nevis. Most hotels offer USA Direct calling service, or they can connect you with a U.S. operator.

Taxes: St. Kitts & Nevis has a US$17.00 airport departure tax, an additional US$1.50 Environmental Levy and a room tax of 7% and service charge of 10%.

Television: Most hotels have 22 cable channels, including CNN, ESPN, the Disney Channel, premium movie channels and local stations.

Electricity: 230 volts, 60 cycles. Most hotels have 110 volts, and converters are available.

Drinking Water: Safe spring water comes from numerous volcanic springs.

Appropriate Attire: Beach attire is appropriate for the beach but not the town, shops or restaurants. Please refrain from short shorts, bikinis and bare chests in these places. Informal, but conservative clothing is the standard.

Time Zone: Atlantic Standard Time, one hour ahead of Eastern Standard Time and the same as Eastern Daylight Time.

Currency/Money: The official currency is the Eastern Caribbean Dollar, which is fixed to the US dollar. Recent exchange rate was US$1.00 = EC$2.70. US currency, travelers checks and major credit cards are welcome everywhere.

Banks: Bank of Nova Scotia, Barclays Bank PLC, Royal Bank of Canada, St. Kitts-Nevis-Anguilla National Bank Ltd., Bank of Nevis Ltd., Nevis Co-Operative Banking Co. Ltd. Banking hours are Monday through Thursday from 8:00 am to 3:00 pm and Friday from 8:00 am to 5:00 pm. The St. Kitts & Nevis National Bank is also open from 8:30 am - 11:00 am on Saturdays.

Medical Facilities: St. Kitts & Nevis has doctors on call at hotels and a 24-hour Casualty Department. Recompression chambers are available by air ambulance at nearby Saba and in St. Thomas. Pharmaceutical services are widely available.

Passports and Immigration: U.S. and Canadian citizens need proof of citizenship: a passport, birth certificate or voters' registration card. U.S. residents need their green card. All others require a valid passport. A return or continuing ticket is also required.

Shopping Hours: Monday through Saturday 8:00 am to noon and 1:00 pm-4:00 pm. On Thursdays, most shops close for the afternoon.

Personal Safety: St. Kitts & Nevis are relatively crime free, but exercise normal precautions. For example, don't leave valuables unattended in rental cars or on the beach.

GETTING THERE:

Jet service is usually to San Juan Puerto Rico, St. Maarten, Guadeloupe, Virgin Islands or Antigua, with transfers to lighter aircraft for the final flight to St. Kitts.

Robert L. Bradshaw International Airport on St. Kitts, located approximately 2 miles from Basseterre, is capable of handling wide-bodied jets.

Newcastle Airport on Nevis is approximately 1/2 mile from Charlestown. It can handle only smaller, twin-engine propeller aircraft.

From the US:

American Airlines Eagle, Continental Express,

From Europe:

British Airways
BWIA
Air France
Lufthansa
KLM

Inter-Island:

Air St. Kitts/Nevis - (869) 469-9241
Carib Aviation - (869) 465-3055
LIAT - (869) 465-2286
Nevis Express - (869) 469-9756
Windward Islands Airways

Approximate flight times:

New York - 4 hours
Miami - 3 hours
London - 8 hours

Antigua - 20 minutes
Puerto Rico - 1 hour
St. Maarten - 20 minutes

GETTING AROUND:

Visitors require a temporary driver's license, valid for one year, which can be obtained from the Police Traffic Department for a fee of EC$50. All traffic keeps to the left (as in England), and international highway signs are used.

Car Rentals:

St. Kitts
Caines Rent-A-Car Tel: 456-2366
Choice Car Rental Tel: 465-4422
Delisle Walwyn Car Rental Tel: 465-8449
Holiday Car Rental Tel: 465-6507
Higgins Car Rental Tel: 465-8080
Island Car Rental Tel: 465-3000
Kitts Car Rental Tel: 465-1665
St. Kitts Taxi Association Tel: 465-4253 or 465-8487
Sunshine Car Rental Tel: 465-2193
TDC Rentals Ltd. Tel: 465-2991
Nevis
D&R Rent-A-Car Tel: 469-1922
Gajor's Car Rental Tel: 469-5367/1439
Nisbett's Car Rental Tel: 469-9211
Noel's Car Rental Tel: 469-5199
Parry's Car Rentals Tel: 469-5917
Skeete's Car Rental Tel: 469-9458
Stanley's Car Rental Tel: 469-1597
Striker's Car Rental Tel: 469-2654
TDC Rentals Ltd. Tel: 469-5690

Taxis:

Fares are fixed, and can be negotiated beforehand. Rates increase 50% between 10:00pm and 6:00am and there is an additional 20% for arranged trips between 6:00pm and 6:00am. Sample fares:

- Robert L. Bradshaw International Airport to Basseterre - $US 7.00
- Robert L. Bradshaw International Airport to Frigate Bay - $US 11.00
- Newcastle Airport to Charlestown - $US 14.00

Ferry Service Between Basseterre, St. Kitts and Charlestown, Nevis:
The ***Caribe Queen*** leaves twice a day Monday, Tuesday, Wednesday, Friday, and Saturday. The trip takes 45 minutes and costs EC$20.00 (or US$8.00).
The ***M.V. Sea Hustler*** goes back and forth twice a day, 7 days per week and also costs EC$20.00 (or US$8.00).

TOURIST OFFICES AND TRAVEL AGENTS

In the US:
New York City
St. Kitts & Nevis Department of Tourism
414 East 75th Street, Suite 5
New York, NY 10021
Tel: (212) 535-1234 / (800) 582-6208
Fax: (212) 734-6511
Manager: Robert Kelly

Washington, DC
St. Kitts-Nevis Tourism Office
8720 Georgia Avenue, Suite 905
Silver Spring, MD 20910-3602
Tel: (301) 587-1555 / (877) 533-1555
Fax: (301) 587-0647
Eml: **info@stkitts-nevis.com**
Tourism Officer: Abdullah Skerritt.

In Canada:
St. Kitts and Nevis Tourism Office
365 Bay Street, Suite 806
Toronto, Ontario M5H2V1
TEL: 416-368-6707
Fax: 416-368-3934
Email: **skbnevcan@sympatico.ca**
Manager: Carolyn James

In the U.K.:
St. Kitts and Nevis Tourism Office
10 Kensington Court
London W8 5DL
TEL: 0171-376-0881
Fax: 0171-937-6742
Email: **stkitts.nevis@btinternet.com**
Manager: Ester Smith

In Germany:
St. Kitts & Nevis Tourism Office
Walter-Kolb Straße 9-11
60594 Frankfiurt, Germany
Tel: 069 96216413
Fax: 069 610637
Tourism Rep: Walter Kolb

In St. Kitts and Nevis:
Department of Tourism
Pelican Mall, Bay Road
P.O. Box 132
Basseterre, St. Kitts, W.I.
TEL: 869-465-2620/4040
FAX: 869-465-8794
Email: **mintc&e@caribsurf.com**

Minister of Tourism:
Hon. G.A. Dwyer Astaphan
Permanent Secretary/Director:
Mrs. Hillary Wattley

Nevis Tourism Bureau
Main Street
Charlestown. Nevis, W.I.
TEL: 869-469-1042
FAX: 869 469 1066
Email: **nevtour@caribsurf.com**
Director of Tourism
Ms. Elmeader Brookes

St. Kitts and Nevis Hotel
and Tourism Association
P.O. Box 438
Basseterre, St. Kitts, W.I.
TEL: 869-465-5304
FAX: 869-465-7746
Executive Director: Mr. Val Henry

TRAVEL AGENTS

For travel arrangements to the Federation of St. Kitts & Nevis, please contact your travel agent or select one from the following list of certifiedSt. Kitts- Nevis Destination Specialists

---

Dagmar Sawyer
Travel Strategies
2480 Black Rock Turnpike
Fairfield, CT 06430
Vox: (203) 335-8119; Fax (203) 374-9687

Dawn M. Loughlin
Dreams & Things Travel
P.O. Box 543043
Dallas, Tx 75354
Vox: (214) 902-4844; Fax: (214) 902-4844
Email: dreams@cyberramp.net

Frances Cearley
Sunset World Travel
4965 Addison Circle
Addison, TX 75248
Vox: (888) 301-3692; Fax: (972) 386-9807
Email: sunset@ont.com

Geraldine Beam
Tourscan, Inc
1051 Boston Post road
Darrien, CT 06820
Vox: (800) 962-2080; Fax: (203) 655-6689
Email: tourscan@ix.netcom.com

Janet Messersmith
Castle Travel
3 Ridge Lane
Colonia, NJ 07067
Vox (800) 425-2983; Fax: (732) 396-2655
Email: castle@compuserve.com

Judi Carosi
Caribbean Connections
4965 Addison Circle
Addison, TX 75248
Vox: (888) 301-3692; Fax: (772) 386-9807
Email: sunset@ont.com

Kristin Cheney
Travel World
427 Broad street
Shrewsbury, NJ 07702
Vox: (800) 637-7677; Fax: (732) 842-1889

Shelly Witter
Uniglobe Destiny Travel
8226 Douglas
Dallas, TX 75225
Vox: (800) 522-7510; Fax: (214) 346-0900
Email: :udtravl@aol.com

Sue Sorrels
Access Travel
4020 North MacArthur, #118
Irving, TX 75038
Vox: (800) 345-8894; Fax: (972) 717-1751
Email: mailto:accessirving@worldnet.att.net

RESTAURANTS ON ST. KITTS

Arlecchino
Italian/European, Basseterre, Tel: 465-9927

The Atlantic Club
West Indian/Continental, Morgan Heights, Tel: 465-8633/9271

B's Bar & Restaurant
West Indian, Sandy Point, Tel: 465-6388

The Ballahoo
West Indian/International, Basseterre, Tel: 465-4197

Bird Rock Beach Resort
Continental, Bird Rock, Tel: 465-8914

Blue Horizon
Continental, Bird Rock, Tel: 465-5863

Charlie's
Bar & Restaurant, Basseterre, Tel: 465-0709

Chef's Place
West Indian, Basseterre, Tel: 465-6176

Circus Grill
P.O. Box 485, Basseterre, Tel: 869-465-0143

Cisco's Place/Yang's Garden
Chinese, Basseterre, Tel: 465-9009

The Fairview Inn
International, Boyds Village, Tel: 465-2472

Fisherman's Wharf
West Indian/International, Fortlands, Tel: 465-2754

Fort Thomas Hotel
International, Fortlands, Tel: 465-2695

Frigate Bay Resort
West Indian/Continental, Frigate Bay, Tel: 465-8935

The Golden Lemon
International, Dieppe Bay, Tel: 465-7260

J's Place
West Indian, Sandy Point, Tel: 465-6264

Kenzie's Bar & Restaurant
West Indian/Basseterre, Tel: 465-7979

Lighthouse Restaurant
West Indian/Continental, Bird Rock, Tel: 465-0739; Fax: 465-3131

Llewellyn's Haven
West Indian, Basseterre, Tel: 465-2941

Manhattan Gardens
West Indian/International, Old Road, Tel: 465-9121

The New Pizza Place
Pizza/West Indian, Basseterre, Tel: 465-2546

Ocean Terrace Inn
West Indian/Continental, Fortlands, Tel: 465-2754/2380

O.T.I. Turtle Beach Bar & Grill
West Indian/Continental, Turtle Beach, Tel: 465-9086

Olivees Bed & Breakfast
West Indian/Continental, Upper Buckley's, Tel: 465-3662

Ottley's Plantation Inn Royal Palm Restaurant
Gourmet, Ottley's, Tel: 465-7234

The Patio Restaurant
International/West Indian, Frigate Bay, Tel: 465-8666

PJ's Pizza Bar & Restaurant
Pizza Parlour/Italian/Vegetarian, Frigate Bay, Tel: 465-8373

QT's Delight
West Indian, Basseterre, Tel: 465-3423

Rafters Restaurant And Lounge
West Indian, Basseterre, Tel: 465-9883

Rawlins Plantation
West Indian/Innovative, Mount Pleasant, Tel: 465-6221

Sun 'n Sand Beach Resort's Village Restaurant
Continental/West Indian, Frigate Bay, Tel: 465-8037

Sunset Café
International/West Indian/Seafood, oceanfront at Timothy Beach Resort,
Tel: 869 465 8597"

Tracy's Corner
West Indian, St. Johnson's Village, Tel: 465-6109

Trinity Inn Poolside Bar & Restaurant
Seafood/West Indian, Palmetto Point, Tel: 465-3226

Victor's
West Indian, Basseterre, Tel: 465-2518

The White House
International, Basseterre, Tel: 465-8162

RESTAURANTS ON NEVIS

C.J.'s Cafe
Coffee Shop, Charlestown, Tel: 469-5389

Callaloo
Creole, Charlestown, Tel: 469-5389

The Carousel
Beach Bar & Restaurant, Pinney's Beach

Cla-Cha-Del
West Indian, Newcastle, Tel: 469-9640

Cliffdwellers
International, Tamarind Bay, Tel: 469-0262/5195

The Courtyard Bar & Restaurant
Continental/Nevisian, Charlestown, Tel: 469-5685

Croney's Old Manor Estate
West Indian/International, Gingerland, Tel: 469-3445

Dick's Bar
Nightclub, Brick Kiln Village, Charlestown

Eddy's Restaurant
West Indian/North American, Charlestown, Tel: 469-5958/VHF 16

Fort Ashby Bar & Restaurant
West Indian, Fort Ashby, Tel: 4690135/3464

The Four Seasons Resort
International, Pinney's Beach, Tel: 469-1111

Golden Rock Estate
International/West Indian, Gingerland, Tel: 469-3346

The Hermitage Inn
West Indian/International, Gingerland, Tel: 469-3477

Jonathan's Villa Bar & Restaurant
Seafood/Caribbean, Mount Lily, Tel: 469-9148

Miss June's
Caribbean, Stoney Grove Plantation, Tel: 469-5330

Montpelier Plantation Inn
International, Montpelier, Tel: 469-3462

Mt. Nevis Hotel
International/West Indian, Newcastle, Tel: 469-9373

Newcastle Bay Marina Restaurant and Watersports Centre
Italian, Newcastle, Tel: 469-9395/9373

Night Cap Restaurant & Bar
West Indian, Pinney's Industrial Site, Tel: 469-0268

Nisbet Plantation Beach Club
Creole/Continental, Newcastle, Tel: 469-9325

Oualie Beach Club
West Indian/Continental, Oualie Beach, Tel: 469-9735

Pemos restaurant & Bar
West Indian, Camp's Road, Tel: 469-9188/9102

Pinney's Beach Hotel
Continental/West Indian, Pinney's Beach, Tel: 469-5207

The S's
West Indian, Newcastle, Tel: 469-9458

Scene II
West Indian/Italian, Newcastle Airport, Tel: 469-9211

Sea Spawn
Seafood, Charlestown, Tel: 469-5239

Sunshines on Pinney Beach

Unella's
West Indian, Charlestown, Tel: 469-5574

SUPPLEMENTS

IMPORTANT WEBSITES

Nevis Press and Public Relations
http://www.gisnevis.com

Nevis Tourism Authority
http://www.nevisisland.com

Nevis Land and Housing Cooperation (Pinney's Estate Development Agency)
http://www.pinneysestate.com

The Government of St Kitts and Nevis
http://www.stkittsnevis.net

Nevis Disaster Management Office
http://www.geocities.com/odpnevis/

Nevis Culturama
http://www.nevisculturama.net/

Private Sector

Morning Star Holding Company Ltd.
http://www.morningstarnev.com

Meridian Trust Company Ltd.
http://www.meridiannev.com

Nevis Historical and Conservation Society
http://www.nevis-nhcs.org

Other

The Eastern Caribbean Central Bank
http://www.eccb-centralbank.org

The Eastern Caribbean Securities Exchange
http://www.ecseonline.com

St. Kitts & Nevis International Ship Registry
http://www.StKittsNevisRegistry.net

SELECTED GOVERNMENT AND BUSINESS CONTACTS

No person has been authorized by the Federal Government to carry on offshore banking, investment, insurance or assurance business in or from within the Federation of St. Kitts and Nevis.

Government Listings

The Hon. Delano F. Bart
Attorney General

Telephone: +1 (869) 465-2127
Telecopier: +1 (869) 465-5040

Mr. Wendell Lawrence
Financial Secretary
Ministry of Finance
Telephone: +1 (869) 465-2127
Telecopier: +1 (869) 465-1532

Mr. Horatio Versailles
Permanent Secretary
Ministry of Trade and Industry
Telephone: +1 (869) 465-2127
Telecopier: +1 (869) 465-1778

Mr. Joseph R.R. Escher
Director General
Financial Services Department
Telephone: +1 (869) 466-5048
Telecopier: +1 (869) 466-5317

TRUST AND CORPORATE BUSINESS

Fidesco Trust Corporation
6 Horizons Villas, Frigate Bay, P.O. Box 898
Basseterre, KN
St. Kitts
Telephone: +1 (869) 466-6989
Telecopier: +1 (869) 466-7355
E-mail: info@fidesco.com

CORPORATE BUSINESS

Lillian V. Benjamin, B.A. (Lond.), H.N.D. Business (Lond.)
Barrister-at-Law and Solicitor
Kennylin House, New Street, P.O. Box 440
Basseterre, KN
St. Kitts
Telephone: +1 (869) 465-2878/7865
Telecopier: +1 (869) 465-6077
E-mail: mitcham@caribsurf.com

Malchus Irvin R. Boncamper, F.C.C.A.
Certified Chartered Accountant
22 Cayon Street, P.O. Box 281
Basseterre, KN
St. Kitts
Telephone: +1 (869) 465-4459 or 466-7049
Telecopier: +1 (869) 465-5983/4417
E-mail: afms@caribsurf.com

Dr. Henry L. Browne, LL.B., L.E.C, Ph.D.
Barrister-at-Law and Solicitor
20A Market Street
Basseterre, KN
St. Kitts
Telephone: +1 (869) 465-2973/9305
Telecopier: +1 (869) 465-1016

Terence V. Byron, C.M.G., B.A. (Cantab.)
Barrister-at-Law and Solicitor
O'Loughlin House, Fort Street, P.O. Box 154
Basseterre, KN
St. Kitts
Telephone: +1 (869) 465-2055
Telecopier: +1 (869) 465-7191
E-mail: infoserv@caribsurf.com

Scott R. Caines, C.P.A.
Certified Public Accountant
Bird Rock and Frigate Bay Road, P.O. Box 398
Basseterre, KN
St. Kitts
Telephone: +1 (869) 465-8385
Telecopier: +1 (869) 465-6191

Robin H. Cotterell, F.C.A.
Chartered Accountant
Barclays Building, Suite 1, Main Street
Charlestown, KN
Nevis
Telephone: +1 (869) 469-0200
Telecopier: +1 (869) 469-0201
E-mail: hanverco@caribsurf.com

Patricia A. Dublin, LL.B. (Lond.), L.E.C.
Barrister-at-Law and Solicitor
Central College Street
Basseterre, KN
St. Kitts
Telephone: +1 (869) 465-2276 or 466-5318
Telecopier: +1 (869) 465-5867

Anthony E. Gonsalves, LL.B., LL.M. (Cantab.)
Barrister-at-Law and Solicitor
Independence Square South, P.O. Box 449
Basseterre, KN
St. Kitts
Telephone: +1 (869) 466-5455
Telecopier: +1 (869) 466-5456

Lindsay F.P. Grant, LL.B., L.E.C., LL.M. (Harv.)
Barrister-at Law and Solicitor
3 Church Street, P.O. Box 481
Basseterre, KN
St. Kitts
Telephone: +1 (869) 465-2795/7825 or 466-7428/7429
Telecopier: +1 (869) 465-1004
E-mail: vgasklaw@caribsurf.com

Glenford R. Hamilton, LL.B., L.E.C.
Barrister-at Law and Solicitor
Miriam House, 5 Lozack Road, P.O. Box 450
Basseterre, KN
St. Kitts
Telephone: + 1 (869) 465-2900/2770
Telecopier: +1 (869) 465-1147
E-mail: hamilton@caribsurf.com

Sir Probyn Inniss, M.B.E., B.A., D.P.A., F.B.I.M.
Barrister-at-Law, Solicitor and Notary Public
11A Cayon Street, P.O. Box 395
Basseterre, KN
St. Kitts
Telephone: +1 (869) 465-4010/3488
Telecopier: +1 (869) 465-3323
E-mail: lyrinnis@caribsurf.com

Claudette Jenkins, LL.B.
Barrister-at-Law and Solicitor
Corner Cayon and Sprott Streets, P.O. Box 510
Basseterre, KN
St. Kitts
Telephone: +1 (869) 465-6809/6459
Telecopier: +1 (869) 465-1190
E-mail: jenkins@caribsurf.com

Damian E.S. Kelsick, LL.B. (Lond.), L.E.C.
Barrister-at-Law and Solicitor
Central Street, P.O. Box 100
Basseterre, KN
St. Kitts
Telephone: +1 (869) 465-2992/0185
Telecopier: +1 (869) 465-4881

Marcella A. Liburd, B.A., LL.B., L.E.C.
Barrister-at-Law and Solicitor
Shear Lane, P.O. Box 923
Basseterre, KN
St. Kitts
Telephone: +1 (869) 465-2756/1047
Telecopier: +1 (869) 465-5519

Patrick E. Patterson, B.A., LL.M. (Lond.)
Barrister-at-Law and Solicitor
Rams Complex, Bird Rock Road, P.O. Box 718
Basseterre, KN
St. Kitts
Telephone: +1 (869) 465-5157
Telecopier: +1 (869) 465-5235

J. D. Quinlan, LL.B., L.E.C.
Barrister-at-Law and Solicitor
Quincott House, 23 Cayon Street West, P.O. Box 208
Basseterre, KN
St. Kitts
Telephone: +1 (869) 465-5221
Telecopier: +1 (869) 465-5221

David W. Rawlings, B.A., L.L.B., L.E.C.
Barrister-at-Law and Solicitor
Central Street at Fiennes Avenue, P.O. Box 222
Basseterre, KN
St. Kitts
Telephone: +1 (869) 465-2887
Telecopier: +1 (869) 465-1317
E-mail: off$hore@caribsurf.com

Vernon S. Veira, LL.B., L.E.C.
Barrister-at Law and Solicitor
3 Church Street, P.O. Box 481
Basseterre, KN
St. Kitts
Telephone: +1 (869) 465-2795/7825 or 466-7428/7429
Telecopier: +1 (869) 465-1004
E-mail: vgasklaw@caribsurf.com

Charles L.A. Wilkin, M.A. (Cantab.)
Barrister-at-Law and Solicitor
Independence Square South, P.O. Box 174
Basseterre, KN
St. Kitts
Telephone: +1 (869) 465-2645/2726/2440
Telecopier: +1 (869) 465-7808
E-mail: lawkwf@caribsurf.com

FINANCIAL INSTITUTIONS

Monetary Authority

Eastern Caribbean Central Bank
Bird Rock Road, P.O. Box 89
Basseterre, KN
St. Kitts
Telephone: 1 (869) 465-2537/2538/2539
Telecopier: +1 (869) 465-1051/9562

RETAIL BANKS

Bank of Nevis Ltd.
Main Street, P.O. Box 450
Charlestown, KN
Nevis
Telephone: +1 (869) 469-5564/5796/1451/1318
Telecopier: +1 (869) 469-5798

Bank of Nova Scotia
Fort Street, P.O. Box 433
Basseterre, KN
St. Kitts
Telephone: +1 (869) 465-4141 or 466-6710/6711
Telecopier: +1 (869) 465-8600

Main Street, P.O. Box 467
Charlestown, KN
Nevis
Telephone: +1 (869) 469-5411
Telecopier: +1 (869) 469-0231

Barclays Bank PLC
The Circus, P.O. Box 42
Basseterre, KN
St. Kitts
Telephone: +1 (869) 465-2519/2510/2449/1081/2264/5981
Telecopier: +1 (869) 465-1041/1618

Main Street, P.O. Box 502
Charlestown, KN
Nevis
Telephone: +1 (869) 469-5467/5309
Telecopier: +1 (869) 469-5106

National Bank Ltd.
Central Street, P.O. Box 343
Basseterre, KN
St. Kitts
Telephone: +1 (869) 465-2204
Telecopier: +1 (869) 465-1050

Prince Williams Street
Charlestown, KN
Nevis
Telephone: +1 (869) 469-5244/5123
Telecopier: +1 (869) 469-0194

Royal Bank of Canada
Fort Street, P.O. Box 91
Basseterre, KN
St. Kitts
Telephone: +1 (869) 465-2259/2409/2389/4374
Telecopier: +1 (869) 465-1040

Insurance Companies, Agents and Brokers

INSURANCE COMPANIES

Barbados Mutual Life Assurance Society
Cayon Street and West Independence Square, P.O. Box 835
Basseterre, KN
St. Kitts
Telephone: +1 (869) 465-9476/9457
Telecopier: +1 (869) 465-6437

British American Insurance Company Limited
Cayon Street, P.O. Box 378
Basseterre, KN
St. Kitts
Telephone: +1 (869) 465-2348/8758
Telecopier: +1 (869) 465-7838

Main Street
Charlestown, KN
Nevis
Telephone: +1 (869) 469-5415
Telecopier: +1 (869) 469-1635

Colonial Life Insurance Company (Trinidad) Limited
Cayon Street and Rosemary Lane, P.O. Box 534
Basseterre, KN
St. Kitts
Telephone: +1 (869) 465-4557/9908
Telecopier: +1 (869) 465-5423

National Caribbean Insurance Co. Limited
Central Street, P.O. Box 374
Basseterre, KN
St. Kitts
Telephone: +1 (869) 465-2694/2689/5345/4027/3718
Telecopier: +1 (869) 465-3659

Main Street
Charlestown, KN
Nevis
Telephone: +1 (869) 469-5456/0424
Telecopier: +1 (869) 469-1158

St. Kitts-Nevis Insurance Company Limited
Central Street, P.O. Box 142
Basseterre, KN
St. Kitts
Telephone: +1 (869) 465-2845 or 466-6330
Telecopier: +1 (869) 465-5410

Main Street, P.O. Box 548
Charlestown, KN
Nevis
Telephone: +1 (869) 469-5430
Telecopier: +1 (869) 469-1329

INSURANCE AGENTS

E. A. Laws Company Ltd.
Agents for
Gulf Insurance Ltd.
Southwell Industrial Park, P.O. Box 283
Basseterre, KN
St. Kitts
Telephone: +1 (869) 465-8832/8833
Telecopier: +1 (869) 465-1390

Delisle Walwyn & Co. Ltd.
Agents for
Sun Alliance Insurance Company (Eastern Caribbean) Ltd.
Liverpool Row, P.O. Box 44
Basseterre, KN
St. Kitts
Telephone: +1 (869) 465-2631
Telecopier: +1 (869) 465-1125

S.L. Horsford & Co. Ltd.
Agents for
N. E. M. (West Indies) Insurance Limited
Independence Square West, P.O. Box 45
Basseterre, KN
St. Kitts
Telephone: +1 (869) 465-9355/2616
Telecopier: +1 (869) 465-1042

Stoney Grove
Charlestown
Nevis
Telephone: +1 (869) 469-5600/1272/1624
Telecopier: +1 (869) 469-5604

INSURANCE BROKERS

S.L. Horsford & Co. Ltd.
Brokers for
HSBC Gibbs, Lloyds Brokers
Independence Square West, P.O. Box 45
Basseterre, KN
St. Kitts
Telephone: +1 (869) 465-9355/2616
Telecopier: +1 (869) 465-1042

Stoney Grove
Charlestown
Nevis
Telephone: +1 (869) 469-5600/1272/1624
Telecopier: +1 (869) 469-5604

Quinlan Walwyn & Associates
Brokers for
American Home Insurance Company
American Life Insurance Company
Quincott House, 23 Cayon Street West, P.O. Box 208
Basseterre, KN
St. Kitts
Telephone: +1 (869) 465-2681
Telecopier: +1 (869) 465-2681

VISA APPLICATION INFORMATION

Saint Christopher and Nevis
Statutory Rules and Orders
1985, No.3

The Visa (Exemption) Order, 1986 made under subsection (2) of section 13 of the Immigration and Passport Act (Chapter 145)

1. SHORT TITLE. This order may be cited as the Visa (Exemption) Order 1985.

2. VISA EXEMPTION. Aliens being citizens of thc countries mentioned in the schedule landing in Saint Christopher and Nevis from any place beyond Saint Christopher and Nevis and in possession of valid passport issued to them by the proper authority of their country of nationality shall be exempt from the provisions of subsection (1) of the Immigration and Passport Act, requiring passport of aliens to be visaed by a Saint Christopher and Nevis Consular Officer or other person duly so authorised.

3. REVOCATION OF ORDER. The Passport Visa (Exemption) Order, 1950 (S.R.&O. (L.I. 13 of XX) as amended is hereby revoked.

SCHEDULE

COMMONWEALTH COUNTRIES

Antigua and Barbuda
Australia
Commonwealth of the Bahamas
Bangladesh
Barbados
Belize
Botswane
Canada
Cyprus
Dominica
Fiji
The Gambia
Ghana
Grenada
Guyana
India
Jamaica
Kenya
Kiribati
Lesotho
Malawi
Malasia
Maldives
Malta
Mauritius
Nauru
Namibia
New Zealand
Nigeria
Papua New Guinea
Saint Lucia
Saint Vincent and the Grenadines
Seycelles
Sierra Leone
Singapore
Solomon Islands
Sri Lanka
Swaziland
Tanzania
Tonga
Trinidad and Tobago
Tuvalu
Uganda
United Kingdom and Dependencies
Vanuatu
Western Samoa
Zambia
Zimbabwe

ORGANIZATION OF AMERICAN STATES (OAS) COUNTRIES

Argentina
Bolivia
Brazil
Chile
Colombia
Costa Rica
Dominican Republic (a visa is required)
Ecuador
El Salvador
Guatemale
Honduras
Mexico
Nicaragua
Panama
Paraguay
Peru
United States of America
Uruguay
Venezuela

OTHER COUNTRIES

Austria
Bahrain
Belgium
Denmark
Egypt
Federal Republic of Germany
Finland
France
Greece
Iceland
Ireland
Israel
Italy
Jordan
Kuwait
Liechtenstein
Suriname
Luxembourg
Monaco
Netherlands (Holland)
Netherlands Antilles (Aruba, Bonaire, Curacao, St. Maarten, St. Eustatius, Saba)
Norway
Oman
Puerto Rico and the U.S. Virgin Islands

Quatar
Republic of China (Taiwan)
Republic of Korea
Saudi Arabia
Spain
Sweden
Turkey
United Arab Emirates

Made by the Minister this 25th day of January, 1985.

Kennedy A. Simmonds, Minister of Home Affairs

VISA APPLICATION INSTRUCTIONS

Embassy of St. Kitts & Nevis
OECS Bldg.
3216 New Mexico Avenue, N.W.
Washington, D.C. 20016
Tel. 202-686-2636
Fax. 202-686-5740

Dear Sir/Madam:
This Visa Application form should be completed in its entirety, signed and returned to this office with:

1. Two (2) recent colour passport sized photos;
2. The applicant's valid passport;
3. A visa fee of $20.00;
4. Mailing fee of $5.00, if registered postage is required; or
5. Mailing fee of $10.00, if express overnight service is required.

You might also want to note:

1. Passport must be valid for at least six (6) months after the termination of visit to St. Kitts and Nevis.
2. Fees are payable by CERTIFIED CHECKS OR MONEY ORDERS and should be payable to THE EMBASSY OF ST. KITTS AND NEVIS.
3. Processing time is approximately two (2) working days.
4. All visitors to St. Kitts and Nevis must be in possession of a return or onward ticket and sufficient funds to cover the cost for his/her stay in the country.

CARRIBIAN COMMONWEALTH: BASIC TREATIES AND PROTOCOLS

1.	Treaty establishing the CARIBBEAN COMMUNITY Chaguaramas, 4th July 1973 (This is the official Text of the Treaty, the Final Act and the Agreement establishing the Common External Tariff)
2.	Protocol I amending the Treaty of Chaguaramas.
3.	Protocol II: Establishment, Services, Capital amending the Treaty of Chaguaramas.
4.	Protocol III: Industrial Policy amending the Treaty of Chaguaramas.
5.	Protocol IV: Trade Policy amending the Treaty of Chaguaramas

6.	Protocol V: Agricultural Policy: amending the Treaty of Chaguaramas.
7.	Protocol VI: Transport Policy : amending the Treaty of Chaguaramas.
8.	Protocol VII: Disadvantaged Countries, Regions and Sectors: amending the Treaty of Chaguaramas.
9.	Charter of Civil Society for The Caribbean Community.
10.	CARICOM Agreement on Social Security
11.	Agreement for the establishment of an Assembly of Caribbean Community Parliamentarians
12.	Agreement establishing the Regional Justice Protection Programme
13.	Agreement establishing the Caribbean Court of Justice
14.	Agreement establishing the Seat of the Caribbean Court of Justice and the Offices of the Regional Judicial and Legal Services Commission between the Government of Trinidad and Tobago and the Caribbean Community
15.	Proposed Code of Judicial Conduct
16.	Draft Enabling Bill to implement the Agreement establishing the Caribbean Court of Justice
17.	Protocol on the Privileges and Immunities of the Caribbean Court of Justice
18.	Regulations of the Regional Judicial and Legal Services Commission (Rev.2)
19.	Rules of Court of the Caribbean Court of Justice (Appellate Jurisdiction)
20.	Consensus of Chaguaramas

WORLD BUSINESS LAW HANDBOOK VOLUME 1 STRATEGIC AND PRACTICAL INFORMATION LIBRARY

Ultimate directories for conducting export-import operations in the country. Largest exporters and importers, strategic government and business contacts, selected export-import regulations and more...

Price: $149 each

Afghanistan Business Law Handbook Volume 1 Strategic and Practical Information
Aland Business Law Handbook Volume 1 Strategic and Practical Information
Albania Business Law Handbook Volume 1 Strategic and Practical Information
Algeria Business Law Handbook Volume 1 Strategic and Practical Information
Andorra Business Law Handbook Volume 1 Strategic and Practical Information
Angola Business Law Handbook Volume 1 Strategic and Practical Information
Anguilla Business Law Handbook Volume 1 Strategic and Practical Information
Antigua and Barbuda Business Law Handbook Volume 1 Strategic and Practical Information
Antilles (Netherlands) Business Law Handbook Volume 1 Strategic and Practical Information
Argentina Business Law Handbook Volume 1 Strategic and Practical Information
Armenia Business Law Handbook Volume 1 Strategic and Practical Information
Aruba Business Law Handbook Volume 1 Strategic and Practical Information
Australia Business Law Handbook Volume 1 Strategic and Practical Information
Austria Business Law Handbook Volume 1 Strategic and Practical Information
Azerbaijan Business Law Handbook Volume 1 Strategic and Practical Information
Bahamas Business Law Handbook Volume 1 Strategic and Practical Information
Bahrain Business Law Handbook Volume 1 Strategic and Practical Information
Bangladesh Business Law Handbook Volume 1 Strategic and Practical Information
Barbados Business Law Handbook Volume 1 Strategic and Practical Information
Belarus Business Law Handbook Volume 1 Strategic and Practical Information
Belgium Business Law Handbook Volume 1 Strategic and Practical Information
Belize Business Law Handbook Volume 1 Strategic and Practical Information
Benin Business Law Handbook Volume 1 Strategic and Practical Information
Bermuda Business Law Handbook Volume 1 Strategic and Practical Information
Bhutan Business Law Handbook Volume 1 Strategic and Practical Information
Bolivia Business Law Handbook Volume 1 Strategic and Practical Information
Bosnia and Herzegovina Business Law Handbook Volume 1 Strategic and Practical Information
Botswana Business Law Handbook Volume 1 Strategic and Practical Information
Brazil Business Law Handbook Volume 1 Strategic and Practical Information
Brunei Business Law Handbook Volume 1 Strategic and Practical Information
Bulgaria Business Law Handbook Volume 1 Strategic and Practical Information
Burkina Faso Business Law Handbook Volume 1 Strategic and Practical Information
Burundi Business Law Handbook Volume 1 Strategic and Practical Information
Cambodia Business Law Handbook Volume 1 Strategic and Practical Information

Cameroon Business Law Handbook Volume 1 Strategic and Practical Information
Canada Business Law Handbook Volume 1 Strategic and Practical Information
Cape Verde Business Law Handbook Volume 1 Strategic and Practical Information
Cayman Islands Business Law Handbook Volume 1 Strategic and Practical Information
Central African Republic Business Law Handbook Volume 1 Strategic and Practical Information
Chad Business Law Handbook Volume 1 Strategic and Practical Information
Chile Business Law Handbook Volume 1 Strategic and Practical Information
China Business Law Handbook Volume 1 Strategic and Practical Information
Colombia Business Law Handbook Volume 1 Strategic and Practical Information
Comoros Business Law Handbook Volume 1 Strategic and Practical Information
Congo Business Law Handbook Volume 1 Strategic and Practical Information
Congo, Democratic Republic Business Law Handbook Volume 1 Strategic and Practical Information
Cook Islands Business Law Handbook Volume 1 Strategic and Practical Information
Costa Rica Business Law Handbook Volume 1 Strategic and Practical Information
Cote d'Ivoire Business Law Handbook Volume 1 Strategic and Practical Information
Croatia Business Law Handbook Volume 1 Strategic and Practical Information
Cuba Business Law Handbook Volume 1 Strategic and Practical Information
Cyprus Business Law Handbook Volume 1 Strategic and Practical Information
Czech Republic Business Law Handbook Volume 1 Strategic and Practical Information
Denmark Business Law Handbook Volume 1 Strategic and Practical Information
Djibouti Business Law Handbook Volume 1 Strategic and Practical Information
Dominica Business Law Handbook Volume 1 Strategic and Practical Information
Dominican Republic Business Law Handbook Volume 1 Strategic and Practical Information
Ecuador Business Law Handbook Volume 1 Strategic and Practical Information
Egypt Business Law Handbook Volume 1 Strategic and Practical Information
El Salvador Business Law Handbook Volume 1 Strategic and Practical Information
Equatorial Guinea Business Law Handbook Volume 1 Strategic and Practical Information
Eritrea Business Law Handbook Volume 1 Strategic and Practical Information
Estonia Business Law Handbook Volume 1 Strategic and Practical Information
Ethiopia Business Law Handbook Volume 1 Strategic and Practical Information
Falkland Islands Business Law Handbook Volume 1 Strategic and Practical Information
Faroes Islands Business Law Handbook Volume 1 Strategic and Practical Information
Fiji Business Law Handbook Volume 1 Strategic and Practical Information
Finland Business Law Handbook Volume 1 Strategic and Practical Information
France Business Law Handbook Volume 1 Strategic and Practical Information
Gabon Business Law Handbook Volume 1 Strategic and Practical Information
Gambia Business Law Handbook Volume 1 Strategic and Practical Information
Georgia Business Law Handbook Volume 1 Strategic and Practical Information
Germany Business Law Handbook Volume 1 Strategic and Practical Information
Ghana Business Law Handbook Volume 1 Strategic and Practical Information
Gibraltar Business Law Handbook Volume 1 Strategic and Practical Information
Greece Business Law Handbook Volume 1 Strategic and Practical Information
Greenland Business Law Handbook Volume 1 Strategic and Practical Information
Grenada Business Law Handbook Volume 1 Strategic and Practical Information
Guam Business Law Handbook Volume 1 Strategic and Practical Information
Guatemala Business Law Handbook Volume 1 Strategic and Practical Information
Guernsey Business Law Handbook Volume 1 Strategic and Practical Information
Guinea Business Law Handbook Volume 1 Strategic and Practical Information
Guinea-Bissau Business Law Handbook Volume 1 Strategic and Practical Information
Guyana Business Law Handbook Volume 1 Strategic and Practical Information
Haiti Business Law Handbook Volume 1 Strategic and Practical Information

Honduras Business Law Handbook Volume 1 Strategic and Practical Information
Hungary Business Law Handbook Volume 1 Strategic and Practical Information
Iceland Business Law Handbook Volume 1 Strategic and Practical Information
India Business Law Handbook Volume 1 Strategic and Practical Information
Indonesia Business Law Handbook Volume 1 Strategic and Practical Information
Iran Business Law Handbook Volume 1 Strategic and Practical Information
Iraq Business Law Handbook Volume 1 Strategic and Practical Information
Ireland Business Law Handbook Volume 1 Strategic and Practical Information
Israel Business Law Handbook Volume 1 Strategic and Practical Information
Italy Business Law Handbook Volume 1 Strategic and Practical Information
Jamaica Business Law Handbook Volume 1 Strategic and Practical Information
Japan Business Law Handbook Volume 1 Strategic and Practical Information
Jersey Business Law Handbook Volume 1 Strategic and Practical Information
Jordan Business Law Handbook Volume 1 Strategic and Practical Information
Kazakhstan Business Law Handbook Volume 1 Strategic and Practical Information
Kenya Business Law Handbook Volume 1 Strategic and Practical Information
Kiribati Business Law Handbook Volume 1 Strategic and Practical Information
Korea, North Business Law Handbook Volume 1 Strategic and Practical Information
Korea, South Business Law Handbook Volume 1 Strategic and Practical Information
Kosovo Business Law Handbook Volume 1 Strategic and Practical Information
Kurdistan Business Law Handbook Volume 1 Strategic and Practical Information
Kuwait Business Law Handbook Volume 1 Strategic and Practical Information
Kyrgyzstan Business Law Handbook Volume 1 Strategic and Practical Information
Laos Business Law Handbook Volume 1 Strategic and Practical Information
Latvia Business Law Handbook Volume 1 Strategic and Practical Information
Lebanon Business Law Handbook Volume 1 Strategic and Practical Information
Lesotho Business Law Handbook Volume 1 Strategic and Practical Information
Liberia Business Law Handbook Volume 1 Strategic and Practical Information
Libya Business Law Handbook Volume 1 Strategic and Practical Information
Liechtenstein Business Law Handbook Volume 1 Strategic and Practical Information
Lithuania Business Law Handbook Volume 1 Strategic and Practical Information
Luxembourg Business Law Handbook Volume 1 Strategic and Practical Information
Macao Business Law Handbook Volume 1 Strategic and Practical Information
Macedonia Business Law Handbook Volume 1 Strategic and Practical Information
Madagascar Business Law Handbook Volume 1 Strategic and Practical Information
Madeira Business Law Handbook Volume 1 Strategic and Practical Information
Malawi Business Law Handbook Volume 1 Strategic and Practical Information
Malaysia Business Law Handbook Volume 1 Strategic and Practical Information
Maldives Business Law Handbook Volume 1 Strategic and Practical Information
Mali Business Law Handbook Volume 1 Strategic and Practical Information
Malta Business Law Handbook Volume 1 Strategic and Practical Information
Man Business Law Handbook Volume 1 Strategic and Practical Information
Marshall Islands Business Law Handbook Volume 1 Strategic and Practical Information
Mauritania Business Law Handbook Volume 1 Strategic and Practical Information
Mauritius Business Law Handbook Volume 1 Strategic and Practical Information
Mayotte Business Law Handbook Volume 1 Strategic and Practical Information
Mexico Business Law Handbook Volume 1 Strategic and Practical Information
Micronesia Business Law Handbook Volume 1 Strategic and Practical Information
Moldova Business Law Handbook Volume 1 Strategic and Practical Information
Monaco Business Law Handbook Volume 1 Strategic and Practical Information
Mongolia Business Law Handbook Volume 1 Strategic and Practical Information

Monserrat Business Law Handbook Volume 1 Strategic and Practical Information
Morocco Business Law Handbook Volume 1 Strategic and Practical Information
Mozambique Business Law Handbook Volume 1 Strategic and Practical Information
Myanmar Business Law Handbook Volume 1 Strategic and Practical Information
Namibia Business Law Handbook Volume 1 Strategic and Practical Information
Nauru Business Law Handbook Volume 1 Strategic and Practical Information
Nepal Business Law Handbook Volume 1 Strategic and Practical Information
Netherlands Business Law Handbook Volume 1 Strategic and Practical Information
New Caledonia Business Law Handbook Volume 1 Strategic and Practical Information
New Zealand Business Law Handbook Volume 1 Strategic and Practical Information
Nicaragua Business Law Handbook Volume 1 Strategic and Practical Information
Niger Business Law Handbook Volume 1 Strategic and Practical Information
Nigeria Business Law Handbook Volume 1 Strategic and Practical Information
Niue Business Law Handbook Volume 1 Strategic and Practical Information
Northern Mariana Islands Business Law Handbook Volume 1 Strategic and Practical Information
Norway Business Law Handbook Volume 1 Strategic and Practical Information
Oman Business Law Handbook Volume 1 Strategic and Practical Information
Pakistan Business Law Handbook Volume 1 Strategic and Practical Information
Palau Business Law Handbook Volume 1 Strategic and Practical Information
Palestine (West Bank & Gaza) Business Law Handbook Volume 1 Strategic and Practical Information
Panama Business Law Handbook Volume 1 Strategic and Practical Information
Papua New Guinea Business Law Handbook Volume 1 Strategic and Practical Information
Paraguay Business Law Handbook Volume 1 Strategic and Practical Information
Peru Business Law Handbook Volume 1 Strategic and Practical Information
Philippines Business Law Handbook Volume 1 Strategic and Practical Information
Pitcairn Islands Business Law Handbook Volume 1 Strategic and Practical Information
Poland Business Law Handbook Volume 1 Strategic and Practical Information
Polynesia French Business Law Handbook Volume 1 Strategic and Practical Information
Portugal Business Law Handbook Volume 1 Strategic and Practical Information
Qatar Business Law Handbook Volume 1 Strategic and Practical Information
Romania Business Law Handbook Volume 1 Strategic and Practical Information
Russia Business Law Handbook Volume 1 Strategic and Practical Information
Rwanda Business Law Handbook Volume 1 Strategic and Practical Information
Saint Kitts and Nevis Business Law Handbook Volume 1 Strategic and Practical Information
Saint Lucia Business Law Handbook Volume 1 Strategic and Practical Information
Saint Vincent and The Grenadines Business Law Handbook Volume 1 Strategic and Practical Information
Samoa (American) A Business Law Handbook Volume 1 Strategic and Practical Information
Samoa (Western) Business Law Handbook Volume 1 Strategic and Practical Information
San Marino Business Law Handbook Volume 1 Strategic and Practical Information
Sao Tome and Principe Business Law Handbook Volume 1 Strategic and Practical Information
Saudi Arabia Business Law Handbook Volume 1 Strategic and Practical Information
Scotland Business Law Handbook Volume 1 Strategic and Practical Information
Senegal Business Law Handbook Volume 1 Strategic and Practical Information
Serbia Business Law Handbook Volume 1 Strategic and Practical Information
Seychelles Business Law Handbook Volume 1 Strategic and Practical Information
Sierra Leone Business Law Handbook Volume 1 Strategic and Practical Information
Singapore Business Law Handbook Volume 1 Strategic and Practical Information
Slovakia Business Law Handbook Volume 1 Strategic and Practical Information
Slovenia Business Law Handbook Volume 1 Strategic and Practical Information
Solomon Islands Business Law Handbook Volume 1 Strategic and Practical Information
Somalia Business Law Handbook Volume 1 Strategic and Practical Information

South Africa Business Law Handbook Volume 1 Strategic and Practical Information
Spain Business Law Handbook Volume 1 Strategic and Practical Information
Sri Lanka Business Law Handbook Volume 1 Strategic and Practical Information
St. Helena Business Law Handbook Volume 1 Strategic and Practical Information
St. Pierre & Miquelon Business Law Handbook Volume 1 Strategic and Practical Information
Sudan Business Law Handbook Volume 1 Strategic and Practical Information
Suriname Business Law Handbook Volume 1 Strategic and Practical Information
Swaziland Business Law Handbook Volume 1 Strategic and Practical Information
Sweden Business Law Handbook Volume 1 Strategic and Practical Information
Switzerland Business Law Handbook Volume 1 Strategic and Practical Information
Syria Business Law Handbook Volume 1 Strategic and Practical Information
Taiwan Business Law Handbook Volume 1 Strategic and Practical Information
Tajikistan Business Law Handbook Volume 1 Strategic and Practical Information
Tanzania Business Law Handbook Volume 1 Strategic and Practical Information
Thailand Business Law Handbook Volume 1 Strategic and Practical Information
Togo Business Law Handbook Volume 1 Strategic and Practical Information
Tonga Business Law Handbook Volume 1 Strategic and Practical Information
Trinidad and Tobago Business Law Handbook Volume 1 Strategic and Practical Information
Tunisia Business Law Handbook Volume 1 Strategic and Practical Information
Turkey Business Law Handbook Volume 1 Strategic and Practical Information
Turkmenistan Business Law Handbook Volume 1 Strategic and Practical Information
Turks & Caicos Business Law Handbook Volume 1 Strategic and Practical Information
Tuvalu Business Law Handbook Volume 1 Strategic and Practical Information
Uganda Business Law Handbook Volume 1 Strategic and Practical Information
Ukraine Business Law Handbook Volume 1 Strategic and Practical Information
United Arab Emirates Business Law Handbook Volume 1 Strategic and Practical Information
United Kingdom Business Law Handbook Volume 1 Strategic and Practical Information
United States Business Law Handbook Volume 1 Strategic and Practical Information
Uruguay Business Law Handbook Volume 1 Strategic and Practical Information
Uzbekistan Business Law Handbook Volume 1 Strategic and Practical Information
Vanuatu Business Law Handbook Volume 1 Strategic and Practical Information
Vatican City Business Law Handbook Volume 1 Strategic and Practical Information
Venezuela Business Law Handbook Volume 1 Strategic and Practical Information
Vietnam Business Law Handbook Volume 1 Strategic and Practical Information
Virgin Islands, British Business Law Handbook Volume 1 Strategic and Practical Information
Wake Atoll Business Law Handbook Volume 1 Strategic and Practical Information
Wallis & Futuna Business Law Handbook Volume 1 Strategic and Practical Information
Western Sahara Business Law Handbook Volume 1 Strategic and Practical Information
Yemen Business Law Handbook Volume 1 Strategic and Practical Information
Zambia Business Law Handbook Volume 1 Strategic and Practical Information
Zimbabwe Business Law Handbook Volume 1 Strategic and Practical Information

Basic Laws and Regulations for conducting business and investment activity in the countries with special offshore status

Andorra Offshore Business Law Handbook
Anguilla Offshore Business Law Handbook
Bahamas Offshore Business Law Handbook
Barbados Offshore Business Law Handbook
Belize Offshore Business Law Handbook
Bermuda Offshore Business Law Handbook
British Virgin Islands Offshore Business Law Handbook
Cayman Islands Offshore Business Law Handbook
Cook Islands Offshore Business Law Handbook
Costa Rica Offshore Business Law Handbook
Cyprus Offshore Business Law Handbook
Dubai Offshore Business Law Handbook
Gibraltar Offshore Business Law Handbook
Grenada Offshore Business Law Handbook
Guernsey Offshore Business Law Handbook
Hong Kong Offshore Business Law Handbook
Ireland Offshore Business Law Handbook
Isle of Man Offshore Business Law Handbook
Jersey Offshore Business Law Handbook
Labuan Offshore Business Law Handbook
Liechtenstein Offshore Business Law Handbook
Luxembourg Offshore Business Law Handbook
Madeira Offshore Business Law Handbook
Malta Offshore Business Law Handbook
Mauritius Offshore Business and Investment Opportunities Handbook
Mauritius Offshore Business Law Handbook
Monaco Offshore Business Law Handbook
Nauru Offshore Business Law Handbook
Netherlands Antilles Offshore Business Law Handbook
Panama Offshore Business Law Handbook
Seychelles Offshore Business Law Handbook
Switzerland Offshore Business Law Handbook
Turks & Caicos Islands Offshore Business Law Handbook
Vanuatu Offshore Business Law Handbook

To order and for additional analytical and marketing information, please contacrt
International Business Publications, USA at:
P.O. Box 15343, Washington, DC 20003, USA. Phone: (202) 546-2103. Fax: (202) 546-3275.
E-mail: rusric@erols.com

WORLD CUSTOMS AND TRADE REGULATIONS LIBRARY
(PRICE $149.95)

0739757075	Afghanistan Customs, Trade Regulations and Procedures Handbook
0739757109	Albania Customs, Trade Regulations and Procedures Handbook
073975713X	Algeria Customs, Trade Regulations and Procedures Handbook
0739757148	Angola Customs, Trade Regulations and Procedures Handbook
0739757164	Antigua and Barbuda Customs, Trade Regulations and Procedures Handbook
0739757172	Antilles (Netherlands) Customs, Trade Regulations and Procedures Handbook
0739757199	Argentina Customs, Trade Regulations and Procedures Handbook
0739757210	Armenia Customs, Trade Regulations and Procedures Handbook
0739757229	Aruba Customs, Trade Regulations and Procedures Handbook
0739757245	Australia Customs, Trade Regulations and Procedures Handbook
0739757253	Austria Customs, Trade Regulations and Procedures Handbook
073975727X	Azerbaijan Customs, Trade Regulations and Procedures Handbook
0739757296	Bahamas Customs, Trade Regulations and Procedures Handbook
0739757318	Bahrain Customs, Trade Regulations and Procedures Handbook
0739757350	Bangladesh Customs, Trade Regulations and Procedures Handbook
0739757377	Barbados Customs, Trade Regulations and Procedures Handbook
0739757385	Belarus Customs, Trade Regulations and Procedures Handbook
0739757407	Belgium Customs, Trade Regulations and Procedures Handbook
0739757423	Belize Customs, Trade Regulations and Procedures Handbook
073975744X	Benin Customs, Trade Regulations and Procedures Handbook
0739757466	Bermuda Customs, Trade Regulations and Procedures Handbook
0739757490	Bhutan Customs, Trade Regulations and Procedures Handbook
0739757512	Bolivia Customs, Trade Regulations and Procedures Handbook
0739757539	Bosnia and Herzegovina Customs, Trade Regulations and Procedures Handbook
0739757555	Botswana Customs, Trade Regulations and Procedures Handbook
0739757598	Brazil Customs, Trade Regulations and Procedures Handbook
073975761X	Brunei Customs, Trade Regulations and Procedures Handbook
0739757636	Bulgaria Customs, Trade Regulations and Procedures Handbook
0739757652	Burkina Faso Customs, Trade Regulations and Procedures Handbook
0739757679	Cambodia Customs, Trade Regulations and Procedures Handbook
0739757725	Cameroon Customs, Trade Regulations and Procedures Handbook
0739757741	Canada Customs, Trade Regulations and Procedures Handbook
0739757849	Chile Customs, Trade Regulations and Procedures Handbook
0739757865	China Customs, Trade Regulations and Procedures Handbook

To order and for additional analytical and marketing information, please contacrt
International Business Publications, USA at:
P.O. Box 15343, Washington, DC 20003, USA. Phone: (202) 546-2103. Fax: (202) 546-3275.
E-mail: rusric@erols.com

0739757881	Colombia Customs, Trade Regulations and Procedures Handbook
0739757911	Comoros Customs, Trade Regulations and Procedures Handbook
0739757942	Costa Rica Customs, Trade Regulations and Procedures Handbook
073975601X	Croatia Customs, Trade Regulations and Procedures Handbook
0739756044	Cuba Customs, Trade Regulations and Procedures Handbook
0739756079	Cyprus Customs, Trade Regulations and Procedures Handbook
0739756117	Czech Republic Customs, Trade Regulations and Procedures Handbook
0739756141	Denmark Customs, Trade Regulations and Procedures Handbook
0739756222	Ecuador Customs, Trade Regulations and Procedures Handbook
0739756249	Egypt Customs, Trade Regulations and Procedures Handbook
0739756265	El Salvador Customs, Trade Regulations and Procedures Handbook
073975632X	Estonia Customs, Trade Regulations and Procedures Handbook
0739756370	Fiji Customs, Trade Regulations and Procedures Handbook
0739756400	Finland Customs, Trade Regulations and Procedures Handbook
0739756435	France Customs, Trade Regulations and Procedures Handbook
0739756486	Georgia (Republic) Customs, Trade Regulations and Procedures Handbook
0739756516	Germany Customs, Trade Regulations and Procedures Handbook
0739756540	Ghana Customs, Trade Regulations and Procedures Handbook
0739756575	Gibraltar Offshore & Customs, Trade Regulations and Procedures Handbook
073975677X	Greece Customs, Trade Regulations and Procedures Handbook
0739756893	Haiti Customs, Trade Regulations and Procedures Handbook
0739756915	Honduras Customs, Trade Regulations and Procedures Handbook
073975694X	Hungary Customs, Trade Regulations and Procedures Handbook
0739756966	Iceland Customs, Trade Regulations and Procedures Handbook
0739756990	India Customs, Trade Regulations and Procedures Handbook
0739755013	Indonesia Customs, Trade Regulations and Procedures Handbook
0739755048	Iran Customs, Trade Regulations and Procedures Handbook
0739755072	Iraq Economic Sanctions, Customs, Trade Regulations and Procedures Handbook
0739755080	Ireland Customs, Trade Regulations and Procedures Handbook
0739755102	Israel Customs, Trade Regulations and Procedures Handbook
0739755137	Italy Customs, Trade Regulations and Procedures Handbook
0739755153	Jamaica Offshore Customs, Trade Regulations and Procedures Handbook
0739755188	Japan Customs, Trade Regulations and Procedures Handbook
073975520X	Jordan Customs, Trade Regulations and Procedures Handbook
0739755226	Kazakhstan Customs, Trade Regulations and Procedures Handbook
0739755242	Kenya Customs, Trade Regulations and Procedures Handbook
0739755269	Korea, North Customs, Trade Regulations and Procedures Handbook
0739755285	Korea, South Customs, Trade Regulations and Procedures Handbook
0739755331	Kuwait Customs, Trade Regulations and Procedures Handbook
0739755358	Kyrgyzstan Customs, Trade Regulations and Procedures Handbook
0739755374	Laos Customs, Trade Regulations and Procedures Handbook
07397554404	Latvia Customs, Trade Regulations and Procedures Handbook
0739755439	Lebanon Customs, Trade Regulations and Procedures Handbook
0739755471	Libya Customs, Trade Regulations and Procedures Handbook

073975551X	Lithuania Customs, Trade Regulations and Procedures Handbook
0739755544	Macao Customs, Trade Regulations and Procedures Handbook
0739755587	Macedonia Customs, Trade Regulations and Procedures Handbook
0739755609	Madagascar Customs, Trade Regulations and Procedures Handbook
0739755633	Malaysia Customs, Trade Regulations and Procedures Handbook
0739755684	Malta Customs, Trade Regulations and Procedures Handbook
0739755730	Mauritius Customs, Trade Regulations and Procedures Handbook
0739755757	Mexico Customs, Trade Regulations and Procedures Handbook
0739755854	Moldova Customs, Trade Regulations and Procedures Handbook
0739755889	Mongolia Customs, Trade Regulations and Procedures Handbook
0739755900	Morocco Customs, Trade Regulations and Procedures Handbook
0739755943	Myanmar Customs, Trade Regulations and Procedures Handbook
0739755986	Nepal Customs, Trade Regulations and Procedures Handbook
0739754009	Netherlands Customs, Trade Regulations and Procedures Handbook
0739754025	New Zealand Customs, Trade Regulations and Procedures Handbook
0739754068	Nicaragua Customs, Trade Regulations and Procedures Handbook
0739754091	Nigeria Customs, Trade Regulations and Procedures Handbook
0739754130	Norway Customs, Trade Regulations and Procedures Handbook
0739754165	Oman Customs, Trade Regulations and Procedures Handbook
0739754211	Pakistan Customs, Trade Regulations and Procedures Handbook
0739754246	Panama Customs, Trade Regulations and Procedures Handbook
0739754289	Peru Customs, Trade Regulations and Procedures Handbook
0739754327	Philippines Customs, Trade Regulations and Procedures Handbook
0739754386	Philippines National Police Force Handbook
0739754408	Poland Customs, Trade Regulations and Procedures Handbook
0739754424	Portugal Customs, Trade Regulations and Procedures Handbook
0739754467	Qatar Customs, Trade Regulations and Procedures Handbook
0739754491	Romania Customs, Trade Regulations and Procedures Handbook
073975453X	Russia Customs, Trade Regulations and Procedures Handbook
0739754602	Saudi Arabia Customs, Trade Regulations and Procedures Handbook
0739754629	Scotland Customs, Trade Regulations and Procedures Handbook
0739754696	Singapore Customs, Trade Regulations and Procedures Handbook
0739754750	Slovak Republic Customs, Trade Regulations and Procedures Handbook
0739754726	Slovak Republic Customs, Trade Regulations and Procedures Handbook
0739754807	South Africa Customs, Trade Regulations and Procedures Handbook
0739754858	Spain Customs, Trade Regulations and Procedures Handbook
0739754874	Sri Lanka Customs, Trade Regulations and Procedures Handbook
0739754912	Sudan Customs, Trade Regulations and Procedures Handbook
0739754939	Suriname Customs, Trade Regulations and Procedures Handbook
0739754963	Sweden Customs, Trade Regulations and Procedures Handbook
0739754998	Switzerland Customs, Trade Regulations and Procedures Handbook
0739759019	Syria Customs, Trade Regulations and Procedures Handbook
0739759043	Taiwan Customs, Trade Regulations and Procedures Handbook
0739759086	Tajikistan Customs, Trade Regulations and Procedures Handbook

To order and for additional analytical and marketing information, please contacrt
International Business Publications, USA at:
P.O. Box 15343, Washington, DC 20003, USA. Phone: (202) 546-2103. Fax: (202) 546-3275.
E-mail: rusric@erols.com

0739759116	Thailand Customs, Trade Regulations and Procedures Handbook
0739759167	Tunisia Customs, Trade Regulations and Procedures Handbook
0739759183	Turkey Customs, Trade Regulations and Procedures Handbook
0739759221	Turkmenistan Customs, Trade Regulations and Procedures Handbook
0739759264	Ukraine Customs, Trade Regulations and Procedures Handbook
0739755280	United Arab Emirates Customs, Trade Regulations and Procedures Handbook
0739759310	United Kingdom Customs, Trade Regulations and Procedures Handbook
0739759485	United States Customs, Trade Regulations and Procedures Handbook
0739759663	Uzbekistan Customs, Trade Regulations and Procedures Handbook
0739759779	Vietnam Financial and Trade Policy Handbook
0739759736	Serbia Customs, Trade Regulations and Procedures Handbook

To order and for additional analytical and marketing information, please contacrt
International Business Publications, USA at:
P.O. Box 15343, Washington, DC 20003, USA. Phone: (202) 546-2103. Fax: (202) 546-3275.
E-mail: rusric@erols.com